THE INFERNO

THE INFERNO

A SOUTHERN MORALITY TALE

Joseph B. Ingle

PUBLISHED BY WESTVIEW, INC.
P.O. Box 605
Kingston Springs, Tennessee 37082
www.publishedbywestview.com

ISBN 978-1-937763-1-25-1

First edition, March 2012

Photo credits: Cover photograph as well as photographs on pages xviii, 2,6,23,28,46,50,64,92,96,114,150,156,162,166. are by Gigi Cohen and are used by permission. Gigi Cohen can be reached at *www.southerninferno.com.* Photo page 119 by Eric England is used by permission.

The author gratefully acknowledges permission from Robin Kirkpatrick to quote from his translation of *The Inferno.*

The author gratefully acknowledges permission from Kenny Campbell to print from his correspondence with Philip Workman as well as the official memorandum he received regarding exercise restriction for daring to watch the sunset.

The author gratefully acknowledges assistance from the lawyers and investigators in the Federal Public Defenders Office in Nashville regarding their filings on Philip Workman's behalf.

The author gratefully acknowledges Robert Hutton, a defense lawyer in Memphis, for his *error coram nobis* filing and for conversations about the case.

TO THE MEMORIES OF

Marie Deans, Minda Lazarov, William Styron, Tom Wicker, and Harmon Wray

Con la più sincera gratitudine per nostra amicizia

Contents

TIMELINE OF EVENTS

August 5, 1981

10:22 P.M.   Philip Workman takes the cash receipts from Memphis Wendy's restaurant and directs the employees to a back room.

10: 33 P.M.   Philip leaves the restaurant with cash in a bag under his sweatshirt with a .45-caliber pistol in his pants. He encounters Memphis police lieutenant Ronald Oliver. They chat. Philip sees other police cars arriving and runs. He trips on a curb and falls, then surrenders with hands raised. Lieutenant Oliver strikes Philip on the head from behind with a blunt object, probably a flashlight. Philip's gun discharges in the air. With blood running down his face, he rises and flees. Other shots are fired. Oliver lies mortally wounded.

11:55 P.M.   Police apprehend Philip Workman. He is taken to John Gaston Hospital for treatment of head wound, dog bites, and shotgun pellets to buttocks.

August 6, 1981

4:00 A.M.   Police officers go to the morgue and take Polaroid photographs of Oliver's wounds.

5:00 A.M.   Police officers convene at the Violent Crimes Unit. They review the photos of Oliver's wounds, Workman's gun, Oliver's clothing, and the shell casings and live round found at the crime scene. Afterward an "exchange of information" takes place.

6:00 A.M.   Police officers return to the crime scene to look for additional evidence.

11:30 A.M.   Dr. James Spencer Bell performs an autopsy on Ronald Oliver.

12:25 P.M.   Itinerant drug addict Harold Davis calls the Memphis Police Department from a Memphis motel claiming to have seen the Oliver shooting. Police officer Curry Todd picks Davis up and brings him to police headquarters.

1:25 P.M.   Terry Willis, employed next door to the Wendy's, discovers what he thinks is a ball bearing in the parking lot. Without looking at it, he puts it in his toolbox. After a friend tells him about the shooting, he looks at the object again, realizes it is an aluminum-jacketed .45-caliber bullet, and calls police.

2:25 P.M.   Memphis police log in to the property room the pristine .45-caliber bullet Willis discovered in the parking lot.

2:30 P.M.   From an array of photographs (i.e., without a lineup), Harold Davis identifies Workman as the man he claims to have seen shoot Oliver.

August 18, 1981   Grand jury issues an indictment against Philip on two counts: (1) felony murder of Lt. Ronald Oliver, and (2) premeditated murder.

March 22, 1982	Philip's trial begins with jury selection.
March 24, 1982	Jury is sworn in. Philip pleads not guilty.
March 25, 1982	Opening statements are delivered; testimony from prosecution witnesses Sandra Oliver, Dr. James Bell, Wendy's employees, clean-up man at Wendy's, police officers Aubrey Stoddard and Stephen Parker, and Harold Davis. Police officers Larkin and T. L. Cobb also testify.
March 26, 1982	Trial continues with testimony from prosecution witnesses Terry Willis, Gerald Wilkes, and police officers Stephen Parker and T. L. Cobb. Philip Workman testifies on his own behalf after being instructed by his court-appointed lawyers not to contradict the police.
March 27, 1982	The crime scene diagram is introduced through the testimony of police officer Franklin. Crime scene diagram is interpreted to explain how crime happened. Memphis Crime Scene Squad member C. A. Russell testifies that at approximately midnight he found Workman's gun in the vicinity of his arrest. Terry Willis testifies about finding the ball bearing that "turned out to be a round." FBI agent Gerald Wilkes testifies that the bullet Willis found could not have been the fatal bullet, because it exhibited no mutilation and no blood, fiber, or material was on it.
March 29, 1982	Philip testifies about his actions as he left the Wendy's. Prosecution closes with a description of the crime and how Workman "cooly and deliberately pulled the trigger and sent the bullet down this barrel and into the body of [Oliver]."
March 30, 1982	
10:50 A.M.	Jury retires for deliberation.
12:05 P.M.	Jury finds Philip guilty of felony murder. Sentencing hearing begins. Prosecution describes aggravating circumstances. Defense presents no mitigating circumstances despite indicating they would do so in their opening statement.
March 31, 1982	Philip sentenced to death by electrocution.
March 1, 1985	First post-conviction appeal filed by Howard Wagerman.
June 1989	Paul Morrow of the Capital Case Resource Center ensures that all death row prisoners file pro se petitions for a second post-conviction appeal under newly passed legislation.
November 1990	Chris Minton, of the Capital Case Resource Center, assumes lead lawyer role for Philip Workman. Judge Colton dismisses Philip's post-conviction appeal.
March 20, 1992	Criminal Court for Shelby County dismisses petition for post-conviction relief.

November 29, 1993 Tennessee Supreme Court denies Philip's application for permission to appeal the Court of Criminal Appeals' decision affirming the trial court's dismissal.

February 28, 1994 U.S. Supreme Court denies Philip's certiorari petition.

July 18, 1994 Habeas corpus petition, *Philip R. Workman v. Ricky Bell, warden* is filed in federal court.

October 18, 1994 State responds to petition but argues to dismiss the new claims.

May 2, 1995 State moves for summary judgment, asking to dismiss the opposition on its face.

September, 18, 1995 Philip's lawyers file a response to the state.

October 29, 1996 Judge Julia Gibbons grants summary judgment, thus denying Philip a chance to present his claims of not shooting Lieutenant Oliver on the basis of newly discovered evidence.

November 1, 1996 Judge Julia Gibbons swears in her husband, William Gibbons, as district attorney of Shelby County, Memphis.

June 17, 1998 Philip's case is argued in front of a three-judge panel in the Sixth Circuit Court of Appeals in Cincinnati, Ohio.

October 30, 1998 Sixth Circuit Court's opinion is delivered.

November 12, 1998 Petition for rehearing is filed by Philip's lawyers.

October 4, 1999 U.S. Supreme Court denies Philip's certiorari review.

November 29, 1999 U.S. Supreme Court denies rehearing petitions from Philip and Robert Coe.

December 9, 1999 Tennessee Supreme Court removes attorney general Paul Summers from working against Robert Coe due to his prior involvement as an appellate judge.

January 3, 2000 State supreme court sets an execution date for Philip Workman and Robert Coe of April 6, 2000.

January 2000 Joe Ingle visits with Justin Wilson, the governor's senior policy adviser.

January 27, 2000 Philip files for clemency.

March 2000 Tennessee legislature changes method of execution from electrocution to lethal injection.

April 3, 2000 First clemency hearing is held before governor's appointee Justin Wilson. Philip packs his belongings and is transferred from death row to the death house.

April 4, 2000 Philip receives his first stay of execution from the U.S. Court of Appeals of the Sixth Circuit and is transferred back to his cell on death row.

April 6, 2000 Robert Coe is executed by poisoning through lethal injection.

September 5, 2000   Sixth Circuit dissolves its stay of execution after a 7–7 vote, the "tie you die" vote.

October 5, 2000   Tennessee Supreme Court sets a second execution date for Philip of January 31, 2002, even though a stay of execution is in effect from the U.S. Supreme Court

January 25, 2001   Second clemency hearing is held at Riverbend Maximum Security Institution before the Board of Probation and Parole, which functions as the clemency board in capital cases.

January 26, 2000   Sixth Circuit Court of Appeals stays Philip's execution.

January 28, 2001   Despite the stay, Philip is instructed to pack up his belongings, is shackled, and taken to deathwatch again.

January 30, 2001   Despite the state's efforts to dissolve the stay of execution, it holds and Philip is transferred back to death row.

February 28, 2001   Tennessee Supreme Court sets a third execution date for Philip of March 30, 2001.

March 27, 2001   Philip once again boxes up his belongings and is transferred to the death house. This is his third trip there.

March 29, 2001   Chancellor Ellen Hobbs Lyle presides over *Workman v. Bell*. Philip's brother Terry and Joe Ingle both visit him on death row. Tennessee Supreme Court stays Philip's execution forty-five minutes before it is to occur; orders Shelby County Criminal Court to hold an *error coram nobis* hearing to determine innocence claims.

April 6, 2001   Judge Colton of Shelby County Criminal Court issues a gag order in Philip's case.

April 17, 2001   Tennessee Court of Criminal Appeals postpones the *error coram nobis* hearing Colton has scheduled for April 23.

May 2, 2001   Appellate court remands Philip's case to trial court.

July 31, 2001   Philip's lawyers file a motion for a default judgment.

August 1, 2001   Shelby County Criminal Court issues a letter that no proof will be taken at the hearing on August 13, 2001, but that arguments will be heard on the motion for default judgment.

August 3, 2001   Harold Davis is arrested for shoplifting in Jacksonville, Florida, and booked into jail. Shelby County Criminal Court reverses its decision and orders that proof be taken at the August 13 hearing.

August 13, 2001   *Error coram nobis* hearing takes place before Judge Colton; Davis testifies that he did not see Philip Workman shoot Lieutenant Oliver.

August 16, 2001	Vivian Porter testifies in *error coram nobis* hearing that Davis was with her on the night of the crime.
October 16, 2001	Dr. Cyril Wecht testifies in the continued *error coram nobis* hearing that "within a reasonable degree of medical certainty" Philip's bullet did not kill Lieutenant Oliver.
November 5, 2001	Trial juror Wardie Parks testifies in continued *error coram nobis* hearing that he would not have voted to convict Philip if he knew Harold Davis was not there and that forensic evidence revealed it was not Philip's bullet that killed Ronald Oliver.
January 7, 2002	Judge Colton rules against Philip Workman, denying relief, despite the fact that the only proof offered by the state was the trial court record.
June 1, 2002	Dr. O. C. Smith bomb incident occurs. Philip's birthday.
June 2, 2002	Dr. Smith discovered wrapped in barbed wire with an "explosive device" strapped to his chest.
December 30, 2002	Tennessee Court of Criminal Appeals affirms the Shelby County Criminal Court's denial of the *error coram nobis* petition.
May 19, 2003	Tennessee Supreme Court denies Philip's request for appeal.
June 2, 2003	Tennessee Supreme Court denies Philip's request for reconsideration of its denial of the appeal; sets a fourth execution date of September 24, 2003, for Philip.
August 12, 2003	Results of polygraph test taken by Harold Davis reveal he did not see Philip shoot Oliver. Philip's clemency team files clemency papers.
September 9, 2003	Philip is interviewed by Dr. George Woods, who determines he suffers from post-traumatic stress disorder.
September 10, 2003	Philip packs and prepares to wash down his cell in preparation for moving to death row for September 24 execution.
September 15, 2003	Governor Bredesen announces a 120-day reprieve for Philip pending the outcome of a federal criminal investigation related to the case. Federal judge Bernice Donald of Memphis holds a hearing on Philip's case and decides to await conclusion of the federal criminal investigation.
January 9, 2004	Governor Bredesen extends Philip's reprieve until April 15, 2004.
February 10, 2004	O. C. Smith is indicted by a grand jury in Memphis for illegal possession of a destructive device and lying to federal investigators.
April 15, 2004	Philip's reprieve expires.
August 2004	Chris Minton files a request for a stay of execution.
September 22, 2004	Philip's fifth execution date.

Mid-September 2004 Stay of execution is granted by Judge Donald.

October 18, 2004 Judge Donald denies Philip's 60(b) petition after previously granting a stay of execution to consider it.

January 2005-2006 Litigation proceeds on 60 (b) issue in several cases throughout the country, and the issue is ultimately resolved by the U.S. Supreme Court. Lethal injection issues litigated in California, North Carolina, and Ohio. Florida halts executions pending review of lethal injection problems. O. C. Smith prosecution continues.

October 31, 2006 Philip's lawyers file a "Motion to Alter or Amend" citing the *Demjanjuk* case.

December 2006 Judge Donald denies Philip's motion to reconsider.

January 16, 2007 Tennessee Supreme Court sets Philip's sixth execution date for May 9, 2007.

February 1, 2007 Governor Phil Bredesen announces he is halting executions until the execution protocol has been reviewed.

April 5, 2007 Public hearing is held on the state's lethal injection protocol.

April 2007 Judge Donald denies Philip's stay of execution request but issues a certificate of appealability indicating the appeal has merit.

April 30, 2007 Tennessee Department of Corrections revises its lethal injection protocol but ingredients remain the same.

May 1, 2007 Philip's lawyers file 60 (b) petition to the Sixth Circuit Court of Appeals.

May 2, 2007 Report on execution protocol; moratorium on executions in Tennessee ends.

May 4, 2007 Sixth Circuit Court of Appeals panel votes 2–1 against Philip's 60 (b) appeal. Federal district court judge Todd Campbell issues a stay of execution based on a review of the lethal injection protocol.

May 7, 2007 Sixth Circuit Court of Appeals panel, composed of two Republicans and one Democrat, vote 2–1 to lift the stay of execution.

May 9, 2007 Philip is executed at Riverbend Maximum Security Institution.

May 9-12, 2007 Litigation takes place on whether Philip's request to maintain his religious belief that "the body is the temple of the Lord" will be respected and thus prohibit an autopsy.

May 12, 2007 Agreement is reached among parties to a partial autopsy, and Philip's body is released for burial.

May 14, 2007 Philip's funeral is held in Nashville with family and friends. He is buried surrounded by people who loved him and are filled with tears of rage and grief.

Cast of Characters

Anderson, Townie	Clemency board member
Ball, Officer	Memphis police officer on the security squad at the crime scene
Ballard, Jay	Governor Sundquist's legal counsel
Bell, James Spencer	Shelby County medical examiner in Memphis at the time of the crime
Bell, Ricky	Warden of Riverbend Maximum Security Institution
Blackmun, Harry	U.S. Supreme Court justice
Bonnyman, Claudia	Chancellor, Chancery Court, Part IV, Davidson County, Nashville
Bredesen, Phil	Governor of Tennessee 2003–2011
Campbell, Donal	Commissioner, Department of Corrections, under Governor Sundquist
Campbell, John	Assistant district attorney in Memphis
Campbell, Kenny	Death row prisoner and close friend of Philip Workman
Campbell, Will	Director of Committee of Southern Churchmen and founder of Southern Prison Ministry
Cavanaugh, Jim	Alcohol, Tobacco and Firearms agent involved in O. C. Smith investigation
Cobb, T. L.	Memphis police officer, one of the first officers on Workman crime scene
Colton, John P.	Criminal court judge in Shelby County, Memphis
Conte, Andrea	Wife of Governor Phil Bredesen
Cooley, Dave	Deputy governor for Governor Phil Bredesen
Craig, Steve	Citizen witness to events at the crime scene, friend of Aubrey Stoddard
Dalton, Bill	Clemency board member
Davis, Harold	Supposed eyewitness to Lt. Ronald Oliver's shooting
Dawson, Don	Clemency attorney for Philip Workman
DeBerry, Lois	Speaker pro tem of the House of Representatives of the General Assembly, from Memphis
DeSente, Lacey	Investigator in Phoenix with the federal public defender's office who helped locate Harold Davis
Dills, Don	Clemency board member
Dodillet, Paula	Ronnie Oliver's daughter, who believed Philip's version of events
Donald, Bernice	Federal district judge in Memphis, currently serving on the Sixth Circuit Court of Appeals
Dorsey, Jefferson	Co-counsel for Philip Workman

Drowota, Frank	Justice on the Tennessee Supreme Court
Dunbar, Tony	Director of Southern Prison Ministry
Dysinger, John	Seventh Day Adventist, friend of Philip Workman
Fackler, Martin L.	Conducted bullet studies providing evidence of Philip's innocence
Fleming, Mike	Host of a radio show in Memphis
Gamble, Dixie	Produced the film on Robert Coe
Gibbons, Julia	Federal district court judge in Memphis, currently serving on Sixth Circuit Court of Appeals, wife of William Gibbons
Gibbons, William	District attorney for Shelby County, Memphis, currently Safety and Homeland Security commissioner for the state of Tennessee and husband of Julia Gibbons
Harbison, E. J.	Death row prisoner
Hassell, Larry	Clemency board member
Hayes, J. R.	Memphis police officer in charge of Workman crime scene
Henry, Kelley	Lawyer for the federal public defender's office in Nashville
Hess, Inspector	Inspector for the Memphis police involved in the "exchange of information meeting" on August 6, 1981
Hollie, Sergeant	Memphis police sergeant involved in the "exchange of information meeting" on August, 6, 1981
Hutton, Robert	Defense lawyer in Memphis who assisted in Workman case
Jackson, Captain	Memphis police captain involved in the "exchange of information meeting" on August, 6, 1981
Johnson, Don	On death row with Philip before his execution
Kahan, Gerald	Defense lawyer in Memphis
Keenan, Clyde	Memphis police officer, led the "shoot team" that checked police weapons after incident of August 5, 1981
Kill, Kerry Scott	Cleaning the Wendy's restaurant at closing time on August 5, 1981
Kitchens, Jerry	Assistant district attorney during trial and clemency; moved on to work in U.S. Attorney's office in Memphis
Larkin, Officer	Memphis police officer who drove Officer Stoddard to the hospital
Lawson, Jim	Minister who visited Philip on death row before execution
Lax, Ron	Private investigator, Memphis
Leuchter, Fred	Rehabilitated the Tennessee electric chair and created lethal injection paraphernalia

Levy, Bruce	Medical examiner for Davidson County, Nashville, and state of Tennessee, later dismissed after being apprehended in Mississippi with marijuana, which probably came from Nashville crime lab
Lewis, Captain	Memphis police captain, attended the "exchange of information" meeting on August 6, 1981
Lyle, Ellen Hobbs	Chancellor, Chancery Court, Division III, Davidson County, Nashville
Marquez, Gene	ATF agent involved in O. C. Smith case
Marshall, Larry	Head of the Northwestern University Innocence Project
McCleskey, Warren	Death row prisoner in Georgia and friend of Joe Ingle
Minton, Chris	Lead lawyer for Philip Workman on appeal
Moore, Mike	Lawyer in the attorney general's office, attended capital punishment meeting
Morante, Kathy	Prosecutor in the Nashville district attorney's office
Morrow, Paul	Lawyer with the Capital Case Resource Center, filed pro se appeals for all death row prisoners
Music, Lieutenant	Memphis police officer who was at the "exchange of information meeting" on August 6, 1981
Nelson, David	Republican appointee to the Sixth Circuit Court of Appeals
Nixon, John	Federal district court judge in Nashville
Null, Garvin	Citizen witness to the events at the crime scene
Oliver, Ronald	Memphis police lieutenant who was shot and killed August 5, 1981 at the Wendy's restaurant in Memphis
Oliver, Sandra	Lieutenant Oliver's widow; testified at trial against Philip Workman
Parker, Stephen	Memphis police officer at the crime scene; moved on to work in U.S. Attorney's office in Memphis
Parks, Wardie	Juror on Philip Workman's trial in 1982
Peterson Eddie	Assistant district attorney at Workman's trial
Pierotti, John	Former Memphis district attorney who joined the clemency team for Workman
Porter, Vivian	Friend of Harold Davis and witness to his whereabouts the night of the crime
Pruden, Glenn	Lawyer for the attorney general's office
Rickard, Jeff	Citizen witness at the crime scene
Ryan, James L.	Republican appointee to the Sixth Circuit Court of Appeals
Scruggs, Harry	Second post-conviction appeal lawyer for Workman
Siler, Eugene E., Jr.	Republican appointee to the Sixth Circuit Court of Appeals

Singletary, Victor	Baptist minister who officiated at Philip Workman's funeral
Smith, O. C.	Shelby County medical examiner who testified at two clemency hearings
Sperry, Kris	Medical examiner for the state of Georgia; testified for defense about Oliver's wounds
Spitz, Werner	Forensics doctor and author of the leading text in the field, *Medicolegal Investigation of Death: Guidelines for the Application of Pathology to Crime Investigation*.
Stoddard, Aubrey	Memphis police officer who shot at Workman and was wounded in the arm by return fire
Strother, Don	Prosecutor in the trial of Philip Workman
Summers, Paul	Attorney general for the state of Tennessee
Sundquist, Don	Governor of Tennessee, 1995–2003
Swearingen, Sheila	Clemency board member
Tarkington, Amy	Lawyer in the attorney general's office
Todd, Curry	Police officer who brought Harold Davis to police headquarters on August 6, 1981; later elected to the House of Representatives of the General Assembly of Tennessee. He introduced the legislation that allowed guns in bars and restaurants. In October 2011, he was arrested for DUI with a deadly weapon in his car.
Tomashevsky, Steve	Philip's lawyer in his civil case against O. C. Smith
Trauger, Aleta	Federal district judge in Nashville
Traughber, Charles	Chairman of the clemency board
Wagerman, Howard	Court-appointed appeal lawyer for Workman in state court
Wecht, Cyril	Preeminent forensics doctor
Welborn, Jerry	Chaplain at Riverbend Maximum Security Institution
Whalen, Joe	Lawyer in the attorney general's office
Wilkes, Gerald	FBI agent, ballistics expert, testified for prosecution at Workman trial
Willis, Terry	Holiday Auto Parts employee who found the "magic bullet"
Wilson, Justin	Senior policy adviser to Governor Sundquist, currently comptroller for the state of Tennessee
Woods, George	Psychiatrist with internationally recognized expertise in trauma
Workman, Philip	Death row prisoner

The Inferno

Canto I

At one point midway on our path of life,
I came around and found myself
Now searching through a dark wood,
The right way blurred and lost

How hard it is to say
What that wood was,
A wilderness, savage, brute
Harsh and wild

Only to think of it renews my fear!
So bitter, that thought, that
Death is hardly worse
      —Dante Alighieri

    (Translated by Robin Kirkpatrick)

Joe Ingle outside Riverbend Maximum Security Institute (RMSI).

INTRODUCTION

When in my life pilgrimage "I came around and found myself / Now searching through a dark wood," I did so in a prison while visiting on death row. This may seem an odd place to encounter a guide as Dante found Virgil for his journey into the Inferno, but death row is where my guide presented himself. Of course, he did not know he was a guide, and I did not know I was about to descend into the Inferno.

My guide, Philip Workman, resided on death row in Nashville, Tennessee. We grew close after I had already encountered what the author William Styron described in the conclusion of *Darkness Visible: A Memoir of Madness*: "For those who have dwelt in depression's dark wood, and known its inexplicable agony, their return from the abyss is not unlike the ascent of the poet, trudging upward and upward out of hell's black depths and at last emerging into what he saw as 'the shining world.' There, whoever has been restored to health has almost always been restored to the capacity for serenity and joy, and this may be indemnity enough for having endured the despair beyond despair."

After profound melancholia for three consecutive autumns (1988–1990), I felt as Dante described his exit from the Inferno: *E quindi uscimmo a riveder le stelle* [And so we came forth, and once again beheld the stars]. The reasons for my melancholia are outlined in my previous work *Last Rights: 13 Fatal Encounters with the State's Justice*. I had spent sixteen years working with the condemned across the South and had lost many friends to the state killing machinery. Yet a decade had passed since then, and Bill Styron and I had become close through our mutual fight against the death penalty. It seemed that what he had shared with me in conversation in 1989 was indeed the case: I could endure the depression and never have it return.

So when my visits with Philip Workman began in earnest in 1999, I believed I had learned valuable lessons about my own ability to cope with melancholia and that I had put it behind me. Those lessons had come at a significant cost to my well-being, so I did not underestimate the power of the killing machinery in this country nor the collateral damage it inflicted on people like me who drew near it.

Hence I began my friendship with Philip in a manner that was not naïve. More than almost anyone in the country, I knew full well what realm I was entering by visiting death row. However, my reckoning of the geography of my soul proved to be in error. Rather than leaving the Inferno behind me, I had entered "the dark wood" and lost my way. And the only way out proved to be through the Inferno. So, as Dante did with Virgil, I would descend with Philip through the circles of Hell.

Philip Workman makes a fist to accentuate a point in conversation in Unit 2 RMSI.

THE FIRST CIRCLE

On August 5, 1981, it was hot in Memphis, Tennessee. Of course, it's almost always hot in August in Memphis, which rests on a bluff over the Mississippi River. The day was unusual, though, in that the high temperature came at night, near 10:00 P.M., when the weather service recorded 93 degrees in the muggy atmosphere.

Philip Workman noticed the heat, but he was a Southern boy and accustomed to it. He had grown up in the South—Georgia, Texas, Tennessee, Missouri, Kentucky—the son of a military man. Abandoned by his mother, he was raised by his German stepmother, whom his father had brought home to Texas after being stationed in the U.S. Army in Germany. At age seventeen, desiring to get away from home, Philip chose the same career route as his father and joined the army. But after receiving his honorable discharge, he came back to the South. No career military life for him. Instead, he returned a different young man, bringing home with him a drug addiction he acquired while in the military in Germany.

It was that jonesing, the intense craving for more cocaine, that brought him to Memphis as he wandered about the South. It led him into a Wendy's restaurant that Wednesday at 9:45 P.M., just before closing time. The cool of the air-conditioned eatery was a relief as he munched his burger in the back corner. But it was neither the cool air nor a hunger for food that brought Workman into the restaurant. His real hunger was for the money in the restaurant's cash register drawer.

Although Philip Workman was strung out and needing a fix, he had no intentions of hurting anyone. It was not in his nature. He figured he would get the money from the cash register by waving his .45-caliber pistol to intimidate the help, and then he would get out. That was as much of a plan as his drug-addled mind could come up with at the time. The four hollow-point bullets he had would remain nestled in the gun.

Kerry Scott Kill arrived at the Wendy's to clean the carpets. The employees locked the restaurant door at 10:00 so that no new customers could enter. Workman continued to eat his burger and fries. He even chatted with an employee. Finally mustering his nerve, at 10:22 he stood up, produced the .45 automatic pistol from his waistband, and informed everyone they must move to the back office. He herded the employees and Kerry Kill into the back room and told them to sit down.

The presence of the gun galvanized the scene. The employees offered their own money, but Workman told them he was only interested in the money in the restaurant's cash register. He told them to remain calm and no one would be hurt. "Keep cool," he kept repeating. He directed a female employee to gather up the day's proceeds. She placed the money in a canvas sack and gave it to Workman. Everyone else remained on the floor. After a few minutes, one of the employees complained of a cramp and asked if he could stand for a moment to stretch his legs. Workman allowed him to get up. The employee triggered a silent alarm at 10:31 P.M.

Responding to the dispatch sent out in reaction to the alarm, police officer Ronald Oliver parked his car facing west in the Wendy's north parking lot and, after observing the restaurant, radioed that it was a false alarm. Workman spied the police car from the north doors of the fast-food emporium.

The Memphis police dispatcher radioed everyone to disregard the call except for Officer Aubrey Stoddard, who was nearby. Police officer Stephen Parker radioed back that he too was close to the Wendy's and would also respond to the call. Stoddard's friend Steve Craig, who enjoyed the excitement of Stoddard's police life, had seen Stoddard driving and followed him to the Wendy's in his car. All of this occurred at approximately 10:32 P.M. Meanwhile, Garvin Null and Jeff Rickard were drinking beer inside Null's pickup truck, which was parked at a service station across from the Wendy's.

Philip Workman walked to the north door of the eatery at 10:33. He tucked his pistol into his pants, covered the money bag with a blue sweatshirt, and walked out of the Wendy's. He encountered Lieutenant Oliver walking toward the restaurant and asked Oliver if there was a problem. All police officers had been briefed at roll call about an African American male robbing fast-food restaurants in the area. Having seen no blacks at the scene, and disarmed by the polite inquiry of a white male who was apparently a customer, Lieutenant Oliver did not hesitate to talk with Workman. He still believed the alarm was a false one, since there was no sign of unusual activity.

Meanwhile, Officer Stoddard had driven around to the back of the restaurant and parked his car, facing Oliver's, in the north parking lot. Stoddard's friend Craig parked his car in the adjacent parking lot of the Holiday Auto Parts store. Officer Parker drove into the Wendy's south parking lot, facing west.

When Lieutenant Oliver took his eyes off Philip Workman to note the arrival of Stoddard's police cruiser, Workman realized he was trapped among policemen. He sprinted toward the Holiday Auto Parts parking lot but tripped over the curb separating the Wendy's parking lot and the Holiday Auto Parts lot.

After falling to the ground with his back to Oliver, Workman pushed himself up to a kneeling position and yelled, "Don't shoot! I give up!" Oliver asked, "Where is your gun?" Workman reached into his waistband and lifted the pistol out and up over his head. Lieutenant Oliver responded to the sight of the gun with a blow to Workman's head with a blunt object, most likely a police flashlight. As Workman was struck, his gun discharged into the air. Stunned, he stood up. He was concussed and bleeding from the blow to his head. He racked his pistol, forgetting it was an automatic. This move ejected a live round harmlessly onto the pavement.

Once Workman was on his feet, Officer Stoddard fired a round at him. Reflexively responding to the flash from Stoddard's gun, Workman fired back. The shot hit Stoddard in the arm, which flew up, and he went down.

Officer Parker, responding to the gunfire, ran across the front of the Wendy's restaurant and into the north parking lot. He saw Oliver falling to the ground and Stoddard spinning from Workman's return of fire. Parker fired a shotgun at Workman, striking him in the buttocks. Steve Craig saw Parker fire the shotgun two or three times at Philip Workman.

Across the street, Garvin Null and Jeff Rickard heard the gunfire and drove into the north parking lot of the Wendy's. Rickard saw Workman fleeing across the Holiday Auto Parts parking lot holding his bleeding head. Workman continued behind the north corner of the parking lot, stumbled, and discharged another shot into the air. He then hid in a neighboring field and tried to collect his thoughts.

Officer Stoddard radioed that he had been shot at the Wendy's and all units should respond. Police officer T. L. Cobb was one of the first among many police officers to arrive in response to the "officer down" call.

At 10:44 P.M. the Memphis police crime scene officers arrived at the Wendy's, and Officer J. R. Hayes took charge of the crime scene. Crime scene officers found three .45-caliber shell casings, one live .45 round, and a number of bullet fragments.

After an hour-long search by police using dogs, helicopters, cruisers, and on-foot officers, Philip Workman was found at 11:55 P.M. and arrested. He was taken to John Gaston Hospital for suturing of his head wound, treatment for dog bites, and removal of shotgun pellets from his buttocks. As Workman was treated at the hospital, he learned from a television report that Lieutenant Oliver was dead. Workman did not recall killing anyone.

At 12:06 A.M. on August 6, 1981, the police found Philip Workman's empty gun next to a truck parked near the field in which he had hidden and been arrested.

After returning to police headquarters, officers went to the morgue at 4:00 A.M. They took Polaroid pictures of Lieutenant Oliver's wounds. The entrance wound was slightly below the lieutenant's left nipple, and the corresponding exit wound, smaller than the entrance wound, was below his right shoulder blade. The officers returned to headquarters with the photographs for a meeting.

In the Violent Crimes Unit at 5:00 A.M., the following police personnel gathered: Inspector Hess, Captain Jackson, Captain Lewis, Lieutenant Music, Lt. Clyde Keenan, Sergeant Hollie, Sgt. Rick Wilson, and Officer Ball. The policemen reviewed the photographs of Lieutenant Oliver's mortal wound and Workman's gun, as well as the three shell casings and one live round from Workman's .45 that were recovered at the crime scene. They also examined Oliver's clothing. The police log for that date makes the vague description that "an exchange of information [took] place."

In the course of reviewing the assembled evidence it became apparent that the size of the wounds in Lieutenant Oliver's body did not correspond to the ammunition from Workman's .45 automatic pistol. Aluminum-coated .45-caliber hollow-point bullets, which Workman used, would expand upon entering the body and exit with a larger wound than entrance wound, if they exited at all. But Oliver's body had a larger entrance wound than exit wound. This was consistent with a bullet from another police officer's pistol. Thus, it appeared that Lieutenant Oliver had been the victim of "friendly fire."

***

The political dynamic of Memphis in the summer of 1981 served as the context for the discussion in the Violent Crimes Unit in the early morning hours of August 6. Previously that year two police officers had been slain; Lieutenant Oliver made a third dead policeman. There was no doubt that Philip Workman had committed the robbery of the Wendy's fast-food establishment. Nor was there any doubt he had wounded Officer Stoddard. Finally, he was a strung-out drug addict without local ties to the community. So what if his bullets were not actually the ones that killed Ronnie Oliver? He was just another druggie scumbag who needed to be put away. And, who, pray tell, wanted to try to explain to the public how one Memphis policeman had accidentally shot and killed another Memphis cop?

So it came to be that Philip Workman was indicted for killing Lt. Ronald Oliver. On August 18, 1981, the grand jury issued an indictment on two counts: (1) felony murder of Lt. Ronald Oliver, and (2) premeditated murder. Workman was appointed public defenders to represent him in his capital trial.

Light shining into the holding cell on death watch.

The Shelby County jail housed fourteen hundred prisoners in the spring of 1982. It was one of the new mass incarceration facilities that were springing up throughout the South in response to the civil rights movement. Philip Workman awaited trial in the Shelby County jail from August 6, 1981, until March 22, 1982. The trial began with group voir dire, or preliminary questioning, for jury selection.

The opening argument by prosecutor Don Strother in voir dire included the statement that they were looking for jurors who could "put totally out of their mind any sympathy." He reiterated that desire with another panel of prospective jurors, urging them "to put aside any sympathy." The jury panel was completed and sworn in on March 24, 1982. The indictment was read to the court and Philip Workman pled not guilty.

On March 25, 1982, assistant district attorney Eddie Peterson delivered his opening statement. It was a description of what happened at the scene of the crime. He re-created the scene for the jury. In doing so, he enhanced the state's theory which featured a need to prove that it was Workman's bullet, not "friendly fire" from a fellow policeman that killed Lt. Oliver. This statement was not challenged by defense.

> Officer Stoddard will tell you that as he went to the ground he was looking at Workman, who was still in the grasp of Lieutenant Oliver. Mr. Workman aimed the pistol at him and fired again, but missed. Then Officer Stoddard was on the ground and he does not see what happens for the next few seconds.
>
> What happens though is that he does hear something. That's another shot. [This would be a third shot from Workman.] Then there are a series of shots and [an] exchange of gunfire. Officer Parker is out of his car on the other side.
>
> You will . . . hold in your hand the bullet . . . that entered Officer Oliver and eventually killed Officer Oliver as well. The pathologist will testify that although Oliver was mortally wounded, he could still pull off six shots, although his marksmanship would be compromised.

The defense's opening argument by the public defender consisted of the following: Workman "was high on drugs, really messed up on drugs . . . That is simply it."

Sandra Oliver, Lt. Ronald Oliver's widow, took the stand. She described their last day together and their final contact through a telephone call at 6:00 P.M. The state introduced a photograph of Lieutenant Oliver.

The chief Shelby County medical examiner, Dr. James Bell, was the state's second witness. He testified that at 11:30 A.M. on August 6, 1981, he performed an autopsy on Lieutenant Oliver. "The bullet passed through the left lung, through the diaphragm, through the stomach, through the diaphragm again, through the heart, through the right lung, exited the right chest . . . The entry wound was 57/100ths of an inch in diameter. The exit wound was 21/100ths by 24/100ths of an inch. The wound was caused by a bullet from a weapon above a .22 or .25 caliber." The wound resulted from a distant gunshot, one fired twenty-four inches or more away from Oliver. Oliver could have fired six shots from his pistol in the estimated four minutes of time before he died. On cross-examination, Dr. Bell admitted that a person could also go right into shock after such a wound as Lieutenant Oliver suffered.

The next witnesses were Wendy's employees who recounted the events leading up to the shooting. None of them were witnesses to the shooting, and their testimony simply described the events that took place inside the Wendy's throughout the robbery and Philip's leaving the restaurant.

Then there was the testimony of Officer Aubrey Stoddard. His testimony described a struggle between Workman and Oliver, but he said he did not actually see Lieutenant Oliver shot. Although Stoddard was wounded in the arm and then shot at again by Workman, he said he never fired his own weapon. This accounting was unchallenged by defense counsel.

Upon cross-examination by the public defender, Stoddard said he had no knowledge of Oliver striking Workman with a flashlight. He also thought Officer Parker came around later, but he didn't remember if Parker had a weapon. Stoddard did remember Steve Craig coming over to help him after he was wounded.

It had become clear at this point that the state was operating on the theory that only two shooters were involved in the crime—and the two shooter theory became the *only* one considered. According to the state's proposition, the only persons firing weapons were Lieutenant Oliver and Philip Workman. This theory was promulgated despite indications from Wendy's employees and other witnesses at the crime scene, who were not called to testify, that *a lot of shots* were fired. The problem with the two shooter theory was that no police officer actually saw Lieutenant Oliver get shot. Hence the testimony of a man named Harold Davis seemed critical.

Harold Davis, an African American male, took the witness stand after Stoddard's testimony and before that of Officer Steve Parker. He revealed that he had actually seen Philip Workman shoot Oliver from a distance of no more than three feet. His testimony was critical to the prosecution's case, since neither Stoddard nor Parker had seen Workman shoot Lieutenant Oliver; they merely heard shots fired.

Unbeknownst to the jury, Harold Davis had contacted the Memphis police about the slaying of Ronald Oliver at 12:25 p.m. on August 6, 1981. Police asked Davis to come in to talk, a police officer named Curry Todd brought him down to the precinct, and at 2:30 P.M. that day he gave a statement to the police: "As I got out of the car and went up to the door, I saw this man coming out of the back coming toward the door with a gun in his hand." Davis retreated to his car and climbed into it. "I heard the policeman tell the man to stop, and then I saw the man turn around and start shooting at the police. I saw the police return fire and I saw one policeman go down. Then I heard some more shots, and I saw the guy who shot the policeman run across the auto parts lot and he was holding his head. Then a bunch of police showed up at the crime scene." Harold Davis was not cross-examined by the defense after repeating his statement to the jury.

At the time of Workman's trial, Tennessee was four years into the administration of its new death penalty law passed by the state legislature in 1977. (The death penalty had been declared unconstitutional from 1972 to 1976 but had recently been reinstated in Tennessee.) Several of the cases prosecuted under that law and sent to death row involved prisoners who were tried in Memphis: Richard Austin, Bill Groseclose, Ronald Rickman, and, in July 1982, Gary Cone. The decisions on all of these cases were reversed on appeal due to ineffective trial lawyers, but Philip Workman was not so fortunate. As he watched his defense lawyers in action (or perhaps more accurately, non-action), he had a feeling of growing alarm.

Philip Workman had seen no black person in the Wendy's restaurant or in the parking lot during or after the robbery. Nor had his defense team questioned Dr. Bell or challenged him with their own forensic expert. They had not even conducted a vigorous cross-examination of the medical examiner. Indeed, it appeared to Workman that his lawyers had accepted the state's hypothesis that he killed Officer Oliver even though he could not recall doing it. By not challenging Dr. Bell or the mysterious Harold Davis, Workman's lawyers were conceding the state's case. Their counsel to him—to admit his drug use and ask for mercy—seemed a meager defense when faced with the state's relentless effort to seek the death penalty.

The trial resumed on March 26, 1982, with the testimony of Officer Steve Parker. He described how after receiving the call from dispatch and arriving at the Wendy's, he went to the south doors and found them locked. He looked in the drive-in window to see if he could see anyone: "I was mainly looking for—they had just read out on roll call that day that there was a man—a black male robbing only Wendy's and McDonald's and who hid in the bathroom at closing time and took an employee hostage when they come in to clean the bathroom."

Officer Parker then told of hearing gunshots. He described running around the restaurant and discovering Lieutenant Oliver, saying, "It looked like he was just falling back and hitting the ground. I just saw his shoulder and head hit the ground and he just kind of bounced, you know, just a little bit, arched his back and settled real still."

Parker then recalled seeing Workman and Stoddard struggling. He saw Stoddard shot, and he yelled at the shooter. "I was trying to pull my pistol out, but my holster had slid forward and I had missed a thumb snap on my holster, so I started yelling at the white male [meaning Workman]."

According to Parker, despite the presence of three police officers and being struck on the head, Workman escaped with bullets flying from only Oliver's gun. Neither Stoddard nor Parker admitted firing their weapons. The two shooter theory, Oliver and Workman, was completed with Parker's testimony.

Officer T. L. Cobb testified that he arrived at the Wendy's and had been there a minute or less when he heard one shot that sounded like a truck backfiring. Cobb said there was a "slight pause, maybe half a second or so, then I heard two more. It sounded like maybe a muffled sound, still a loud sound and then a series of shots after that, approximately eight or ten, twelve shots altogether."

Officer Cobb went to Stoddard, who was lying on his back in the parking lot. Stoddard gave Cobb a description of Workman, and Cobb broadcasted that information and requested an ambulance. He then ran over to Lieutenant Oliver and performed first aid until the ambulance arrived. Cobb rode with Oliver in the ambulance to the hospital with Oliver's gun at his feet. He kept the gun with him until he arrived at the hospital and determined that all six rounds had been shot. While at the hospital, he was given Oliver's and Stoddard's clothes. He also eventually obtained Philip's clothing.

After Officer Cobb's testimony concluded, the defense asked the court to force the state to reveal evidence that Workman had been hit on the head with a flashlight by Lieutenant Oliver. The defense lawyer handed a document to the court, saying:

> [This is] an interview with a witness on the indictment . . . Garland Null, and according to Mr. Null, and I think he's probably a teenager who was nearby and heard the shots, went to the scene and actually saw the defendant running away with his hand to his head, and according to Mr. Null, a blond-headed man in a pickup truck [Steve Craig] saw this, involving the struggle between Lieutenant Oliver, Officer Stoddard, and the defendant, and this man also stated that he saw the shooting.
>
> Null stated that he heard either from people on the scene or from the blond-headed man that the shooting resulted from a struggle between the defendant, Officer Stoddard, and Lieutenant Oliver in which the defendant was struck by a flashlight by one of the officers.

The court ruled against the admissibility of any of this testimony, because it was deemed hearsay. Craig was in the hospital with appendicitis and refused to talk to the defense. The district attorney stated that neither Jeff Rickard nor Garland Null was at the scene at the time of the crime but showed up later. The remainder of the prosecution's testimony came from officers who had arrived at the scene of the crime and described what they did upon arrival.

Then the testimony of Terry Willis was presented. Willis was employed by Holiday Auto Parts, located next door to the Wendy's restaurant. Willis was the assistant manager and had worked there "for four years." He described his discovery of August 6, 1981: "At first I thought it was an automotive type bearing, but it turned out to be a round [of ammunition]. I found it between the parking lots of Holiday and Wendy's, just middle ways between the buildings. At the time, I was checking a car to see what problem it had." Willis identified the round he found about a foot or less from the curb. "At first I put it in my toolbox and then I contacted the North Precinct and they sent an officer out there again."

Although the entire crime scene had been staked out the previous night and morning, complete with yellow tape and markers where evidence was found, no police officer had found this bullet. The pristine bullet was logged in to the property room at 2:25 P.M. on August 6, 1981. Mr. Willis was not cross-examined by the defense.

FBI agent Gerald Wilkes testified that the bullet Willis found had been fired from Philip Workman's gun. Wilkes also stated that if the bullet had gone through Oliver's body, it would exhibit mutilation and not be in pristine condition. The fact was that there was no blood, tissue, or fabric on the bullet.

Philip Workman then took the stand, having been instructed by his lawyers to be contrite for a murder he could not recall committing. He described leaving the restaurant, talking to Lieutenant Oliver, fleeing when he saw additional police cars, stumbling over the curb and falling, and surrendering with his hands in the air and his back to Oliver. He said that when Lieutenant Oliver had asked, "Where is your gun?" he pulled it from his waistband and raised it up in a surrender motion. He was struck on the head and the gun discharged. "The next thing I know, I just heard the noise, the gunfire, the flame from the barrel, and I turned to it, and I guess I shot again . . . It was coming from my right."(This was determined to be the shot that struck Stoddard in the arm).

In the state's closing argument, prosecutor Peterson announced:

> What I'm going to do with Lt. Oliver's [picture] so [he] can perhaps look at you all and listen what we're saying, I'll just set his picture right there, because I feel that he has an opportunity to be here just as much as Mr. Workman.
>
> And what did Mr. [Harold] Davis say in regards to the tussle that he saw took place? Mr. Stoddard gets shot and spins away, Lt. Oliver and the defendant . . . [Mr. Workman] coolly and deliberately pulled this trigger and sent the bullet down this barrel and into the body of that man right there [referring to the Oliver picture while aiming the gun at the picture].

According to prosecutor Strother, Philip's testimony was that he had indeed shot Officer Oliver. (Actually, the closest Workman came to such a statement was from lack of memory and when under hostile cross-examination he stated that he "guessed" he did it.) There were only two shooters, Strother asserted, two people who fired weapons: Oliver and Workman. "Officer Stoddard never fired his weapon. Officer Parker never fired his weapon. Did Lt. Oliver take and turn his revolver around and shoot himself? Well, that's ridiculous. That's ridiculous. So who shot and killed Lt. Oliver? Philip Workman."

Peterson reminded the jury that in his opening argument he had told them they would hold the bullet that killed Lieutenant Oliver. Harold Davis, he said, had corroborated that this bullet was the one, because he saw Workman shoot Oliver. Peterson then passed to the jury the pristine bullet that Terry Willis had found. This was the bullet that FBI agent Wilkes had testified was from Philip's gun but showed no indication of passing through someone because it displayed no fiber, blood trace, or hair. It was a clean bullet. Peterson closed his argument by urging the jury to make a decision without sympathy to anyone.

Once the state concluded its case and had no more witnesses, it was possible to objectively consider the level of proof that had been offered, if one had defense counsel who were inclined to do so. Unfortunately for Philip Workman, his court-appointed defense counsel had accepted the state's theory of the case, done no investigation, brought in no expert witnesses, and left unchallenged a number of important points that were certainly worth pondering:

1. The prosecution's careful orchestration of placing the testimony of the sole eyewitness to the shooting, Harold Davis, between that of Officers Stoddard and Parker made for good dramatic impact. But who was Harold Davis? And where had he been at the Wendy's? No witness had seen an African American at the scene of the crime. Not even the police testified to seeing him there, and surely they would have noted the presence of an African American male after their alert at roll call. Nor was Davis's car observed by anyone or included in either the crime scene diagram or pictures taken of the scene.

2. The bullet found by Terry Willis was truly a magic bullet. It had been unobserved by crime scene investigators, although Willis testified that it was clearly visible near the curb. And despite the state's allegation that it was the fatal bullet that had killed Lieutenant Oliver, FBI agent Wilkes testified to its pristine condition. Although it supposedly came from Philip's gun, there was no blood, hair, cloth, or any indication that the bullet had penetrated a human being.

3. If there were only two shooters, how did shotgun pellets get into Philip's buttocks? And what about Steve Craig, who saw Parker fire his shotgun several times at Workman?

4. If Workman was not struck in the head by the police, why did he need seven sutures to his head at the hospital? And why was Garvin Null, who saw Philip bleeding and holding his head, never called as a witness?

5. A photo of the crime scene taken by a *Memphis Commercial Appeal* photographer showed a cup covering an unknown object. This could have been the fatal bullet fired by a policeman shooting at Philip but accidentally killing Oliver. However, this cup was never mentioned in police reports as being in the scene, and the only indication it actually was there came from the picture taken by an independent photographer.

6. Where was the shell casing from Philip's gun that Parker had stated was fired at him as Workman fled? Philip had only four bullets. One was ejected, and the other three casings were found elsewhere.

7. What about the crime scene witnesses who were not police officers and not interviewed or deposed and hence did not testify: Steve Craig, Jeff Rickard, and Garvin Null?

8. Two pieces of "evidence" had been entered in the police log book at 2:25 P.M. on August, 6, 1981: (1) the statement made by the mysterious Harold Davis, who claimed he had witnessed the homicide, and (2) the magic bullet that had suddenly appeared courtesy of Terry Willis, who claimed he initially thought what was obviously a bullet was a "ball bearing," only to later realize it was a bullet. Rather than new pieces of evidence, this seems to be the weaving together of an explanation for Lieutenant Oliver's killing that steers inquiring minds from a "friendly fire" explanation by pointing the finger at Philip Workman.

If there had been a diligent defense effort and prosecution not dedicated to proving "friendly fire" was not an option in the police officer's death, these and other elements of the case against Philip would have exploded the case against him. Unfortunately, he had ineffective counsel who accepted the prosecutors' theory of the case as fact, even though much of it was created out of whole cloth. Hence Philip's later appeals would be circumscribed by the trial court record, which was largely a story created to hide the unpleasant fact that one Memphis policeman had accidentally shot and killed a colleague.

***

Philip's trial consisted of two stages: (1) the guilt/innocent phase, and (2) the sentencing phase. He was found guilty of capital murder at the conclusion of the first phase of the trial after the jury retired at 10:50 A.M. on March 30, 1982. The jury returned the guilty verdict at 12:05 P.M., a mere seventy-five minutes after they had started deliberating about Philip's life. The sentencing phase began immediately.

The district attorney reiterated the state's theory, now substantiated as fact by the guilty verdict: "Two members of the Memphis Police Department halt, trying to take him into custody, having him in custody in their grasp, and he breaks away and shoots and kills."

In the opening statement by the defense counsel in the sentencing phase, the lawyer asked the jury to withhold judgment, saying, "The proof will show mitigating circumstances." However, the defense presented no proof to the jury in the sentencing phase. The only testimony was from police officers. Officers Parker and Stoddard testified that Workman had shot at Parker, thereby providing a basis for the aggravating circumstance of the "great risk of death." In contradiction to an earlier statement given to police, Parker testified that he saw Stoddard trying to get away from Workman.

The prosecutor closed his presentation in the sentencing phase with these words:

> The defense could have brought in, they could have testified, they could have brought in anything in the world to prove mitigation. They're not limited by those statutory creations. We are. Anything in the world, and what did they give you? Nothing. Nothing. It's not there.
>
> Go back there, ladies and gentlemen, with no sympathy, no prejudice, and bring back the verdict that truth dictates and justice demands.

After the jury found five aggravating factors and no mitigating circumstances, on March 31, 1982, at 2:35 P.M. Philip Workman was sentenced to death by electrocution.

The Tennessee State Prison opened in western Nashville in 1898. The prison was built with funds authorized by the 1893 legislature in response to the abuse in the convict lease system, which proved to be a form of neo-slavery. By locating a central facility in Nashville where the state's worst prisoners could be sent, convict leasing could be lessened and the antiquated prison on Church Street in downtown Nashville closed. Hence a prison was designed with single cells, one that would put prisoners to work in a safe and secure environment. The population of the new prison in 1898 was 1,403, which consisted of the following: "377 White males, 985 Colored males, 3 White females and 38 Colored females." In time, single cells gave way to double-celling, and in some cases as many as four to a cell, as the model prison of 1898 became an overcrowded, antiquated facility.

By the time Philip Workman arrived at the Tennessee State Prison, known to prisoners as "the Walls," it was an overcrowded and violent place. The facility, an imposing, castle-like edifice, physically resembled the Magic Kingdom of Disney World. An 1898 newspaper description of the prison remained accurate in 1982 when Philip arrived:

> The cells are built of Pikesville sandstone and white brick. Each row of cells [is] fifteen feet from the other walls in either direction, and facing the windows, so that there is not a dark hole in the building. The cells are built of vitrified brick, non-absorbent, and laid in cement and plastered inside and out with cement and alabastine. The floor is cement, laid on arches and steel beams. Each cell has a lattice door, made in one quarter inch steel mesh, for light and ventilation. The cells are of an average size of 6'x8'x8'.

Many citizens went to bed easier knowing that the prisoner was in his cell and could not escape. More important, they could forget about the prisoner—out of sight, out of mind.

In 1975 the prisoners conducted a major rebellion against prison conditions (recounted in *Last Rights*) and thus were no longer out of sight or out of mind. Litigation resulted from the woeful conditions and the violence in the overcrowded facility, one of the most violent in the United States. Ultimately, the entire prison system and the Tennessee State Prison would be declared unconstitutional and placed under the supervision of the federal court with a "special master," someone appointed by a judge to ensure that judicial orders are followed. It was into this milieu that Philip Workman was transported after his sentence of death in Memphis on March 31, 1982.

Although Philip did not recall killing anyone, he was nevertheless guilt-ridden for "creating the scene," as he put it. He knew it was his act of robbery that had sparked the ensuing events. What he did not know was that under Tennessee law, following the case of *State v. Severs*, he was not guilty of felony murder if he did not fire the bullet that killed Lieutenant Oliver.

When Workman arrived at the Walls, death row had moved to a single-story, stand-alone structure in the main yard—Unit 6. Unit 6 was a former honor dorm that had been retrofitted to house death row and the electric chair. The initial men sent to death row in 1977 were put in "the hole" in Unit 1 with nothing but a Bible. Then they were moved to Unit 6 when its renovation was completed.

Unit 6 was subject to its own lawsuit in the mid-1980s—*Groseclose v. Dutton*—in which federal court judge John Nixon found the conditions in the unit unconstitutional. Unit 6 consisted of four corridors, or "walks," in the parlance of the prison. The two exterior walks had several small openings at the top of the exterior concrete walls, which allowed for fresh air in the summer but also frigid air in the winter. The openings also allowed a measure of natural light to enter the unit. The interior walks, however, were without natural light and thus dungeon-like in their darkness. On these four walks the condemned of Tennessee were housed.

The electric chair was housed at the end of 1 Walk, so that walk provided two fewer cells for prisoners. Each of the other three walks had thirteen cells. The electric chair and adjacent temporary morgue, where the body would be kept after execution until removed by the medical examiner, were snugly configured into 1 Walk.

Exercise was provided for in a large caged area behind Unit 6. The men could go outside in small groups from their walk for a specified time. Meals were served to each prisoner in his cell.

Philip Workman was the twentieth prisoner to become part of Tennessee's death row since the state law bringing the return of the death penalty had been enacted in 1977.

The Fourth Circle

I first met Philip Workman while he was housed on death row at the Tennessee State Prison. The meeting was not noteworthy, and we did not really connect until years later when the Walls was closed and Riverbend Maximum Security Institution opened in 1989. He was one of the guys I talked with as I visited the walks of the prison's death row. I did not do this often, since my responsibility as director of the Southern Coalition on Jails and Prisons(SCJP) took me to every death row across the South. The Tennessee project of the SCJP, the Southern Prison Ministry, with which I initially affiliated with in 1974, was responsible for death row in Tennessee.

Kenny Campbell, who had come to death row in 1981, befriended Philip Workman. Kenny was from eastern Tennessee and had an easy personality. He was established on the row by the time Philip arrived in the spring of 1982 and was placed next to Kenny on 3 Walk, one of the interior walks.

When Kenny had passed by Philip's cell, he introduced himself and they shook hands through the bars. Philip had a big smile on his face. When they discussed their situations, Philip told Kenny he'd been wrongly convicted of killing a police officer in Memphis. He also told Kenny that police had beaten him on the head and that he had no memory of the shooting.

Kenny noticed that Philip was a deeply caring man. He helped out other prisoners when he could and was sensitive to others' needs. As Philip and Kenny became close friends, they shared their lives.

By 1984 Kenny and Philip had been on death row for about two years. Kenny later wrote about his experiences with his friend.

> I watched Philip go from bad to worse as time progressed. I mean in the sense of emotional despair. I'm sure he wasn't the only one, I wasn't very happy myself, but sometimes it's easier for us to see the condition of others than we can see our own condition. He would talk about how he never shot that officer in Memphis, about how he missed his family, especially his young daughter at the time [Michelle]. I felt sorry for him, but what could I do? I thought of one thing I could try—making wine. [Prisoners often made wine out of various ingredients they could obtain through the commissary.] I figured I could cheer alot [*sic*] of us up around there. I proceeded to make ten gallons a month and, for the times we were drinking, at least the troubles were more tolerable. We had so much wine that they use [*sic*] to let us carry two liter bottles of water to the yard, so we would get the green liter bottles of 7 Up or Sprite because the bottles were green in color and not see through so when we would go to the yard instead of our bottles filled with water they would be filled with wine. We never did get busted for that.

One of the funnier events Kenny described happened when he was sharing his wine with the other guys on death row. One prisoner, Ron, became quite tipsy. Kenny tells the story:

> We were all pretty tipsy, all of a sudden I hear Ron telling two officers that he needed to go to the hospital. I thought, oh no, their [*sic*] going to bust him, then the rest of us. I still had about five gallons of wine left. I was thinking—Ron please! just lie down! Let those

officers go! But I'll be darn if they weren't escorting him to the hospital. Here he came out of his cell with only pajamas and a blue house coat on, smoking a pipe and had a 16 ounce glass of wine in his hand. I couldn't believe it! Here they came past my cell, Ron grinning like a possum. "See ya later, brother," he yelled. When they left I hollered to Ron's friend Gerald. I said hey Gerald they just took Ron out of here to go to the hospital. I said he was dressed like Hugh Hefner and had a 16 ounce glass of wine. That Yankee bastard! . . . Well, about a half hour later, here they come back, same officers, same Ron, pajamas, housecoat, slippers, pipe and wine. He got to my cell door and whispered, as if the guards right behind couldn't hear, "Good wine, bro. You got any more?" I said, "Ron, please just go lay down!" The guards put him back in his cell, they were just smiling—they knew that Ron was drunk and that there was a whole lot of us drinking, but they never said a word. I reckon they figured, they're in cells by themselves and, they're all waiting to die, let them drink a little.

Another story involving Kenny and his wine found him with Philip drinking steadily in the afternoon.

By about 4:00 P.M. we were pretty well three sheets to the wind. Just about the time I decided it was time for me to call it quits and lie down, here comes Philip with an officer. "What's going on?" I said. Philip said, "I'm going out to do an interview (with a local TV station)." I said, "Are you okay?" I new [*sic*] I wasn't, I could barely stand, much less do an interview, and I knew he was about the same. "How do I look?" he said. Now part of me wanted to talk him out of it, but the other part wanted to watch him on T.V. so I could see him drunk doing this interview. That second part of me won out, "Oh, you look good man," I said. He said, "Do I?" I said, "Oh, yeah, they'll never notice." Off he went. I thought, Oh Lord, what have I done? But I couldn't help smiling. I started drinking black coffee, forcing myself to stay awake. I had to see that interview on the news. In about half an hour, Philip comes back, still lit up, but he's mad and fussing a bit. I didn't know what that was about until I heard Philip say "I'm taking this fan in my cell."

We didn't have any windows or air conditioning in the unit so it did get unbearably hot! The only thing we had was this big giant fan that set on a metal stand. So the next thing I know, Philip unplugs the fan and drags it in his cell. To my amazement the guards never stopped him. I was thinking, I wonder if he's going to plug that thing in—just about that time I hear the whir of that Big Giant Fan. I stuck my mirror out the bars to see. It looked like an F-5 tornado was in Philip's cell. I saw papers, all kinds, blowing through the bars. I saw toilet paper—I saw bandanas, pencils, pens etc. etc. I saw Philip trying to grab stuff through the bars. Then I heard him say, "Ah, s—. I don't give a damn!" He left that fan going and went to sleep, all that stuff lying in the hall everywhere!

Well, that night on the ten o'clock news they announced an interview with death row inmate Philip Workman . . . Philip was still asleep and missed it. I waited, half smiling, half afraid to look. Well, they showed the interview and to my surprise, what Philip was saying actually made sense. He was talking mostly about the injustice of the Justice System and, he was correct. I was surprised by the lucidness of his speech, but I still got a laugh because "I" knew how drunk he really was. Plus, in the interview, he kept leaning further and further back as if he was in a Lazy Boy lounge chair or something. I was cracking up! After the interview, Philip had gotten angry thinking about what he was saying in that interview about the so called "Justice System"—that's why he was mad when he came back and the big fan incident occurred.

The next day, Philip asked, "Was I on the news?" "Yeah, I watched it," I said. "How did I do?"he said. I said, "Actually you made good sense," I said. "How did I look?" he said. "Could you tell I was drunk?" I said, "Oh, no, you looked good, straight as an arrow." I wasn't about to tell about the Lazy Boy look! . . .

After that, a few started getting busted for wine here and there, and by 1985 it just seemed to come to an end. I guess we'd all had our fill by then.

By 1985 Philip had made friends and was part of the community of death row at the Walls. But he was also full of despair, because his case—a conviction for killing a cop—meant certain execution. His mind began to think of alternatives to that end. Kenny Campbell recalls the time clearly:

It was the summer of 1985, three years now for Philip and I on death row. A few more laughs, but, mostly, a little more despair, a little more depression, and a little more desperation. When one is on death row, it is different than the regular guy doing time. Let's say a person has ten years to do—well, it seems a ways off; however, every day he wakes up he knows he's one day closer to getting out, that ten year sentence will eventually run out. It is not like that for a death row inmate because each day you wake up, part of you is glad you're still around, but the other part of you says your [sic] one day closer to your day of death—not a release date.

I remember that at that time Philip's television was on the blink, so I was letting him use mine. He hollered at me later that night, "Hey, Kenny! I'm going to court in Memphis tomorrow," he said. I said, "You'll probably be gone for awhile, won't you?" He said, "Yeah, I probably will." I said, "Well, leave your cell door open so I can go in and out and get my television." He said, "Okay, I will." The next day I woke up and Philip was already gone . . .

I was watching the local news that night and, to my surprise, it said death row inmate Philip Workman tried to escape from custody. I thought, well, at least they didn't say he was killed . . . The news showed an old picture of Philip, the vehicle they were in, and the transportation officers, who looked pretty shook up. Well, they didn't bring Philip right back . . . probably the police took him on to Memphis for court. When Philip came back a few weeks later he told me the whole story.

When Philip left [for court], among some other items he also had a double barrel .32 cal. derringer. Now I know someone reading this would say, See, he had a gun, he was violent, he was a killer. But that's because like the radio legend Paul Harvey use [sic] to say, they didn't know "the rest of the story." I do, because I was there myself. The real story is that there was an inmate there at the time being housed on death row, [who] wasn't under sentence of death. That inmate had the gun originally, and his intention was to kill three or four other inmates with that gun. This man had already killed more than one in prison, so it wasn't a joke. Anyway, when Philip found out about it, he went to the guy and convinced him to let him hold the gun. Philip told him, "That way, if anyone gets busted, it will be me and not you, and when you're ready to use it, I'll give it to you. Philip only told him that to keep him from killing those other inmates. Then later Philip told the guy the guards had found the gun. It wasn't true, but it worked, the guy believed it. So that is the real story of how the gun came to be and how Philip ended up with it.

Back to Philip coming back from court. I said, "Philip, what the heck happened? . . ." He said, "Kenny, I'm sorry about that . . .when I left here . . . I knew I wasn't going to hurt anyone. But I told myself that I would either be free or dead," he said. "I'd either get away or they would kill me." He told me he his plan was to bluff the officers with the gun, have them to pull the car over, then have the officer driving to handcuff the lady officer to the steering wheel, then come back and let him out.

Well, somewhere on the way to Memphis, Philip got out of his handcuffs, pulled the gun out just like he said, and told them to pull over. He told me that as they started to pull over, instead of coming to a stop, he said, they just kept rolling real slow. He said, "I was telling them to stop, but they still didn't . . . I knew they were up to something but what could I do, I wasn't really going to shoot anybody . . ." The officers ended up bailing out of the car and rolling away from it, leaving Philip trapped in the car . . . The State Police came [Kenny couldn't recall the details of how they'd been notified], and they never ask [*sic*] Philip to give up or anything else. They just started firing his gun at Philip . . . Philip said, "I was hollering, 'I surrender. I surrender,' but they just kept firing," he said. "What could I do? The windows [wouldn't come down and the doors wouldn't open] . . . All I could do was duck for cover . . ." He said, "Kenny, I don't know how they missed me," he said. "There was bullet holes from the ceiling to the floorboard," he said. "God had to be watching over me."

Well, after it was over they made the officers out to be hero's [*sic*], they both got promoted. Philip said, " I noticed they left out the part where one of them was so scared, they threw up all over the car and the part where I could have shot them if I'd really wanted to."

. . . [Later on Philip] looked at me and said, "I've thought of another escape plan for you and me this time." I said, "Oh, yeah." He said, "Yeah, but it involves you loosing [*sic*] about sixty pounds." I said, "Philip, I love you but that's too desperate." I said, "I like to eat too much. I'm not going. Besides, it's fried chicken night." He said, "I'll be damned!" But he let it go. From then till 1987 there would be times that we would discuss various way's [*sic*] of trying to escape, but we never did attempt it. Like the wine making, it just seemed to taper off, then come to a complete halt.

On August 8, 1986, Kenny and Philip made ready to go out to the yard for exercise. Philip told Kenny, "I'm going to watch the sunset tonight." Kenny looked at Philip intently. "Man, you can't do that. They always lock us back up before the sunset." Philip just repeated, "I'm gonna watch the sunset."

Since it was summertime, when the sun set late, this meant Philip was intending to observe the sun going down behind the walls of the castle-like prison, a sight he had not seen in the five-plus years he had been on death row. The men on 3 Walk who wanted to exercise left their cells for the yard.

On the yard, everything went normally. Some guys lifted weights, others shot basketball, still others just talked, enjoying the sunshine after the dungeon-like oppression of 3 Walk. The guards called out to everyone that it was time to come in. The prisoners began assembling near the door that would lead them back to 3 Walk. Kenny looked at Philip, who didn't move.

"Kenny, I'm staying, like I told you. I want to see the sunset. You go on ahead," Philip said.

"Philip, man, the goon squad will come and beat the hell out of you," Kenny responded.

A third prisoner, overhearing the conversation, decided he would stay as well. Soon all of 3 Walk had headed back to their cells except Philip, Kenny, and the other man who had decided to stay. The guards returned and called out, "Okay, you three, come on. It's time to go."

Philip eyed the sun shining brightly, not yet setting, and said, "I'm staying for the sunset." Kenny and the other prisoner both said, "Me, too."

The guard repeated, "Come on, here. If you don't come, I'll get the tactical squad. You know what that means." But the three prisoners stayed put.

By the time the tactical squad assembled outside the door to the yard, the third prisoner had changed his mind. He hollered, "I'm coming." He then headed toward the door to the yard, which was unlocked, and disappeared toward 3 Walk. Philip and Kenny remained. Once the other prisoner was locked down, the squad reassembled. "Workman, Campbell, this is your last chance. Come out or we're coming in." The goon squad was equipped with billy clubs, a large shield, and enough personnel to whip Philip and Kenny within an inch of their lives.

Philip kept looking at the sun. It was disappearing behind the walls of the prison. As it finally dropped out of sight, he turned and said, "I'm ready. I'm coming in." Kenny accompanied him.

Philip Workman had seen the sunset.

STATE OF TENNESSEE
DEPARTMENT OF CORRECTION
DIVISION OF ADULT SERVICES

Tennessee State Penitentiary

STATION A
NASHVILLE, TENNESSEE 37219-5255

August 11, 1986

MEMORANDUM

TO: Kenneth Campbell, #96392

FROM: Michael Dutton, Warden

RE: Exercise Restriction (8-11-86 to 8-16-86)

On August 8, 1986, you and two (2) other inmates refused to come off the exercise yard in Unit VI. Because of this reason, you are being restricted from the exercise yard for a period of five days beginning August 11, 1986, and extending through August 16, 1986.

At the end of this period of time, I will review your behavior and make a decision as to whether this restriction should be continued.

Michael Dutton

MD/ba

cc: Institutional File
     Unit VI OIC
     File

THE FIFTH CIRCLE

On December 30, 1986, Kenny Campbell was a lonely and despondent man. After contemplating his mother's death for seven months, he had no energy to continue to live, since he had told himself he was staying alive for his mother's sake. He had carefully harbored razor blades to slit his wrists just after midnight. He did not want to see a new year.

As he prepared to kill himself, Kenny knelt for one last prayer. His mother had been devoutly religious, and he felt he owed one last prayer for her sake. But there was no answer to his imploring God as to whether he should live or die. He had just begun to rise when suddenly he felt like his soul was seized and lit with fire. Later he described the experience by quoting from the Bill Gaither gospel song "He Touched Me": "Shackled by a heavy burden beneath a load of guilt and shame / then the hand of Jesus touched me and now I am no longer the same."

The next day when he went to the yard, Kenny carried a small New Testament with him. He could hardly wait to share his experience with Philip. But when he saw Philip, he could see that his friend was acutely depressed. He called to Philip, "Come over here."

As Philip approached Kenny, he noticed that Campbell was weeping. Not knowing they were tears of joy rather than sorrow, Philip asked, "What's wrong?"

Kenny responded, "Nothing is wrong." Then, because Kenny felt like Philip's depression might make him unwilling to hear about his religious experience, he decided to cast it into the form of a dream and said, "I had a dream about you last night."

Philip's response was brief: "You did?" Kenny started to tell Philip about what God had told him, to share it with Philip, but Philip said, "Good, I don't want to hear about it."

Kenny was crushed that his friend would not listen, and Philip stopped speaking to him. When Kenny went by Philip's cell, Philip would pull the curtains on him. (Prisoners were allowed to make curtains out of blankets at the Walls.) This routine of Philip closing Kenny out went on for four months, until sometime in the spring of 1987.

One evening Kenny was lying on his bunk when he heard a call: "Kenny!" Stunned, he lay there. "Kenny!" the voice came again. Campbell thought of Samuel's being called by God, not knowing where the call was coming from (I Samuel 3:8). A third time, louder, the voice called, "Kenny!" This time Kenny jumped up and ran to the back of his cell, climbed up on the commode, and called out to the voice he finally recognized as Philip's.

"How you doing?" Kenny called.

Philip responded, "Where you at? . . . Come to your cell door."

Kenny peered out the bars and saw Philip in the adjacent cell.

Philip said, "I bet you don't know what I've been doing over here."

"I don't know.," Kenny replied. "There's no telling what you've been doing."

Philip chuckled and told his friend, "I've been reading the Bible."

Kenny instantaneously responded, "No, you haven't!"

"Yes, I have. I read the whole New Testament last night."

Incredulous, Kenny said, "Philip, if you're telling the truth, then I'm glad. But if you're trying to just make fun, it's not funny."

"No, Kenny, I'm serious," Philip insisted. "I had a vision of Jesus last night . . . I was praying last night, and when I looked up I saw a vision of Jesus on the wall . . . Jesus spoke and told me if I wanted to be with Michelle [Philip's daughter], then he was the Way, to come and follow him . . . Kenny, I'll tell you the truth. You know I've been obsessed with the idea of escape and wanting to be with Michelle . . . Jesus made it clear the only way I would see her is if I followed him. From now on, that's what I'm going to do."

Later that day, Kenny and Philip went out to the yard. They were working out with weights. As they did their repetitions, they would call off the name of someone from the Bible and count: "One for Abel—one for Noah—one for Abraham—and so on and so on." They were both on fire for the Lord.

In looking back at that time, Kenny recalled:

> I could see on Philip's face—just as I'm sure he could see on mine—a new hope, a new way to cope with our loneliness, a shared faith in our blessed Saviour. Does that mean we never had another worry? Of course not, we were still human. Does that mean we were perfect from then on and never sinned against God or man? Of course not, to say such a thing would make us a liar, but, what it did mean and it's alot [*sic*]—it meant that we were not just alone with our worries, our fears, our hurts, such as loosing [*sic*] family members, etc. For Jesus promised never to leave us or forsake us, and he doesn't. And when we sinned . . . , it didn't just remain that way. We would go to the Lord in prayer seeking His forgiveness . . . We were no longer alone in our dark and lonely world, we got strength and encouragement from each other and from the Holy Spirit of God.

Philip later detailed his conversion in his self-published book, *Though You Slay Me*:

> After my escape attempt, there wasn't any hope left in me of ever leaving death row alive. I was bottoming out during the year that followed. I had given the escape attempt my best shot and no one had gotten hurt, which I felt good about, and I was still somehow alive. Still, life looked like dead men walking. Death was on my mind a lot. I thought about committing suicide, and about my appeals running out and having to be executed. I even considered dropping my appeals just so I could get it over with. It was a continual raging battle over death and dying. And with all of the other thoughts, I wondered if there really might be some kind of life after death.
>
> During that next year and a half, I had the same dream three times. The first two times were like a nightmare, but the third time turned into an eternal charm. I dreamed that I was trying to build an escape tunnel. It seemed like even though I dug and dug, I could only go straight down and, no matter which other direction I might try to dig, it always continued downward. It kept getting deeper, too, like a deep well. Finally, I gave up digging and from where I was, I sat hunkered down closed in by the sides of the tunnel. As I looked up, a long, thick rope began snaking its way down toward me and stopped right in front of my face a couple of feet away. Of course, in the dream, I thought to myself that this was obviously a trick being played on me by someone and I wasn't going to fall for it. I knew that if I reached out for the rope that it would immediately be yanked back up. I remember smirking to myself at the thought of some nut thinking that I would go for such a game. Then I woke up, and of course, I was still in my cell.

The dream came the second time about six to eight months later and it was exactly the same as the first time. After about eight more months had passed, I had the dream for the third time. That time, again, I was at the bottom of the tunnel, tired, frustrated and bewildered. That stupid trick rope was let down again from the top where my cell was located.

That time, however, the dream lasted longer than the previous two had. I began to study the rope. My attention was caught by it, even though I knew that it was only a trick. I began contemplating the idea of snatching the rope. All at once, without further thought, I grabbed it with both hands and held on. Slowly the rope started pulling me up toward the top on the tunnel and my cell. As I traveled upward, to my amazement, the rope transformed into the arm and hand of JESUS CHRIST.

Immediately upon arriving back at my cell, I woke up from the dream. I literally woke up, I guess we could say. After that experience, I began searching through the Bible that I had before derided and mocked. Some people had claimed that the Bible is a holy book inspired by the Holy Spirit and that God speaks to us through that book. I know that I was drawn by God to discover whether that was true or not.

THE SIXTH CIRCLE

As a result of two lawsuits about conditions of confinement, the initial one statewide and the second one focused on death row—*Grubbs v. Bradley* and *Groseclose v. Dutton*—the Tennessee State Prison was ordered to close. Indeed, the entire prison system was deemed unconstitutional by the federal court. The new Riverbend Maximum Security Institution opened in the fall of 1989 less than ten miles down Cockrill Bend Industrial Road from the Walls.

The prisoners were transferred from the Walls to Riverbend. Death row was the last segment of prisoner population to move. Kenny Campbell and Philip Workman were on 3 Walk, cells 13 and 12. The antiquated death row, a former honor dorm, with no interior light for 2 and 3 Walks and openings in the walls on 1 and 4 Walks that allowed for hot air in the summer and freezing air in the winter to penetrate death row, was history as of October 27, 1989. And so was the indelible smell of dried urine that greeted anyone who walked those death row walks at the Tennessee State Prison.

The old, castle-like facility was swapped for a brave new world of the penitentiary experiment. The units at Riverbend did not have cell blocks or walks. Rather, the men were held in "pods." A vertical strip of sealed plastic, the window for each cell, accounted for a prisoner's only contact with the outside world. The cell door could be closed and was made of solid metal instead of iron bars.

Riverbend used a behavior modification system that divided the prisoners into levels. "A" level allowed for maximum out-of-cell time, which could include working a job, going to the law library or school room, contact visits without shackles, access to the yard (a large cage outside where the wire-mesh roof prevented a high arc on a shot at the basketball goal), and group meals. "B" level was a step down—not as much out-of-cell time, handcuffed during visits, not eligible for a job. "C" was the lowest level, and it was a virtual lockdown. There were no contact visits for the bottom level, and the only out-of-cell time was for recreation. Each prisoner was reviewed after one year to determine if he could move up a level. Infractions would result in a write-up and a trip to the disciplinary board, where it would be decided if the prisoner would lose a level.

Although the new facility was air-conditioned and heated, the hermetically sealed environment of Unit 2, death row, at Riverbend was more formal and restricted than the old death row at the Walls. The recycled air, the total isolation from the remainder of the prison, the inability to touch grass or dirt, and the level system, which was all too easily manipulated by guards with an agenda against a prisoner, led to the general consensus of the prisoners that the old death row at the Walls was preferable to that of Riverbend. It was hard to imagine making wine and having a drunken prisoner parading to the infirmary with a cup of wine in hand at the new death row.

No executions had taken place in Tennessee since 1960, so the electric chair that was transported to Riverbend from 1 Walk at the old death row had to be repaired and reconstructed. The state of Tennessee hired Fred Leuchter to do the job. Leuchter had done work for a lot of Southern death rows, rehabilitating execution equipment, after the U.S. Supreme Court brought back the death penalty. Although he represented himself as an engineer, in reality he had a bachelor's degree in history. He also was someone who did not believe Jews had been killed in the Holocaust. In a trial in Canada of a fellow Holocaust denier, Leuchter testified as an expert witness that he had visited Auschwitz and believed that the claims of mass extermination of Jews were false or exaggerated.

This man was paid seventy-five thousand dollars by the state of Tennessee to rehabilitate the execution equipment at Riverbend. (In 1999 Errol Morris made a fascinating documentary of Leuchter titled *Mr. Death: The Rise and Fall of Fred A. Leuchter Jr.*, and as someone who has visited both Auschwitz and Madjanek, I have no doubt that Leuchter's denial of the Holocaust is erroneous.)

The move from the Walls to Riverbend separated Kenny and Philip. In the new prison, Kenny was in C pod and Philip was in D pod. They did get to exercise at the same time, although they were not in the same large outdoor cages. The D pod prisoners were on one side and those from C pod were on the other, but prisoners could converse through the cage while on the yard. One day, during the course of a conversation in the recreation cage, Philip mentioned to Kenny that he was probably going to get jumped by some guys who were jealous of his phone use and of his visits from his fiancé, a woman he had met when she was visiting another prisoner. Kenny volunteered to transfer into D pod to watch Philip's back. They agreed it would be good if it could be worked out.

In working with a corporal who had transferred from the Walls and whom both Kenny and Philip knew, a meeting was set up several days later to discuss the possibility of Kenny transferring to Philip's pod. The corporal asked Kenny, "So you want to move to D pod?" Kenny nodded his assent and asked, "When can I move?" The corporal replied, "Tonight," and Kenny said, "I'm ready."

Then, to Kenny's surprise and bewilderment, Philip spoke up, saying, "No, I don't think he's ready."

Kenny stared at his friend in disbelief. He then reiterated that he was ready to move.

But Philip held firm, saying, "I think we need to think about it some more. I use the phone a lot and so does he, and that might create a conflict."

Kenny knew that the phone issue was a simple matter the two could work out, so he sensed there must be some other reason Philip did not want him in D pod. Kenny told the corporal, "We probably would have problems over the phone, so I had better stay." The meeting was over and the two men returned to their respective pods.

The next evening on the yard, Kenny asked Philip why he had changed his mind about the move. Philip responded, "I didn't want you to get involved. It's my problem [handling the prisoners who had threatened him] and I have to deal with it."

When Kenny later reflected on this episode, he said he realized that "I was more important to him than his own safety. He was [more] willing to face his ordeal alone than to risk a friend's possible troubles." Kenny went on to say, "There's not a lot of people that would do that or even think of the *other* person like that." It really revealed the quality of Philip's character. Fortunately, the matter that concerned Philip was ironed out without a fight.

***

Philip Workman had decided to marry again. He invited Kenny to the ceremony, which was held in the visiting gallery of Unit 2. The service went as expected until the final prayer after the couple had been pronounced man and wife. As the minister was about to pray, Philip requested, "I'd like my friend Kenny to say a prayer." Although surprised, Kenny was honored and offered a prayer for the newlyweds.

Regular Wednesday and Thursday night worship services for death row were conducted by volunteer ministers from outside the prison. Philip and Kenny attended these services in 1990. While attending one of the services, there was an opportunity to offer prayer. Kenny spoke up and said, " I would like to offer a prayer for my brother, Philip." And he prayed. When he finished the prayer, he looked at Philip, who was moved to tears by Kenny's gesture. It was one of only two times in eighteen years in prison together that Kenny saw Philip weep.

Philip Workman gazes through the non-contact visiting booth on Unit 2 RMSI.

Philip's appeal of his conviction and sentence of death was filed on March 1, 1985, and chugged along through the state system with court-appointed counsel. For the state-level post-conviction appeal—Philip's first opportunity to correct the record of what had occurred at trial—Howard Wagerman was appointed to represent Philip. During the appeal process, however, Philip never met Wagerman, and the appeal brief consisted of a mere ten pages. The argument portion of the brief, wherein a case is made for reversal, consisted of just four pages.

In 1986 the Tennessee legislature enacted a three-year statute of limitations on state post-conviction appeal, so time was of the essence. Paul Morrow, a lawyer at the Capital Case Resource Center of Tennessee, filed pro se appeals (those made on prisoners' behalf without individual lawyers) for all death row prisoners the last week before the new legislative statute took effect, hence ensuring a second state post-conviction proceeding for the prisoners.

Harry Scruggs was appointed for Philip's second post-conviction appeal, which was filed on June 22, 1989. Scruggs had been convicted of money laundering and lost his law license. He reacquired it with the stipulation that he no longer practice criminal law. Indeed, Scruggs had stated in his disciplinary hearing before the bar that he had no desire to practice criminal law and that he would confine his practice to civil law. Nonetheless, he was appointed in 1989 to represent Philip on a death penalty appeal.

If "the machinery of death," as U.S. Supreme Court Justice Harry A. Blackmun put it, churned along spitting out incompetent lawyers to represent death row prisoners, who cared? Certainly no one had cared about Philip's trial and appeal from 1982 through 1989. However, in 1990 the roulette wheel of capital case appointment came to a stop in favor of Philip. After nine years of incompetent and uncaring litigation carried out on his behalf, a new lawyer came on board as co-counsel: Chris Minton. He came to the Capital Case Resource Center in November 1990 and filed an amended state post-conviction petition to Morrow's original pro se petition. One of Minton's first acts was to make a public records request seeking access to the police file, district attorney file, and any other pertinent information concerning Philip's trial. This was one of the first requests made under the new Tennessee Public Records Act (TPRA), so the prosecution did not know how to respond except to provide what was asked for. Based on the information he found in the TPRA request, Minton amended the post-conviction petition in state court, before Judge John P. Colton Jr. in Memphis. When Minton journeyed to Memphis for a status conference on the petition before Judge Colton, he was handed the decision in the case. Assistant district attorney John Campbell was also present.

By this time, Minton was impressed by the fact that his client's story was consistent whereas the stories of the police, district attorney, and judges involved in the case kept changing. The information obtained through the public records act revealed contradictions in the police log and trial statements. It also raised questions about the so-called eyewitness, Harold Davis, whose presence was not recorded in police notes or crime scene drawings. But it was also clear from Judge Colton's preemptory dismissal of the appeal that Memphis authorities would grant no relief to Philip.

The next alternative for Philip was federal court. On July 18, 1994, a federal habeas corpus petition was filed upon completion of the appeal in state court. If a "colorable claim" of innocence or a material fact that would have affected Philip's conviction could be found, he was entitled to a hearing in federal court. Chris Minton had unearthed enough contradictory claims and inconsistencies in the state's position to deserve such a hearing in federal court. By the time Minton filed Philip's federal court petition, he had established the following issues from trial court proceedings:

- Memphis police officer Parker's testimony at trial—a graphic description of Lieutenant Oliver dying from what he believed to be a shot from Philip's gun—contradicted his initial statement at 2:10 A.M. on the night of the crime when he stated he did not see Philip shoot Oliver but did see him shoot Stoddard in the arm.
- The medical examiner for the state of Georgia, Dr. Kris Sperry, provided an expert report that Lieutenant Oliver's wounds were dramatically inconsistent with wounds created by ammunition that Philip shot.
- Witness statements and police reports demonstrated that Harold Davis was not present to witness Lieutenant Oliver's shooting.
- Witness statements, police reports, and medical records demonstrated that persons other than Lieutenant Oliver and Philip fired weapons.
- Witness statements, police reports, and medical records demonstrated that Philip ran into the Holiday Auto Parts lot, where police bludgeoned him.
- The defense's evidence demonstrated that Davis, Stoddard, and Parker had testified falsely.
- Substantial evidence existed that prior to the shooting of Lieutenant Oliver, Philip surrendered and was bludgeoned by police, and in the ensuing confusion another police officer, not Philip, shot Lieutenant Oliver.
- The state withheld evidence and knowingly presented perjured testimony to obtain Philip's conviction.

THE EIGHTH CIRCLE

After the prisoners' move from the Walls to Riverbend, the process of adapting to their new living environment began. It was an adjustment for everyone except the death row prisoners, who already knew each other well. For them, it was like moving from one village location to another: the social structure remained intact; it was just the living conditions that changed. The guys would joke about some of the guards trying to adjust. The veteran guards for the most part had developed a "been there, done that" attitude at the Walls. For some of the newer guards, however, it was a more difficult adjustment, and the prisoners spoke about not only "breaking the unit in" but "breaking the guards in" as well.

Philip Workman was nearing the end of a decade of death row incarceration. He was confined to his second death row. He dealt with the ups and downs of death row living as well as most. Yet for almost ten years he had felt guilty for the death of Lt. Ronald Oliver. Then, one day in 1991, a visit from his lawyer Chris Minton totally altered Philip's understanding of what happened on the night of August 5, 1982, in Memphis, Tennessee.

Minton went out to the prison to detail for Philip the evidence that had been uncovered showing that his client did not shoot Lieutenant Oliver. Philip sat there listening. Not happy, not joyous, just absorbing the information. Minton later recalled an almost quizzical expression on Philip's face, "kind of like a dog that cocks his head to the side when he hears an unexpected noise."

Kenny Campbell recalled talking to Philip shortly after Minton's visit. It was out in the exercise cage at Riverbend. Philip told Campbell, "Kenny, I didn't kill that police officer. He was shot by one of his own." Kenny wanted to hear more, and Philip filled him in on what Minton had told him the investigation had uncovered. Now it was just a matter of finding a court to set the record straight and trying to obtain some justice in the case—a task each of them knew was no easy matter, since the trial court record almost always controlled the outcome of death penalty cases.

The filing of the federal habeas corpus petition—*Philip R. Workman v. Ricky Bell, warden*—in July 1994 triggered the best hope for Philip to win relief on the newly discovered evidence. The petition was filed before Judge Julia Gibbons, a Republican appointee, and based on the discovery of material facts that would have possibly altered the decision of the jury, a hearing was requested in order to determine the validity of the claims.

Proving that the wheels of justice indeed move slowly, the state took its time in responding to the petition, and on October 18, 1994, argued to dismiss the new claims. On May 2, 1995, the state moved for summary judgment, asking the federal court to dismiss the opposition on its face. On September 18, 1995, Philip's lawyers filed a response to that motion.

For laypeople, the ins and outs of capital litigation remain a mystery. Those who actually review the course of such litigation from the U.S. Supreme Court cases of July 1976 (*Gregg v. Georgia, Proffitt v. Florida*, and *Jurek v. Texas*) to the present day, find that case law is littered with mid-course corrections, rules changing on the fly, and increasingly desperate attempts by those who support the death penalty to hold the entire ball of twine together despite its constant unraveling that reveals one injustice after another. Unbeknownst to Philip, his case would become a classic example of judicial discretion and deceit thwarting a claim for justice.

As noted previously, Philip's lawyers had met the material evidence standard for an evidentiary hearing on his claims of exculpatory evidence in federal court. As the brief put it, "Workman's evidence that (1) his ammunition did not cause Oliver's mortal wounds; (2) Davis was not present to witness the Oliver shooting; (3) persons other than Workman and Oliver fired weapons; (4) Workman was bludgeoned as he attempted to surrender" succinctly supported his claims demanding a hearing.

In order to make the summary unmistakably clear, the argument of the newly discovered evidence followed:

> Workman alleges that contrary to the State's case against him, he did not wrestle with Stoddard and Oliver from the Wendy's lot onto the Holiday lot, produce a gun, and shoot them. Rather, Workman alleges that he ran from the Wendy's lot onto the Holiday lot, tripped and fell, offered his surrender, was bludgeoned, and in the resulting confusion a fellow police officer, not Workman, shot Oliver.

> Workman asserts a Fourteenth Amendment claim that the prosecution withheld evidence of events surrounding Oliver's death while it knowingly presented false testimony. This claim requires Workman to show that (1) the evidence the prosecution presented was actually false; (2) the prosecution knew it was false; (3) the false evidence was material.

One would be inclined to think that if a judge were presented a series of claims alleging a fundamental violation of an individual's rights—in this case, framing someone for a murder he did not commit—a hearing to determine the validity of such claims would be warranted. Indeed, the case law was clear that in such circumstances the merits *should* be weighed in a hearing. However, and not for the last time, it must be pointed out that the proceedings under discussion took place in Memphis, Tennessee. The Memphis police and prosecutors are notorious for the corruption of justice and unethical behavior. They are the belly of the beast of the criminal justice system in Tennessee. So what may be settled case law in the courts of the land does not necessarily translate across the Shelby County line. The distance from the marble halls of the U.S. Supreme Court to the grime of the Shelby County criminal justice system is more than a matter of miles. The two are light-years apart and exist in entirely different constellations of justice.

Judge Julia Gibbons, the federal judge hearing the Workman appeal, was a product of the Memphis establishment. She had been a circuit court judge in Shelby County and served as legal counsel to Republican governor Lamar Alexander before her appointment to the federal bench by President Ronald Reagan. The youngest judge appointed to the bench, she was married to William Gibbons. Mr. Gibbons, serving as county commissioner, had recently been appointed by Republican governor Don Sundquist as district attorney general for Shelby County. On November 1, 1996, he was sworn into office by Judge Julia Gibbons, his wife, in her judicial robes. The official swearing in was preceded on October 29 by Judge Gibbons granting the state's request for summary judgment motion in the Philip Workman case. This decision meant that Philip would be denied an opportunity for a hearing to present his newly discovered evidence of the fact that he did not shoot Officer Oliver but that another Memphis policeman had accidentally done so.

The photograph first published in the *Memphis Commercial Appeal* on November 2, 1996
of Judge Julia Gibbons, in her judicial robe, laughing with her husband, William Gibbons,
at remarks made by a presenter at Mr. Gibbons' swearing in ceremony as district attorney general
for Shelby County, Tennessee, cannot be shown here because of copyright restrictions.

At this critical juncture, the district attorney general, William Gibbons, whose office had previously colluded with police in creating a misleading picture of the crime that targeted Philip Workman for a murder he did not commit, was sworn in by his wife, a federal judge, three days after the dismissal of Philip's appeal by the same Judge Julia Gibbons. The dismissal benefitted Mr. Gibbons and his office because a hearing would have exposed to the public the workings of the district attorney's office and Memphis police in Philip's case. As Workman's petition alleged, this included the manufacturing of a witness, as well as citizen witnesses and police with contradictory accounts of the crime scene. There would be no hearing to lay bare the evidence revealing that prosecutors had presented false evidence, that they knew it was false when presenting it, that the evidence was material to the conviction, and that they had manufactured a witness and his testimony. By granting the summary judgment motion, Judge Gibbons essentially buried from public view the allegations of corruption in a case that her husband's office had previously assembled and pursued in order to cover up the fact that Lieutenant Oliver had been accidentally killed by another police officer. Judge Gibbons passed the matter on to the appellate courts. There would be no fair and impartial consideration of the material evidence of the Workman case on her watch.

In 1998, nine years after the move from the Walls to Riverbend, Kenny Campbell received relief from the courts. His death sentence was reduced to life in prison. This meant he would be leaving death row and saying good-bye to his friend Philip Workman. He recalled his feelings upon learning from his lawyer of the court's decision:

If I said that part of me was not happy and excited, and a big weight of despair was lifted from my shoulders when the threat of being fried in the electric chair was suddenly taken away from me, well, of course I felt good about that. On the other hand, I dreaded telling Philip. A big part of me did not want to leave him there to face death alone. It's the same principle that you hear from soldiers in Vietnam who did not want to leave their buddies. There's "something" that's probably beyond words to describe about the possibility of facing death with another soul, and at that point Philip and I had become great friends and spiritual brothers for almost eighteen years, from young men to middle-aged men.

The night before I left death row for good, I was on one side of the exercise cages and Philip was on the other side. He was just pacing around. Finally, I called Philip over and told him, "Philip, I'm leaving here." He said, "Where are you going? Back to court?" I told him, "No, brother, my death sentence has been overturned and I'm leaving here tomorrow." He said, "Tomorrow?" I said, "Yeah." He then told me, "That's good." Both of us were hiding sadness behind the words.

When it was time to go in, Philip was let out of his cage. He was supposed to go right in, but he came back to where I was and he smiled. He stuck his hand out to shake through the slot in the cage door. When we shook hands we didn't say anything, but we looked each other in the eye, and tears were streaming down our faces.

The next morning I left death row for good. My heart was partly glad and partly very sad that I was leaving behind my best friend and brother of all those years to face death alone. I knew within me he wasn't totally alone, but that's how it felt to me at the time.

***

The next legal step for Philip Workman was the filing of his appeal to the Sixth Circuit Court of Appeals. A three-judge panel of the Sixth Circuit would consider the appeal. Philip's lawyers filed the legal briefs and awaited oral argument. The case was argued in Cincinnati, Ohio, on June 17, 1998.

For most Americans, judicial hearings are believed to be fair and impartial proceedings governed by the facts and the law. The record of the Sixth Circuit Court of Appeals, however, raised some fundamental questions about the accuracy of such a perception. The *Cincinnati Enquirer* undertook a survey of decisions in the Sixth Circuit Court of Appeals from 2000 until 2007. An article by *Enquirer* reporter Dan Horn titled "The Politics of Life and Death: An Inmate's Fate Often Hinges on Luck of the Draw" published on April 15, 2007, clearly revealed the partisan split in the Sixth

Circuit Court of Appeals during that time period: Republican judicial appointees voted to deny death row appeals 85 percent of the time; Democratic appointees voted to grant at least partial relief in 75 percent of those cases. As the title of the article indicated, the outcome of these cases depended not so much on matters of fact and law as on which political party composed the majority of the panel hearing the capital appeal.

The *Enquirer* article highlighted the case of Paul House, a condemned Tennessee prisoner, to illustrate the disparity of justice along party lines. On appeal of a rape and murder conviction, of which House maintained his innocence, he prevailed in the Sixth Circuit in 2002. He would be granted a new trial primarily on the basis of DNA, which exonerated him. Due to procedural twists and turns, the case came back before the Sixth Circuit once again in 2004. The same facts and law were presented in argument. This time the case was put before the entire Sixth Circuit Court, fourteen judges, and four new Republican appointees were on the bench. House lost because of the new Republican votes even though he offered the same case as he had four years earlier. The decision was later appealed to the U.S. Supreme Court, and House prevailed in a decision that stated in part, "any reasonable juror would have found Mr. House not guilty."

So it was into the judicial snake pit of the Sixth Circuit that Philip's appeal proceeded. The roulette wheel of justice was spun, and the names of the judges came up: David A. Nelson, James L. Ryan, and Eugene E. Siler Jr.. All three were Republican appointees. As Chris Minton once said to me, "My son, who is four, can tell how a [death penalty] case in the Sixth Circuit will come out. No matter the merit, if you have a majority of Republicans, you will lose." Philip's oral argument on June 17, 1998, was a pro forma exercise, a formality, for a rapidly delivered opinion on October 30, 1998: a 3–0 vote against relief. Minton's son had foretold the outcome of Philip's case.

The judges, so accustomed to routinely denying death penalty appeals, did not spend much time thinking through Philip's appeal. It was just another death penalty case from a defendant saying he didn't do the crime, it was the police who did it. Granted it was a somewhat unique claim but surely a far-fetched one from the viewpoint of the Republican appellate judges. In order to quickly get to the conclusion of dismissal, a few issues needed to be disposed of initially. First was the matter of Dr. Sperry's affidavit that "he had seen 30 to 40 corpses with wounds from ammunition of the sort Workman used"; that in every one of these cases "the .45 Silvertip hollow-point bullet expanded upon entering the human body involved"; that approximately 90 percent of the time the hollow-point never emerged from the victim's body at all; that "in the remaining instances the exit wound created by the .45-caliber Silvertip hollow-point bullet was significantly larger than the entrance wound the bullet created"; and that it would be inconsistent with the exit wounds seen by Dr. Sperry "for a .45 Silvertip hollow-point bullet to create an exit wound smaller than the entry wound."

Judge Siler, writing for the panel, disposed of Dr. Sperry's affidavit thusly:

> If a .45 caliber hollow point bullet had gone all the way through Lt. Oliver's chest and emerged in one piece, we have no doubt that the exit wound would have been larger than the entry wound. It hardly follows, however, that Lt. Oliver could not have been shot with the type of ammunition Workman was firing—because the record in no way compels the conclusion that the bullet which killed the officer emerged from his body in one piece.
>
> Soft point bullets sometimes shed fragments after entering a human body. See, for example, the paper on "Ballistic Injury" presented by Col. Martin L. Fackler, of the U.S. Army Medical Corps, at the March 1986 Symposium of the American College of

Emergency Physicians. The paper, accepted for publication in the *Annals of Emergency Medicine*, describes one soft point bullet wound where the percentage of bullet fragmentation was calculated at 33.4 percent. Dr. Fackler gives the following description:

> "As the bullet deforms on impact, small pieces of it separate. In this case, 33.4% of the bullet's total weight leaves the main mass in the form of fragments. Each fragment crushes its own path through tissue as the multiple fragments spread out laterally away from the main projectile."

If part of the bullet that killed Lt. Oliver remained in the officer's body, that would be entirely consistent with Dr. Sperry's observation that hollow point bullets remain inside the victim's body about 90 percent of the time. Dr. Bell did not recover any bullet segment, to be sure, but no x-ray was taken and the small piece of metal could simply have been overlooked. Dr. Bell did report a gunshot wound fracture of Lt. Oliver's left seventh rib, so the bullet may have fragmented on striking the rib. But regardless of when any fragmentation may have occurred, the most obvious explanation of the quarter inch "slit-like tear in the skin" on Lt. Oliver's back is that the wound was caused by the exit of a hollow point bullet fragment (possibly part of the aluminum jacket) and not by the exit of an entire bullet. Therefore, there is no reason to conclude that Workman was actually innocent of causing Lt. Oliver's mortal wound, just as there is no reason to conclude that the prosecution knowingly presented false evidence in this connection.

The second issue that needed to be cleared up in order to get Philip's case dismissed was the matter of Harold Davis, who in witness interviews and in police notes and diagrams was not recorded as being present at the crime scene, those materials having registered only white people as being present. Judge Siler's response to this issue was this: "The district court also correctly concluded that the fact that several witnesses did not mention seeing Davis established neither his presence nor absence at the scene. Specifically, it found that Officer Stoddard's failure to see Davis is understandable because he was involved in an altercation with Workman and was ultimately shot by him, the other witnesses Workman produced were busy helping the officers, and therefore it was also understandable that they did not see Davis."

A vote for relief in a capital case for these three judge would be, as they say in the country, as scarce as hens teeth. However, an examination of the panel's interpretation, absent their bias toward the prosecution in capital cases, leads in the opposite direction of their conclusion of Philip's guilt. Judge Siler's first claim involved the fragmenting bullet theory. But at trial Dr. James Bell, the Shelby County medical examiner, made no mention of any bullet fragmenting in Oliver's body. Indeed, no one suggested such a possibility until a law clerk for Judge Nelson unearthed Col. Martin Fackler's study as justification for the fragmentation theory. This elaborate possibility, not suggested by the state or in the record at all, was *created out of thin air* by the panel using Fackler's study. Rules of procedure prevent the introduction in appellate court of new evidence that is not on the trial record, but this was not a problem for a partisan panel determined to mete out the death penalty to a presumed cop killer.

At oral argument, Chris Minton was surprised when the judge confronted him with this unique interpretation ascribed to Colonel Fackler. Minton was also taken aback by the judge's notion that the bullet may have fragmented, even pointing out that there was no evidence to that effect in the record. When Judge Nelson asked if there was an x-ray of the wound, Minton responded that he had subpoenaed all medical records, including an x-ray, but had never received one. Upon returning to Nashville after the oral argument, Minton contacted Colonel Fackler directly to confirm if what Judge Nelson had lectured was indeed fact.

Fackler was astonished that such an interpretation had been made on the basis of his study. He pointed out to Minton that his study had established that high-velocity NATO 7.62mm soft-point rifle bullets, not .45 automatic pistol bullets, regularly shed small fragments upon impact. Fackler did not study .45 bullets, nor was his report applicable to them. Thus, the judges had misapplied the study to Philip Workman's situation. Additionally, a related study by Fackler demonstrated that Philip's bullet would have done exactly what Dr. Sperry's affidavit concluded: the entry wound would have been smaller than the exit wound, which was not what happened with Lieutenant Oliver's wound.

Dr. Bell had testified at trial that "the bullet that entered Officer Oliver and eventually killed Officer Oliver exited Officer Oliver as well." There was no evidence on the record put before the Sixth Circuit panel that the bullet fragmented. Rather, Judge Nelson *invented* an imaginary fragmenting bullet, the possibility vouched for by an erroneous interpretation of Colonel Fackler's study of NATO rifle bullets, in order to justify the wound discrepancy of the exit wound being smaller than the entrance wound, which is *not* a characteristic of the hollow-point ammunition used in Philip's gun.

Courts of appeal are governed by rules. One such rule is that material that has not been put before the district court in the original trial cannot be consulted in the appeal (*Landefeld v. Marion General Hospital, Inc.*). Obviously, Colonel Fackler's ballistic study had not been discussed in district court, since Judge Nelson was the first to bring it into the oral argument, doing so without notice to counsel.

What a strange opinion the Sixth Circuit panel of judges had authored. Without expert testimony anywhere in the record indicating that the bullet had fragmented, the panel made up their own medical theory to explain the wound discrepancy. For supposedly conservative judges, this was an exercise in judicial overreach that defied belief. In effect it was a decision that created a theory ex nihilo, concocted out of nothing, in order to provide a basis for the execution of a man whom the medical facts indicated did not kill Lt. Ronald Oliver. One may wonder why such an extraordinary step was taken.

The "clue of a thread" that runs through the Workman case, just like the string that Greek hero Theseus used for finding his way back from his encounter with the Minotaur, was that Philip's life was considered worthless by police, prosecutors, judges, all the official actors in the system. He was objectified because of his crime—the supposed murder of a policeman when robbing the Wendy's—and because he was a drug addict. His life was granted no value by those who run the system. Rather, the thought processes of Memphis and federal officials went something like this: If he was just a druggie and an armed robber, why should anyone care whether he actually killed a police officer? If he hadn't really done it this time, surely he would do it sooner or later. Better just to dispose of this detritus now and be done with it.

From this perspective the Sixth Circuit panel decision is not a surprise but, rather, consistent with the manner in which Philip was treated from his arrest, trial, state appeal, and now federal appeal. Once Philip was dehumanized, objectified into a category where he was not fully human but just a criminal, anything could be and was done to him by his opponents. Making up a ludicrous theory not based on medical evidence was just the latest event in a process of total dehumanization designed to lead to Philip's extinction, and not for what he had done but because of who he was perceived to be: the outsider. The next step was to file back to the panel and demonstrate how preposterous their contentions truly were. The petition for rehearing was filed on November 12, 1998.

I had begun visiting Philip Workman on a regular basis in the 1990s. After returning from a fellowship at Harvard University in 1990, I began to reintegrate myself into death row visitation once again. I had been emotionally exhausted from working with prisoners on death row throughout the South, losing a number of them to state killing from 1979 to 1989 (my experiences in this are described in *Last Rights*). Hence I was eager to take advantage of a Merrill Fellowship to Harvard so that I could take a break from the killing machinery.

I had known Philip Workman back at the Walls. He had been on 3 Walk, and I talked with him on occasion when I was visiting the Walls. But it was only after his move to Riverbend and the subsequent revelation that he did not shoot Lt. Ronald Oliver that we came to know each other well. I officially became his spiritual adviser in mid-February 2000.

Acquainting myself with Philip's legal situation provided a shock even to me, a veteran of many death row cases and someone who was well aware of how too many innocent people are shipped to death row. The utter contempt for Philip's life demonstrated by the Memphis police and prosecutors during his arrest and trial involved a breathtaking level of deceit, lying, manufacturing witnesses, and creating a complete fiction about the crime. To see the circle of that deception extend not only through the state judiciary but also into the federal district court and the Sixth Circuit Court of Appeals was an infuriating and eye-opening experience.

Philip's lawyers filed the appeal of Judge Siler's opinion back to the panel, pointing out that Colonel Fackler's study did not establish that Philip's bullet would have fragmented and that the study the panel cited involved only NATO-type rifles, not .45 automatic pistols. Perhaps in its haste to move the case along, the judges had not read Fackler's study accurately. The study, attached to the appeal for the rehearing, very clearly revealed that it focused on the "M-16 and the 7.62 NATO bullets." These were high-velocity rifle bullets, not low-velocity pistol bullets. Another study by Fackler determined that hollow-point bullets from a low-velocity handgun, like the .45 Philip used, hardly ever fragmented.

After some months of digesting the fact that the rehearing petition revealed the panel's opinion to be built upon a fundamental error, the question was, how would the judges respond? The entire fragmenting-bullet theory, not established in the trial record, was sustained only by citing Colonel Fackler's study. However, because the reality was that Fackler's study did not establish what the panel purported it to say, there was not even a gossamer thread to maintain the idea that the bullet that killed Lieutenant Oliver had fragmented. How would the Sixth Circuit panel address and correct its error?

One should not wonder but remember the words of children. As Chris Minton's four-year-old son would tell you, once informed of the three Republican judges on the panel, the only possible result could be denial. And so it remained a vote of 3–0.

If the result was predictable, the judges' written opinion itself was astonishing. They simply marked through the words pertaining to Colonel Fackler's study, crossing out the paragraphs. By essentially gutting the rationale for the fragmenting-bullet theory and there being no evidence on the record to support such a theory, the panel opinion was no longer anchored in fact or reason. It had become a wishing and hoping opinion.

What was particularly insolent was the letter to the parties involved that accompanied the revised opinion. Dated May 10, 1999, the letter read simply:

Dear Counsel:

Enclosed are copies of corrected pages from the decision originally sent to you October 30, 1998. Please make corrections in your publication version as indicated on page 8, line 32, thru page 9, line 26.

Thank you for your cooperation in this matter.

Yours very truly,
Leonard Green, Clerk
By (Mrs.) Linda K. Martin
Deputy Clerk

THE ELEVENTH CIRCLE

Philip's appeal went forward after the Sixth Circuit panel opinion, the infamous slashing-of-the-offending-evidence decision. The case carried over to the U.S. Supreme Court's fall certiorari review, in which the lower court's records were called up. On Monday, October 4, 1999, the Supreme Court denied certiorari to two Tennessee cases: Philip's and that of Robert Glen Coe, who had been convicted of the kidnapping, rape, and murder of an eight-year-old girl. The state attorney general's office moved to have the Tennessee Supreme Court set execution dates for Workman and Coe.

In the autumn of 1999, as Philip's case pended review in the state supreme court, Chris Minton went back through all the documentation of the case. A photograph in the *Memphis Commercial Appeal* showed a black man in handcuffs at the hospital to which Philip had been was taken. Minton wondered if this could be the mysterious Harold Davis.

In seeking to find Davis, Minton contacted his family again. He had tried to speak with them previously but with no luck. Now that the execution was in the news, however, the family of Harold Davis was open to talking. After a discussion with Davis's sister, Jackie, she invited Minton to Cordova, outside of Memphis, for a visit. Visiting with the Harold Davis family, Minton learned that the black male in the hospital photo he had seen was not Harold. However, Jackie told the lawyer about a woman named Vivian Porter, who had been with Harold the night of the Wendy's crime. Jackie called Ms. Porter, who agreed to meet with Minton that afternoon.

Ms. Porter, who now ran a Christian drug counseling center in Memphis, informed Minton that she and Harold had been together the night of the Wendy's robbery and Lieutenant Oliver's slaying and agreed to give him a videotaped statement. The information Vivian Porter provided finally clarified the role of Harold Davis in the Wendy's crime.

On the night of August 5, 1981, Porter and Davis had been driving around Memphis while smoking marijuana. A Memphis police officer pulled them over. She recalls thinking, "Oh, no, he's going to smell the marijuana and we'll get busted." The police officer approached the car in which Porter and Davis were sitting, but before he got there he apparently heard a police radio broadcast about an officer being down. He suddenly returned to his car, jumped into the seat, and rapidly drove off. Davis and Porter followed him, audibly repeating, "Thank you, Jesus," to each other, since the officer's quick departure had saved them from a probable arrest for marijuana possession. They drove by the Wendy's restaurant, where the crime scene was already marked off with yellow tape. Returning to Porter's apartment, they partied and watched the news on television. It was through the news reporting that they learned a policeman had been killed at the Wendy's restaurant.

In conversations with Jackie, Minton learned that one way Harold maintained his crack cocaine habit was to be an informant for police. In exchange for money, or for pending charges against him being dropped, Davis would say what police asked him to say in order to incriminate someone. While watching the news about the police slaying at Wendy's, Davis's M.O. had inspired him to take advantage of the event. Even though he had not actually been there, he had been close by, so surely he could be of use to the police in exchange for some remuneration. Vivian Porter confirmed that Harold would likely do something like that. According to police logs, Davis contacted them at 12.25 P.M. By 2:30 P.M. on August 6 he had given a statement describing Philip's killing Oliver without even identifying Philip in a physical lineup.

It had become clear to the defense lawyers that Harold Davis must be found. They had made a trip to California following a lead on his whereabouts, but that trip turned out to be a wild goose chase. However, Chris Minton learned that Davis's mother had her son's telephone number. When he called the number and reached a motel in Phoenix, Arizona, Minton, along with his colleague Jefferson Dorsey, took a chance and flew to Phoenix. After renting a car and checking into a motel, they visited the motel that had been identified by tracing the number Harold Davis's mother had provided. When they knocked on the door where they thought Davis was housed, a white man opened the door to the room—obviously not Harold Davis. In checking with the motel management, however, they learned that Davis had just been there.

The two lawyers traversed a long strip of motels bordering Van Buren Street, about ten miles of motels stretching down the road. The good news was that as they searched for Davis by going motel to motel, they learned the kind of motel he preferred—not the top of the line nor the bottom either, but usually a Days Inn or Motel 6. They were told that Davis had been at one particular motel three weeks earlier. He would wear out his welcome at one and move on to the next one, cobbling together temporary living quarters as he maintained his drug-addled existence. Such was the life of an itinerant drug addict. But afternoon turned to evening, evening to the darkness of night, and there was still no Harold Davis. Finally reaching the end of Van Buren Street with nothing but the darkness of the desert stretching out ahead of them, Minton resigned himself to ending their search for the night, acknowledging that they had given the search a good effort, saying it was like looking for a needle in the haystack anyway and so forth. Dorsey just said, "We're moving on," so the two attorneys kept searching, driving down the road into the dark desert night.

After about a mile or two, lights of a Motel 6 loomed in the night, and the two men decided to stop. They went to the desk, showed the innkeeper the picture of Harold Davis, and the reply came: "Room 240." After twelve hours of numbing and exhausting search, they had finally found the place where Harold Davis was currently residing.

The duo went to room 240 and knocked on the door. Harold Davis was inside, but he was not about to open the door. The lawyers talked to him through the door for twenty minutes. They explained that Philip Workman was about to be executed for a murder he didn't commit and that Harold could save his life. They told him all they knew about the case—about Vivian Porter, about Harold's work with the police, and how they had visited his family—until finally he opened the door. They then audiotaped Davis's account of the events of the Wendy's robbery, and he agreed to participate in a videotaped interview the next day at 10:00 A.M. The lawyers showed up at 9:15 A.M. and obtained the videotaped interview.

When Minton and Dorsey returned to Nashville, they worked with the local CBS affiliate for a weeklong series on the Workman case that aired in December 1999. They also provided the facts of the case to Sonny Rawls, who wrote several long stories on the case for the *Nashville Tennessean*. The stories recounted the events at the Wendy's restaurant, Harold Davis's recantation of his original statement, and the shenanigans of the Memphis police and prosecutors, including a statement from Davis that two white men whom he assumed to be police had come to his motel room in Memphis and told him he had better cooperate with the police or his family would be in trouble.

***

The pieces of the Philip Workman prosecution puzzle were slowly falling into place. But for several reasons, their case was built on faulty and erroneous information:

(1) The prosecution claimed only two shooters, whereas the police journals and witnesses revealed multiple shooters.

(2). Harold Davis had not been at the crime scene; instead he had been manufactured by the prosecution as being an eyewitness to the shooting of Lieutenant Oliver.

(3) The magic bullet, not found by police during the crime scene investigation but amazingly located by a worker at Holiday Auto Parts the next day, was pristine, meaning it was not the bullet that killed Lieutenant Oliver as the state maintained.

(4) The bullet that went through Lieutenant Oliver did not fragment, according to Dr. Bell, the medical examiner, and the federal appellate court had crossed out their fragmenting-bullet theory, thus discarding their own *lex ex machina* crime/creation story.

(5) Dr. Kris Sperry's statement that Philip's hollow-point bullets would leave a larger exit than entry wound, reinforced by Colonel Fackler's work with pistols, was unchallenged.

As the body of evidence emerged—essentially completing the puzzle that revealed the Memphis police had shot one of their own and engaged with prosecutors in a frame-up of a restaurant robber—the haunting question became, would anyone care that Philip Workman did not kill Lieutenant Oliver? Or would events convert Phillip's oft-stated analysis of the case into a prediction of its conclusion: "I'm not innocent enough."

As Tennessee geared up for its first execution since 1960, the state was represented by attorney general Paul Summers. A former criminal court appellate judge, Summers brought a zest to pushing death penalty cases that his predecessors did not manifest. (The attorney general of Tennessee is appointed by the Tennessee Supreme Court, which removed the overt political component of running for election to the office that motivated other Southern attorneys general to advocate a rabid prosecutor-prone position on capital cases to ensure their own election and perhaps propel them to the state executive mansion.) Summers began preparation for the Coe and Workman executions.

On September 30, 1999, Attorney General Summers wrote to Charles Traughber, chairman of the Board of Probation and Parole, which was delegated to hold a clemency hearing on capital cases and make a recommendation to Governor Sundquist. Summers advised Traughber that the role of the attorney general's office "should be that of legal advisor to the board."

After the U.S. Supreme Court's October 4 denial of certiorari on Coe's and Philip's petitions, Summers held a press conference in which he said, "This is a sobering and somber day for the Attorney General's Office . . . It is a serious matter when you are dealing with the taking of life" (*Memphis Commercial Appeal*, October 5, 1999). There was some thinking in political circles that Summers was seeking to position himself into the upcoming gubernatorial race on the basis of a strong execution platform, hence the press conference. Governor Sundquist's office also issued a statement, saying, "The governor takes his responsibility very seriously and will review each case on its merits" (*Memphis Commercial Appeal*, October 5, 1999).

Now that state officials had gone on record with their utmost concern about carrying out their duty, one previously neglected fact was brought to their attention: Coe and Workman could still file rehearing petitions in the U.S. Supreme Court; thus it was premature for the attorney general's office to file for an execution date to the Tennessee Supreme Court. When this matter was brought to the attention of the Tennessee Supreme Court, the court denied the state's request to set an execution date of October 11, 1999. This action prompted a media response by Summers in which he told reporters he was "determined" to see the executions carried out (*Knoxville News Sentinel*, October 12, 1999).

In preparation for a clemency hearing in the Philip Workman case, state officials were in touch with local Memphis officials for a coordinated effort. A key person in the presentation to the clemency board was the Shelby County medical examiner, Dr. O. C. Smith. Indeed, Dr. O.C Smith and his Power Point show would be the chief witness against Philip.

On November 29 the U.S. Supreme Court denied the rehearing petitions for Coe and Workman. Once again the attorney general's office petitioned the Tennessee Supreme Court to set execution dates. Summers also stated publicly that although he had been an appellate judge when Robert Coe's case was ruled upon by that court, he saw no conflict in prosecuting the case now (*Memphis Commercial Appeal*, November 30, 1999). However, about one week later the Tennessee Supreme Court disqualified Summers from further participation in the Coe case for that very reason.

On January 3, 2000, the state supreme court set an execution date for Philip Workman and Robert Coe of April 6, 2000. Attorney General Summers stated, "We will do everything in our power to bring this case to conclusion" (*Memphis Commercial Appeal*, January 4, 2000).

***

Nashville is not a particularly large city. If you don't know someone you would like to meet, you probably know someone who knows that person and can make such a meeting happen. Such was my situation in January 2000. Don Sundquist was Tennessee's governor, and I wanted to meet with Justin Wilson, the governor's senior policy adviser, but I did not know him. Mutual friends made the meeting possible.

By this time it was apparent to me that Philip Workman was being railroaded to the death house by the Memphis police and prosecutors. There was no doubt about Philip's robbing the Wendy's restaurant, but it was clear that he had not killed anyone and that Lieutenant Oliver had been slain by "friendly fire." I sought the meeting with Justin Wilson to review the course of action that had brought Philip to the eve of execution for a murder he did not commit.

By this point in my life, I had been working against the death penalty since 1974. I had met several governors and their assistants throughout the South in conjunction with death cases. I knew how the game was played, but the Workman case revealed an extraordinary callousness for the truth that emanated all the way from the arrest and trial through the appeal. I wanted to meet with Wilson to be sure he understood the elements of deceit and treachery that were so abundant in this case.

Justin Wilson and I met in January 2000. He was polite and gracious. We discussed the case, and I went through the details of prosecutorial malfeasance, manufacturing of testimony, and the creation of a witness who was not even present at the crime scene. As we neared the end of our meeting, he assured me that the governor would be made aware of this knowledge, saying, "The state of Tennessee would not execute an innocent man."

I conveyed the results of my meeting with Wilson to Philip and his lawyers. However, it was hard to be optimistic about any political relief coming through clemency given the utter commitment of the Shelby County authorities to execute Philip. When I told Philip about the meeting, he shook his head in a resigned manner and said, "They won't execute an innocent man. But they will execute me. I'm not innocent enough, Joe. I'm just not innocent enough. I created the scene by committing the robbery, and that's all they care about. They're not about to face the fact that they killed one of their own."

Although I understood Phillip's fears, state law was clear: following *State v. Severs,* if the accused did not kill, or if the person who did the killing was trying to thwart the felony, the individual was not guilty of a capital offense. Thus the felony murder rule did not apply in Philip's case, because he did not kill Lieutenant Oliver, and the person who did so was a fellow police officer trying to prevent a felony, so neither person was eligible for the death penalty.

The setting of the execution date for April 6, 2000, commenced the grinding of the gears for state killing in Tennessee. A capital punishment meeting was held on January 28, 2000. It was the day after Philip Workman filed his application for clemency. Those present at the meeting included: Charles Traughber, chairman of the parole board; Justin Wilson; Donal Campbell (commissioner of the Tennessee Department of Corrections), and from the attorney general's office Andy Bennett, Mike Moore, Kathy Morante, Glenn Pruden, and Amy Tarkington.

On February 1, 2000, Pruden e-mailed Tarkington and Whalen, saying, "Kathy would like to meet w/us at 2:00 P.M. today to discuss what our approach should be and what recommendations we should make to the DA [district attorney]. I asked John Campbell [assistant DA in Memphis] to let me know who will be the spokesperson for their office. He said he would approach Gen. Gibbons on the matter and recommend that he call Gen. Summers with his decision." The same day Chairman Traughber e-mailed Charles Scudder and Teresa Thomas, asking them to meet with them that day to discuss the matters Workman had raised in his clemency materials to support the fact that it must have been another policeman, not Philip, who had killed Lieutenant Oliver. Traughber and his wife, Lois DeBerry, who was the speaker pro tem for the House of Representatives in the General Assembly, were from Memphis.

On February 2, 2000, Ray Maples, a clemency board member and a former policeman, e-mailed the Board of Probation and Parole with the statement: "I am notifying you that I am recusing myself from the Phillip R. Workman #095920, case." That same day, Philip's lawyer Chris Minton and the district attorney of Memphis were notified that a clemency hearing had been set for February 23, 2000.

Don Dawson, from the Office of the Post-Conviction Defender of Tennessee, filed a request for public records regarding the setting of the February 23 clemency hearing and the promulgation of the capital case clemency hearing format. (This request initially had been utilized in discovering the shenanigans of the Memphis police and prosecutors at Philip's trial.)

The clemency hearing was moved to March 9, 2000, and a capital punishment meeting was held on February 11, 2000.

In mid-February I officially registered as Philip's spiritual adviser. This meant I would have access to him at any time during deathwatch—the seventy-two-hour period before the execution when the prisoner was moved to Building 8, which contained four holding cells and the killing machinery.

On February 15, 2000, Glenn Pruden e-mailed John Campbell about finding a doctor who would testify that the wounds in Philip's buttocks were from a dog bite.

Philip Workman and Joe Ingle talk in death row visiting gallery.

Attorney General Summers wrote Charles Traughber: "This is to notify you that, pursuant to Tenn. Code Ann. 8-6-302, I am delegating to the staff attorneys of the Board of Probation and Parole the authority to represent the State of Tennessee at the clemency hearing in the Philip Workman case." (The code says: "The attorney general and reporter, exercising discretion and with the concurrence of the head of the executive agency involved, may permit, by express written authorization, staff attorneys employed by the various departments, agencies, boards, commissions or instrumentalities of the state to appear and represent the state of Tennessee in a certain case or certain classes of cases under the direction and control of the attorney general and reporter.")

On February 23, 2000, notice of a capital punishment meeting scheduled for February 25 was distributed to the following: Jay Ballard, Frances Benefield, Andy Bennett, Sharon Curtis-Flair, Lisa Helton, Debbie Inglis, Mike Moore, Kathy Morante, Charles Scudder, Bettye Stanton, Paul Summers, Amy Tarkington, and Teresa Thomas. FNU Wiffins e-mailed Talana M. Schmitt: "I was informed that I did not have to do a facts offense report on Phillip Workman because the Chairman [of the Clemency Board] stated he had all the needed facts."

On February 25, 2000, the following events occurred:

(1) Another capital punishment meeting was conducted.

(2) The chairman of the clemency board, Charles Traughber, e-mailed board members the schedule of the clemency hearing set for March 9.

(3) ADA John Campbell e-mailed Glenn Pruden with suggestions Campbell had received from Ray Maples, the board member who had recused himself. This included determining who had checked the guns from the crime scene and the time that Officer Keenan and "the shoot team" showed up. Campbell wrote, "I think I will contact Kennon [*sic*] and see if I can get an affidavit about what happened at the scene."

(4) Pruden e-mailed Campbell: "John, does Steve Parker know who checked his gun? I'll have Joe give you a call about the rest." Campbell responded: "I'm sure Steve knows but I will ask him to be sure." Pruden replied: "I was just thinking that this would be good if there is nothing in the file. Then we could get an affidavit from this person."

Apparently satisfied that there was "nothing in the file," ADA Campbell obtained a sworn statement from Clyde Keenan, head of the shoot team, in the attorney general's office in Nashville. Keenan swore he was commander of the shoot team, a group of policemen called to investigate any time the police use deadly force. Keenan stated that he and fellow officer Sgt. Rick Wilson were immediately at the scene of the Wendy's shooting: "We were probably on the scene between a minute and a minute and a half after the time we heard the officer was down." He went on to state:

The first thing that we'd found was two officers down. Both of them were known to me. One of the officers was a former partner of mine by the name of Ronnie Oliver . . . The other police officer, Officer Stoddard, was an officer I was familiar with. He was down also. Stoddard had been hit in the arm. Oliver had been hit somewhere in the torso, was badly injured. And at that particular point, we went to try to aid him in any way we could awaiting the arrival of the paramedic crews . . . Officer Parker was . . . standing actually between Lieutenant Oliver and Officer Stoddard.

Keenan then said he went to Lieutenant Oliver's aid and saw him placed in the ambulance and then began checking "the weapons of the officers at the scene. "[We] needed to . . . make sure that any weapons that were there on the scene were not any danger to anybody. So we actually check officers' weapons at that particular point . . . So the first thing I did, the first weapon I actually checked was Officer Parker's weapon, his service revolver . . . There was no indication at all that the weapon had been fired."

ADA Campbell asked, "What about Officer Stoddard? Was his weapon checked also?"

Keenan replied, "His weapon was checked, and his was a little bit different situation. It was in his holster, and his weapon really ended up being checked at the hospital. So once he got to the hospital, both his weapon and the weapon for Lieutenant Oliver were secured. Lieutenant Oliver's had been fired. Stoddard's had not been fired."

This sworn statement stood in contrast to what the police logs documented as having taken place that night. Officer Keenan had arrived at the scene at 10:41 P.M., three minutes after Lieutenant Oliver had been transported by ambulance to the hospital. Obviously, Keenan's story was inconsistent with the police log note that he arrived three minutes after Lt. Oliver was transported to the hospital.

On February 28, 2000, Glenn Pruden sent an e-mail to John Campbell with the subject line "Workman—Final Draft," saying, "John, Joe [Whalen, of the attorney general's office] asks that you review this ASAP and let him know of any changes right away." Later the same day the clemency board received a document titled "Submission of the District Attorney General for the Thirtieth Judicial District in Opposition to the Application for Commutation of Philip Ray Workman." Philip Workman filed his position statement that day as well.

In the exchange of information between the parties in preparation for the clemency hearing, Philip's lawyers were stunned to learn of the existence of an x-ray of the mortal wound to Lieutenant Oliver. Although the x-ray had been under subpoena for years, the state had not complied with the request to produce it. Hence defense counsel were led to believe there was no x-ray. Indeed, the Sixth Circuit Court of Appeals' bizarre opinion had relied on their belief that there was no x-ray in devising their fragmenting bullet theory. Yet later Dr. O. C. Smith had made reference to the x-ray and his intention to use it in his clemency presentation. On March 2, 2000, Philip's counsel journeyed to Memphis to secure the x-ray.

On March 4, 2000, the defense lawyers obtained an affidavit from Dr. Kris Sperry on the x-ray verifying that Lieutenant Oliver's wound was a "through and through" wound with no fragmentation.

On March 6, 2000, Officer Stoddard, ADA Campbell, and O. C. Smith went to the Wendy's restaurant to re-create the events the state contended occurred. More significantly, Philip's lawyers filed a motion to reopen the case in the Sixth Circuit Court of Appeals based on the new evidence of the x-ray and Harold Davis's recantation.

On March 7 the chairman of the clemency board, Charles Traughber, e-mailed the board members with a request from Philip's lawyers for a two-week delay to allow the Sixth Circuit to decide on the rehearing motion. The chairman commented in the e-mail: "My vote would be to have our hearing 3/7 [*sic*; he meant 3/9] so we can send our report and non-binding recommendation to the Governor." Traughber also wrote, "I have consulted with Ms. Thomas and Mr. Scudder and they advise to go ahead and have the hearing. We plan to have the hearing on 3/9/2000 at 8:30 A.M. at RMSI [Riverbend Maximum Security Institution]."

The *Memphis Commercial Appeal*, which functioned as a house organ for the Memphis prosecutors, ran a story on March 8, 2000, saying, "Prosecutors say that Lt. Oliver's fatal wound was consistent with the ammunition Workman used." Philip's lawyers withdrew his clemency petition, thus mooting the clemency hearing scheduled for March 9, 2000. In response attorney general Paul Summers was quoted as saying, "Frankly, we are disappointed at this turn of events because we had looked forward to his presentation and the opportunity to have the Shelby County District Attorney's Office refute each and every one of his claims" (*Memphis Commercial Appeal*, March 9, 2000).

On March 9, 2000, ADA Campbell deposed Keenan and ADAG Eddie Peterson at the attorney general's office.

On March 16, 2000, ADA John Campbell deposed O. C. Smith, Stoddard, and Parker. Although in the clemency hearing Smith would show how he had shot Silvertip ammunition through a pig's foot to prove a certain point, there was no mention of shooting a pig's foot in Smith's March 16 testimony. Results of this key "demonstration" should have been provided through the deposition that indicated to what Dr. Smith would be testifying.

On March 27, 2000, attorney general Paul Summers commented, "My job as a prosecutor is to make sure the guilty are punished and that the innocent are not treated unfairly . . . It's ludicrous to believe that Paul Summers or the governor or anyone else is trying to execute an innocent man (*Memphis Commercial Appeal*, March 28, 2000).

The Sixth Circuit Court of Appeals panel, composed of the three Republican judges who had ruled against Philip twice before, denied his March 6 motion to reopen his case in light of the Harold Davis recantation and the x-ray revealing a "through and through" bullet. After this decision, Jay Ballard faxed the Office of the Post-Conviction Defender saying that the governor's designee would hold a clemency hearing on Philip's case on April 3, 2000, at 2:00 P.M. Summers reiterated that the state was looking forward to the opportunity to refute each and every one of Philip's claims, adding that he was confident that prosecutors would present clear and convincing evidence that Workman and no one else fired the fatal shot.

Meanwhile, a disagreement had emerged between Philip's defense lawyers. Jefferson Dorsey and Don Dawson wanted to go ahead with the clemency, even if it turned out to be a rigged proceeding. Given that there would be no cross-examination and that witnesses could testify to whatever they wished, bound only by an oath without cross-examination, the proceeding was an ominous one for Philip. Chris Minton wanted to wait and see what the en banc court (the full panel of fourteen judges) of the Sixth Circuit would do with the appeal of the panel's denial before proceeding with clemency. Clemency was supposedly reserved for the end of the appellate process, and they had not reached the end, even though there was an April 6 execution date. The decision was reached that Dorsey and Dawson would handle the clemency proceedings, and Minton would work the papers for the Sixth Circuit Court of Appeals.

Philip Workman gestures during death row visit.

Although Philip's lawyers had not requested a clemency hearing, since it was to be conducted at the end of the appeals and he already had an active appeal before the entire Sixth Circuit Court of Appeals, his defense team had been informed that such a hearing would take place the morning of April 3, 2000, three days before the scheduled execution. The hearing was conducted in a room usually utilized for parole hearings that was adjacent to the main visiting area of the prison in Building 8. Beyond the locked door at the end of the visitation area was deathwatch, with its four holding cells and the killing machinery: the electric chair and lethal injection paraphernalia.

Since Philip's scheduled execution was less than seventy-two hours away, he arrived from deathwatch manacled to a waist chain. He appeared wan and determined. He fully understood the effort that had been made to frame him for Officer Oliver's homicide, and he was aware of the utter lack of relief that would probably be forthcoming from this clemency effort. Nevertheless he was resolved to make his statement and try again to show that he did not kill Lieutenant Oliver.

Jefferson Dorsey began making his case at 2:21 P.M. and was given until 3:51 by Justin Wilson. Dorsey reminded Wilson that at trial his client had been advised by "his attorneys, public defenders, [who] told him he was guilty. They told Mr. Workman not to contest the state's proof. They told him he had a one millimeter of a chance of survival, and that was only if he would own up to this crime, admit that he shot Lieutenant Oliver, and then essentially plead for mercy, say his head was clouded by drugs. Because, we know, in 1981 Philip Workman was a drug addict. He was unemployed and a drifter." Philip's trial lawyers had made no investigation and instead accepted the state's two shooter theory as fact for the trial.

After putting up a diagram of the crime scene, Dorsey continued:

> Mr. Workman's account of what happened that night matches this crime scene and Philip Workman's account was done without benefit of seeing this crime scene or knowing about what the investigating officers found or what any other witness was saying or had seen. In his version of events, his first declaration has not changed in 19 years.
>
> Philip Workman always insisted there were only four bullets in his gun. Now this will become important because Officer Parker and Officer Stoddard said he fired at least five times. We have two shell casings where the scuffle occurred. We've got one live round there and then behind the truck we've got another shell casing. That accounts for the bullets. No other shell casings were found. There's not a shred of evidence that he fired more except the testimony of the officers.
>
> The state said Harold Davis's testimony was inconsequential. [But] Harold Davis is the only direct evidence that Philip Workman committed a murder that night. The State has said perhaps they could have proved it without him. Perhaps he could infer from Officer Parker and Officer Stoddard that Philip was the shooter that night, but both of them say they didn't see it. Now it's absurd to say that a jury would not be moved by that testimony.
>
> Furthermore, that testimony provides the heinous element for the death sentence. It's an aggravating factor. It shows deliberation and purposeful shooting of two police officers.

So not only did it have an impact on the guilt stage of this trial; it had an impact on his sentence of death.

At the end of September [1999], Harold Davis's mother told us finally that she had received a phone call from him in Phoenix, Arizona.

Chris Minton and I flew immediately to Arizona. We knew that there was a wealth of evidence. We had affidavits from all the witnesses at the scene. We had Parker's own testimony. We had a picture of the crime scene showing that Harold Davis's car was not even there. We had crime scene diagrams showing his car wasn't even there. We had a lineup that night where Harold Davis wasn't present, and according to police records, the first time he appears is in a phone call around noon the next day.

Dorsey then laid out Philip's case based on the trial record. He read from the account of 3:15 P.M., August 6, 1981, Philip's initial questioning.

Question: "Did you mean to kill the police lieutenant last night?"

Answer: "No. It was an accident. I tried to give up, and he grabbed me. When I fell and the gun went off, I was scared, I ran again and got to a truck. A man saw me, and I told him I'd give up. My leg was hurting. I thought I had been hit."

. . .

Question: "When did you first see the policeman?"

. . .

Workman: "When I came out the door of the Wendy's, he was there. I asked him what was the problem? I think he thought I was the clean-up man. He looked over at another policeman in a police car, and I started running. I fell down. I had my gun in my hand, and I held it up and said, 'I give up. I give up.' Then the policeman jumped me or tackled me. The gun just started shooting. I don't know how many times. The next thing I remember, I'm hiding under that truck."

Dorsey directed his next comments to Justin Wilson:

Now, one of the reasons this is important is because at the trial, and according to Harold Davis' testimony, which I will discuss in a minute, Philip cold bloodedly shot down both police officers.

Now, as Philip Workman said on August 6, 1981, and as he would say here today, he was attempting to surrender. He fell down. There were two police officers, Lieutenant Oliver and Officer Stoddard right behind him. He attempted to surrender, he put his hands up in the air, and he was struck on the head, and there is evidence of all that.

[Question from the interview]: "Did you shoot the other policeman?"

Answer: "I don't know. I saw him shooting at me. I could see the flashes of his gun. I don't remember shooting at anybody. I just kept hearing shots."

Dorsey elucidated to Wilson: "Now, that's important, also. No one has ever contested that Philip Workman fired his gun that night, and we have shell casings up there to prove it. That's not an issue, and by the way, no one has ever contested his guilt of the robbery or the fact that he should be punished, and the point, obviously, of this clemency hearing is that Philip Workman did not commit a murder that night. There are serious questions about his trial, his defense, and the facts of this case." Then he continued:

> Now, as Philip has said time and time again, his recollection of these events was that he tried to surrender, and that's borne up in what he told his attorneys, and it's borne up in what he told these police officers. He said he had four bullets in his gun. He has stated on numerous occasions and through interviews and to us, when he attempted to surrender and said, "I give up," he was struck in the head. His gunshot went off involuntarily, and that guns began firing around him, and he fired towards the flash of light, and I think we can reconstruct what happened.
>
> Now, there's evidence that he was struck on top of the head. To begin with, he's got a scar on top of his head where he took 7 stitches, and there is also a scar up above his right eye where he was bashed and several other scars. He took stitches in several places that night, and there's no doubt that when the police found Mr. Workman, the dogs were sicked [sic] on him, and he was scuffled up a little bit. [Dorsey then introduced exhibits to back up his statements.]
>
> These are copies of the lineup identification cards from two of the witnesses who were present at the lineup that was held that night after the robbery. Steve Craig is one of them and Jeff Rickert [sic] is the other, and if you turn to the second page and look at the back of Steve Craig's card, he wrote, "I think it's No. 3. The man I saw was holding the right side of his head as if he were injured. No. 3 has an injury on the right side of his head the same approximate height."
>
> So Steve Craig, just passing, a witness to all this, saw Mr. Workman running holding his head.

Dorsey next presented a statement from the state's investigator, which read: "As a result of the struggle between the defendant, Officer Stoddard, and Lieutenant Oliver, in which the defendant was struck by a flashlight by one of the officers. Mr. Nall [sic] states that he did not see the altercation himself, what he is stating is merely hearsay . . . According to Mr. Nall, the incident occurred at night at approximately 10:30 P.M. When he and Mr. Rickert arrived on the scene, the defendant was running away holding his head with the gun in his hand."

Dorsey concluded: "Corroboration, another witness sees Mr. Workman holding his head as he runs from the scene."

> . . .
>
> [Officer Stoddard] testified as he parked his police car in the north Wendy's parking lot directly west of Oliver's car, he saw Oliver and Workman walking toward him . . . When Workman started to run, Aubrey [he meant Oliver] yelled, "Hold it," and he grabbed Workman and fell onto the Wendy's lot. As Workman and Aubrey [again he meant Oliver] struggled, Stoddard ran up and joined the fray. The three struggled 60 feet north onto the parking lot of a neighboring business, Holiday Auto Parts, the Holiday lot. Workman produced his pistol, and Stoddard had ahold of him, and shot Stoddard in the arm. As Stoddard fell to the ground, Workman fired another shot at him. The next thing Stoddard

saw was Oliver laying on the ground. Stoddard testified that he did not see Oliver get shot, and he did not fire a weapon at any time.

Now, Police Officer Parker provided testimony that conflicted with Stoddard's, but was consistent with Workman's. At first Parker testified he arrived at the Wendy's at the same time as Stoddard. He parked his car on the south side of the restaurant, looked inside the restaurant. He heard a loud noise, and when he realized it was a gunshot, he heard another shot. He ran to the north parking lot just as Oliver hit the ground.

Now, contrary to Officer Stoddard's testimony, Parker's first statements were, he saw Workman shoot Stoddard in the arm after, not before, Lieutenant Oliver went down.

Now, the State's official version in the trial record says that Philip Workman fired first and that Lieutenant Oliver emptied his gun, and that those were the only two people on the scene that night who fired their weapons. It also says that the first person that fired was Philip Workman, and no police officer fired until after Mr. Workman had fired his weapon.

So what we have got so far with Officer Parker's first statement of events, running around the restaurant, he's heard two shots, and when he comes out there, he sees from 10 or 15 feet away, according to his statement, he sees Philip shoot towards Stoddard, and Stoddard broke his arm and spin [*sic*] away.

Now, once again, I'll remind you, there are two shell casings at that point, two shell casings.

And, furthermore, he saw Lieutenant Oliver hitting the ground. Now, we've got an unexplained bullet being fired there, and there's no evidence that that's Philip Workman's bullet, and we have an expert here who will tell you that probably was not Philip Workman's bullet.

Dorsey next turned to the finding of the mysterious Harold Davis, the supposed eyewitness to the shooting. He called as a witness Lacey DeSente, the investigator in the Phoenix, Arizona, public defender's office who helped locate Davis. As she testified about how they tracked him down, she vividly described the emotional difficulty Davis had when he realized Philip Workman could be executed because of his statement. "[Mr. Davis] was very emotional, nervous, real fidgety. He kept looking out the window. He started crying, actually sobbing . . . after more crying and being really upset, he finally said there was something, and he was afraid to talk about it, but he agreed to . . . on tape." She said they videotaped Harold Davis on October 1, 1999, and that later, on November 20, they videotaped him again. The witness was excused, and Dorsey again directed his comments to Wilson:

Now it's been suggested that somehow we got to Harold Davis. As Ms. DeSante [*sic*] explained, we didn't coerce him. All we did was present the inconsistencies, and what I've got on the diagram is Harold Davis's purported route. Again, he says that the shooting occurred right in front of the Wendy's. He's up to ten feet away by his car, and he says he ran off through that parking lot. If that were true, Harold Davis would have run through the middle of where he would had to jump over Lieutenant Oliver and run past Philip Workman. Obviously, Harold Davis was not there.

The implications of this are very serious. If Harold Davis was not at the scene, how did Harold Davis know to testify with such specificity?

Harold Davis didn't appear on the scene until the next day at about 12:30 P.M. We know from the records he called the police. Now, there's not a shred of evidence anywhere in this world to demonstrate that Harold Davis was there, nothing, except Harold Davis' own testimony. The officers will tell you they didn't see Harold Davis, and all of the other witnesses, and, actually . . . we have affidavits from several witnesses who declared that had an African American man been on the scene that night, they would have seen him. As a matter of fact, let me refer back to Officer Parker's testimony . . .

"I was mainly looking for, they had just read out on role call that day that there was a man, a black male robbing only Wendy's and McDonald's and who hid in the bathroom at closing time and took an employee hostage when they came in to clean the bathroom. I was looking for a black male possibly inside the store is what we were suspecting, because he had pulled 6 or 7 holdups, one at the McDonald's about half a block up the street about three weeks earlier."

Dorsey concluded, "So, obviously, all the police officers in that precinct had a heightened awareness being at a Wendy's at closing time."

Dorsey then delved into Harold Davis's statement:

Harold Davis testified that he pulled into that Wendy's, and in his statement he was

"in the Wendy's parking lot on the north side of the store . . . As I got out of the car and went up to the door, I saw this man coming out the back, coming towards the door with a gun in his hand. I turned around and ran back to my car, and I saw police, two police cars drive up to the parking lot at Wendy's and as the guy was coming out of the door, I heard the policemen tell the man to stop. Then I saw the man turn around and start shooting at the police. I saw the police return the fire, and I saw one policeman go down. Then I heard some more shots, and I saw the guy who had shot the policeman run across the auto parts [lot], and he was holding his head. Then a bunch of police showed up at the scene."

Dorsey pointed out the conflict in this testimony: "Harold Davis has misstated the facts. If we can refer back to the crime scene, Harold Davis says he's parked in a designated place in that parking lot and that the shooting occurs right in front of the doors of the Wendy's, and he sees Philip Workman shoot these officers. Again, we know [by the location of the shell casings] where the shooting actually occurred." The struggle and shooting had occurred in the Holiday Auto Parts lot, not in front of the Wendy's.

After portraying the inaccuracy of the testimony of Harold Davis, Dorsey introduced a witness who was with Harold Davis the night of the Lieutenant Oliver slaying, Vivian Porter. She recounted how she and Harold were driving around smoking marijuana:

A policeman turned on his lights and was pulling us over . . . and we pulled over, and we were kind of panting and kind of, you know, upset because we knew that we had some drugs on us, and right before the policeman could get to us, he kind of leaned over, and I

55

noticed he was talking into the little mic, the walkie-talkie . . . and he turned around and got back in his car, and he drove off.

So we sat there for a few minutes, and we were like, whew, both of our fathers were preachers, so we just really assumed that God had sent a miracle. We were being covered in our sin. We were just talking about, man, God, this is a blessing, so we kind of sat there because we didn't know if the guy was going to come back or actually what was going on . . .

Then we pulled off, and we made a left on Danny Thomas [Place] off of Frazier [Frayser] Boulevard, and that's when we saw a lot of activity at the Wendy's. We did not stop. There was no reason for us to stop, and we just kept going, and we ended up later at my house or somewhere . . . It is impossible for Harold to have been there to witness that when he was in the car with me, and we had gotten pulled over by a policeman. I don't see how he could have seen that.

Dorsey asked Porter, "What was going on at the Wendy's when you all drove past?"

Porter replied, "There was a lot of activity, a lot of yellow tape, and the policemen were everywhere. I don't know. I assumed somebody had been robbed or somebody had been shot."

In summary, Jefferson Dorsey painted a scene that was very different from the account portrayed by prosecutors and left unchallenged by Philip's court-appointed lawyers during his trial. Philip had fled when he realized he was between Lieutenant Oliver and Officer Stoddard. He tripped over the curb of the parking lot and fell into the Holiday Auto Parts lot. He raised his hands in surrender with his back to the police officers, shouting, "I give up! I give up!" He was struck on the head, later requiring seven sutures, and his gun discharged. Lieutenant Oliver grappled with him, and Officer Stoddard closed on him, firing. Philip fired back at Stoddard, hitting him in the arm. The two shots Workman fired left two shell casings in the parking lot. He wrenched free of Lieutenant Oliver and ran. Other bullets were fired and one mortally wounded Lieutenant Oliver, but it was not Philip's bullet that killed him. And the state's key eyewitness, Harold Davis, was not actually there. He was with his friend Vivian Porter.

Yet the state maintained that Philip Workman had confessed. Jefferson Dorsey read the so-called confession that Philip had given at trial after being advised by his lawyers that he had "one millimeter of a chance for survival" and that was to confess.

Workman: "I guess I pulled the trigger."
Question: "And what happened when you pulled the trigger? Did the gun go off?"
Workman reply: "The gun fired."
Question: "And do you know whether or not anybody was hurt?"
Workman: "No, sir, I don't. I didn't see it. I don't know. I didn't see it."

Dorsey summed up: "Now, that is not a confession, and anybody who's spent any time in a criminal court knows that's not, regardless of what you characterize that as."

Don Dawson called the next witness: Dr. Kris Sperry, medical examiner for the state of Georgia. Dr. Sperry indicated that he usually testified for the prosecution and that he had no moral feelings about the death penalty. He just presented the facts.

Dr. Sperry pointed out that the Memphis police used a .38-caliber copper-jacket hollow-point with a nose of lead. The copper jacket is very hard and has a "greater likelihood of exit" due to the jacket maintaining the shape of the bullet as it travels through the torso.

Philip Workman, on the other hand, used Silvertip hollow-point .45-caliber bullets. The silver jacket of such a bullet is malleable, designed "to mushroom" upon entering the body. Because the bullet "jacket [is] very soft," it very rarely exits from the body. When it does exit, the wound is significantly greater than the entry wound.

After reviewing the x-ray that revealed a "through and through" bullet and a diagram of the bullets, Dr. Sperry concluded "with a reasonable degree of medical certainty" that the bullet that killed Lieutenant Oliver would probably have come from the police weapon rather than from Philip's. He stated that he reached that conclusion as an expert who had examined thirty to forty wounds caused by bullets similar to Philip's and that 90 percent of the time the bullet did not exit the body. When the bullet did exit the body, the wound was significantly larger than the entry wound.

Dr. Cyril Wecht, a renowned forensics specialist who worked on the Robert Kennedy assassination, had also submitted an affidavit, concluding: "It is my professional opinion, based upon a reasonable degree of medical certainty, that the gunshot wound of Police Officer Ronald D. Oliver is not consistent with the type of ammunition used by Mr. Philip R. Workman . . . I do not believe that it was Mr. Workman's gun that fired the shot that fatally wounded Officer Oliver."

Jefferson Dorsey finished by addressing the impossibility of crime scene events as portrayed by the state:

> Now, according to Officer Stoddard, Philip Workman was able to drag two full-grown veteran police officers across the Wendy's lot and into the Holiday Auto Parts lot, which is a distance of at least 60 feet . . . The money bag and the jacket (which was covering the bag) are located right next to the blood and right next to the shell casings . . . the incident occurred anywhere from 70 to 90 feet from the front of the Wendy's . . . That bag was full of over a thousand dollars of money and change. That bag was in Philip's hand with the jacket over it.
>
> Now, I just have to question how Philip Workman could possibly be able to drag two full-grown veteran police officers across two parking lots and over a curb while holding a jacket and money bag. Respectfully, I don't think that is possible. Nowhere in Stoddard's testimony does he account for hitting Mr. Workman in the head, although other dispassionate citizen witnesses said they saw him run from the scene holding his head with his right hand, holding the gun in his left hand. Mr. Workman is right-handed.
>
> Now, this is when he is supposed to be turning and firing at Officer Parker and Officer Stoddard, who both claim there were at least five shots, there were three shell casings out there and one live round. Sir, it's impossible. It doesn't work.

The star for the prosecution in the clemency hearing was Dr. O. C. Smith, the Shelby County medical examiner. Dr. Smith showed a Power Point presentation complete with medical and scientific jargon to Justin Wilson, a lawyer with no scientific, much less medical, background. Since Dr. Smith was not subject to cross-examination, he had leeway to state anything he was inclined to say with impunity. His testimony runs from page 96 to page 142 of the clemency hearing transcripts, well over half of the state's total testimony in the clemency hearing.

As one who attended the hearing and was familiar with the case, I listened with astonishment, incredulity, and anger to the confabulation of a tale that was more appropriate to science fiction than any representation of science in the analysis of the death of Ronald Oliver. The transcript of the hearing revealed the laser-like focus of the state of Tennessee in its attempt to execute Philip Workman.

Justin Wilson, who conducted the hearing and represented the governor, the parole board unable to be present with the changing of the clemency hearing dates, addressed Dr. Smith: "In regards to the issues here regarding the autopsy of Lieutenant Ronnie Oliver, at this point I would like to basically turn it over to you. If you could explain to the Governor what you have discovered regarding this autopsy, what generalizations have been made and what specific comments you can make about this autopsy."

Smith responded:

> The focus of the Medical Examiner's Office is not so much on the principals involved other than the victim, that the death of Lieutenant Oliver is a study into itself . . . Basically, the autopsy is going to be the most important source of information in this entire case . . .
>
> Dr. Bell, Dr. Wicks, and Dr. Sperry, and myself have all looked at this case and I believe are in agreement that the wound profile is such that it suggests a projectile that did not leave any bullet fragments in the body . . . I believe that the ammunition that has been alluded was in Mr. Workman's gun actually did produce the wound to Lieutenant Oliver's body.
>
> In this case, the bullet exited intact. It may be deformed, but it would essentially be intact.

Of course, Dr. Sperry had clearly stated that the wound in Oliver's body did *not* match the .45 hollow-point Silvertip bullets that Philip Workman carried in his gun. There was also a detailed affidavit from Dr. Cyril Wecht establishing that the smaller exit wound would not have corresponded with Philip's bullets. So how did Dr. Smith conclude that Philip's bullet was the fatal shot?

The first task Smith had faced was to discredit the exit wound. Dr. James Bell, the medical examiner who had performed the autopsy and testified at Philip's trial, had described the entry wound as a half inch in diameter and "sort of rounded," and said the exit wound was a "sort of slit-like tear in the skin" less than a quarter inch in length. Dr. Sperry and Dr. Wecht had corroborated the fact that the exit wound was smaller than the entrance wound in their review of the medical record as well. The smaller exit wound was not consistent with a silver-jacketed .45 hollow-point bullet, because that type of bullet would have mushroomed on impact and caused a significantly larger exit than entrance wound.

Despite this record, Dr. Smith found the wound to be "a gaping wound." He provided slides of made-up experiments, measurements, and utter fiction in an attempt to nullify the size of the exit wound. He concocted a story about the FBI that supposedly proved his analysis. Again, all of this was done without benefit of challenge through cross-examination. Indeed, this goes on and on until page 108 of the transcript when Dr. Smith announces the following astonishing "fact": "Bullet Q1 is a bullet recovered at the scene in the parking lot. It was recovered the next day. It is my contention that this bullet that was covered in the parking lot is the one that went through Lieutenant Oliver's body."

This proposition about Q1 refers to the bullet Terry Willis claimed to have found the day after the crime. As described earlier, Willis was assistant manager at the Holiday Auto Parts next to the Wendy's and picked up what he thought was a ball bearing. He realized it was a bullet and called the police. As peculiar as the story is on its face, although the police had already scoured the crime scene, at trial the FBI had discounted the bullet found by Willis as the fatal one . The FBI agent testified that there was no hair, cloth, skin, or any indication that Q1 had traveled through a human being; thus, it was a pristine bullet, not a fatal bullet. But for O. C. Smith, Q1 had somehow become the bullet that killed Officer Oliver: "I think that it is reasonable to expect that this bullet could go through Lieutenant Oliver's body without expanding very much at all, but it did produce a small exit wound as a result of not having expanded or having exited base first or sideways. That it didn't deform significantly after the initial nose deformation and that it could have [done so] either by striking the 7th rib, could have either caused the nose to fold inward or to become plugged with debris and fail to expand as expected with most hollow-points."

For anyone familiar with the trial record, Smith's testimony boggled the mind. It contradicted not only what the FBI agent had testified at trial, but also the work of Smith's own "mentor," Dr. Bell, along with that of Dr. Sperry and Dr. Wecht. However, it did leave one intriguing door open.

Smith mentioned that "the bullet that was covered in the parking lot is the one that went through Lieutenant Oliver's body." The initial reaction was to think the word *covered* should read *recovered* in the transcript. But a newspaper photographer at the crime scene had taken pictures of a bullet *covered by a cup* in the parking lot. Mysteriously, this covered bullet was unaccounted for in the police reconstruction of the crime scene. Smith, in his haste to get everything out about Philip Workman being the shooter, had inadvertently mentioned the "covered" bullet. He conflated it with Q1, the pristine bullet supposedly found by Terry Willis. That bullet covered by the cup could very well have been the fatal bullet, but it could *not* have come from Philip's gun, as his bullets were accounted for elsewhere. It had to have come from a fellow police officer's gun, which was why it never appeared in the police notes or crime scene reconstruction. After this testimony about Q1, a complete fabrication, the defense began calling Q1 the "magic bullet."

Dr. Smith went on to describe shooting into gelatin, shooting into water, discussing his paper on shooting at intermediate targets, shooting into cotton boxes, all accompanied with Power Point slides. Finally he came to the matter of the x-ray.

Smith danced an elaborate minuet around the x-ray. The Sixth Circuit Court of Appeals panel had already choked on one decision (utilizing the Fackler study) due to its certainty that there was no x-ray which showed a "through and through" bullet. But Smith had accidentally provided the x-ray that did substantiate such a bullet. Now the en banc Sixth Circuit Court was weighing this evidence even as Smith razzled and dazzled with his Power Point slide show offering "another reason why the X-ray is not of great importance."

In conclusion, Smith shared his comparison experiment, saying:

> This is the bullet model that went through the shirt, the rib cage, and the gelatin . . . I think that you can take a look at those and see that they have enough similarity to believe as I do that this model adequately duplicated the forces that were present on the bullet that went through Lieutenant Oliver's body producing enough similarity and because it only

went 104 feet beyond the blood pool that contained Lieutenant Oliver's body, that Q1 indeed is the bullet that went through the lieutenant, and that bullet, Q1, was by the FBI testing, shown to come from Mr. Workman's cold pistol to the exclusion of all other pistols in the world.

Smith conveniently seemed to forget the statement made by the FBI agent who testified at trial that Q1 could *not* have been the fatal bullet due to its pristine character.

As preposterous as the testimony of Dr. O. C. Smith was and how utterly implausible it was when compared with the scientific record, it was clear that Justin Wilson had bought the story hook, line, and sinker. Indeed, as we would later discover by obtaining the e-mails leading up to the clemency hearing, the entire proceeding was no more than a show trial in which the decision had already been made ahead of time. Philip Workman might as well have saved his breath rather than repeat his version of the events that underscored his guilt for "bringing all the parties together" but being innocent of homicide. For all practical purposes, the outcome was foreordained before we were all subjected to the O. C. Smith show.

After Smith's testimony, the state called Officer Stoddard. Stoddard recounted his story of the struggle with Philip Workman, looking down and seeing the gun pointed at his belly, being shot and calling for help. He also stated that his gun never left the holster. Stoddard also recalled that Lieutenant Oliver shot wildly, emptying his revolver after he fell to the ground. Stoddard stated that the only two shooters were Philip Workman and Lieutenant Oliver.

Officer Parker was the next witness for the state. He recounted what he saw: Lieutenant Oliver hitting the ground and Officer Stoddard shot. He, too, did not shoot his firearm, he said, and he left his shotgun in the car. Thus, somehow two Memphis police officers had witnessed a fellow officer being shot and did not fire their weapons at the shooter, which seems very unlikely.

The final exhibit offered by the state was a videotape of Officer Clyde Keenan, the head of the shoot team, and assistant district attorney Eddie Peterson. Keenan stated, "I personally checked Officer Parker's service revolver and shotgun. None had been fired. Stoddard's service revolver was damaged from his fall and laying under him. It had never been fired. Only Ronnie Oliver's service revolver had been fired." Peterson testified that the trial record was okay as far as he was concerned. This concluded the fabrication of the scenario at the Wendy's restaurant, its initial presentation at trial and now at clemency, in which Philip Workman was framed for shooting Lt. Ronald Oliver.

***

Philip Workman wanted to tell his side of the story at the April 3 clemency hearing. After some wrangling among lawyers, Justin Wilson allowed Philip to make a final statement after the state concluded its presentation. Shackled, Philip left his seat at the rear of the room and came forward to the table with Wilson. He was drawn, fully realizing after the lies he had heard by the state's witnesses that the hearing was not a genuine attempt to discover the truth. As he spoke, his voice was strained but clear:

First off, I'd like to thank you, and—for allowing us to be here like this, and also apologize that any of us have to be here, and, of course, for my actions in creating the incident that brought all this about almost 19 years ago.

I'd like to apologize to the family, Mrs. Oliver. To this day, I still remember her on the witness stand, and how I wanted to die at that moment just watching her, just because of what I created, but I must say [only] up to a certain point.

And I'd like to thank Lt. Oliver's daughter for just looking at this evidence, not just the ballistics, the perjured testimony, I mean how many perjured testimonies does it take? But I just like to thank her for being courageous and for being—it's just hard to describe, explain how a person could grow up such as her and feel the way she is, but I also believe and know that she looked at it and sees that something is not right here. [After reviewing Dr. Kris Sperry's forensic analysis and Harold Davis's recantation, Paula Dodillet, Lieutenant Oliver's adult daughter, had spoken out against the execution, because she did not believe the evidence pointed to Philip Workman as her father's killer.]

And to the State of Tennessee, I'm sorry. I'm sorry that we're here, sorry it happened, of course. But everything isn't the way that it's presented. There wasn't just a shootout. I did try to surrender. I was struck in the head. There are three witnesses that were never brought to trial. There's a police officer stated that first thing he noticed upon arrest that I had blood on my face from a previous encounter with somebody. All of that I didn't know about, but it validates that it wasn't just my word and just me making this up, and with all due respect, Officer Parker testifying, he testified about the corner of that building that I shot at him, said I turned and fell, discharged the shot straight up in the air, that didn't happen. Just simply didn't happen, and the evidence bears it out on the crime scene diagram, there are no shell casings. An automatic kicks out the shell casings.

With all due respect, Officer Stoddard testified I'm shooting all these shots. Where are the shell casings? They're not there because it didn't happen. I discharged two shots in a daze when I was struck, and I still to this day, although I didn't push it at court because my attorneys led me to believe that if I said anything that would seem like I'm trying to shift anything towards the police, that I would lose that one millimeter of a chance for a life sentence. So, of course, I downplayed it.

But when I was struck, I know that first shot went up in the air, and that bullet that was found the next day that the doctor is saying—O. C. Smith, Dr. O. C. Smith, that was found over there by the curb. The State's witness, FBI testified he analyzed that bullet. That bullet had no signs of blood on it, no signs of tissue. I'd be willing to bet you it was a shot, that first shot that went up in the air and it came down and landed on the side. Therefore, a little dent.

But it's just—of course, I'm just sorry for all of this, but it's just, I mean, is perjured testimony allowed in this country for any sentence, let alone a sentence of death? Why was he [Harold Davis] strategically placed in between two officers [in his testimony at trial]? The man was not there. How did he get the information to collaborate almost 100 percent everything Officer Stoddard said? Said he was 10 feet away. His car is not in the pictures. The man wasn't there. And I know everybody's got to know this. How can anyone go to prison for any type of sentence under such a thing, let alone to their death?

We have been trying for ten years to get an evidentiary hearing. I read an article, with all due respect to Mr. Summers, saying that he was looking forward to this the last time because we felt we had to withdraw it because of the X-ray, and it needed to be finalized in court, but that he was looking forward to the hearing. Well, why has the State then blocked us so diligently at every turn at trying to get an evidentiary hearing where we could get in there not just for a hour-and-a-half or take a few days? Look at the cost of all this. What would have the cost of doing this ten years ago, just let us have it, and let's get in there and find out the facts.

And why has the State—I don't understand. I really don't understand, and I'm sorry. Of course, I'm sorry for everything, but I realized long ago, some years back I couldn't handle it all, and I have to be thankful in ways that I had the time to find out there really is a God and there really is a Jesus Christ, and I did turn it all over to him because I'm not a tough guy, and I have that peace.

Nobody wants to die, but if I have to die, I know where I'm going for the first time in my life, but I'm telling you, this is wrong. You, sir, you've got to know, nobody can go to their death and nobody can spend a life sentence in prison on perjured testimony. This is wrong.

And we need to get in there with the experts in a court where we can have time [to] cross-examine and get down on the ballistics, bring forth the witnesses that was in the record. I didn't even know until 1990. I never saw the records. Under the Public's Record Act, when we got the records and my lawyer finally got me to get in there, I always just assumed I'm dead.

And read those statements from the people that were there right at the scene right after the fact that I was holding my head. I wasn't just holding my head because of no reason. I was holding my head for a reason, because I was in a daze. I discharged two involuntarily blind shots, but I told the truth. Yes, it seems like the second one went towards— seemingly towards some kind of flash, but that's all I know, and yes, at post-conviction, sir, I did say, I know I shot Lt. Oliver, but I didn't know. I just knew that I better not try to make any waves like the lawyers told me at the beginning because if I do, I'll never stand a chance of some mercy somewhere along the line for some other type of sentences because I knew nobody would ever believe me that I was trying to surrender.

But I didn't know what was in the record, those witnesses that were never brought forth, but I'm going to close.

I thank you all. I pray, Mr. Governor, that you will feel that this cannot continue without some something other than my execution. And, again, I apologize that we all have to be here, and I thank all of those who have looked at this evidence and see that there is something to it, and it wasn't just like it was all presented at trial.

Thank you.

The hearing was adjourned shortly after Philip's statement.

***

On the morning of April 4, 2000, the en banc court of the Sixth Circuit Court of Appeals granted a stay of execution to Philip Workman in order to review the newly discovered x-ray. All fourteen judges on the court would determine Philip's fate by evaluating the withholding of the x-ray, the panel decision with the redaction of Colonel Fackler's study from its earlier decision, and Philip's claims of being framed by police and prosecutors.

After a summer of study and discussion, somewhat heated at times, the en banc court issued its opinion on September 5, 2000. It was a 7–7 tie and in Philip's case became known as the infamous "tie you die" decision. According to the rules of procedure, a tied en banc decision reverts back to the panel decision. In this instance, the case was now controlled by the earlier Sixth Circuit panel decision with the slashes through the Fackler study and by a result that was also premised on a fragmenting bullet. Without the Fackler study and with the x-ray revealing a "through and through" bullet with no fragmentation, the panel decision literally made no sense now. It was no longer anchored in fact, reason, or law. However, it was anchored in enmity, since the three Republican judges on the panel were three of the seven Republicans on the Sixth Circuit Court of Appeals. Thus seven Republican appointees voted against Philip, and seven Democratic appointees voted for relief. And so it goes.

Philip Workman reading his Bible in his death row cell. Photo by Eric England with permission.

Charles Traughber convened the second Philip Workman clemency hearing on January 25, 2001, at 8:30 A.M. The hearing was held in the same room at the prison used for the previous clemency hearing with Justin Wilson. Traughber explained that the board would act in an advisory capacity to Governor Sundquist. In effect, the parole board had become a clemency board. Ray Maples, a former Memphis police officer, had recused himself. The other board members present for the hearing were Townie Anderson, Bill Dalton, Don Dills, Larry Hassell, and Sheila Swearingen. Each side was allowed two hours to make their presentation.

In an interesting development since the previous clemency hearing, attorney John Pierotti had come aboard Philip's clemency team. Pierotti was a former Memphis associate district attorney who later became head district attorney. He was now in private practice in Memphis and had joined the clemency effort for Philip because he believed Philip had been framed by the perjured testimony of Harold Davis.

During the hearing Pierotti began by mentioning five members of the trial jury who had sworn affidavits stating that if they had known about Harold Davis's not being at the scene, they would have not voted for the death penalty. Pierotti pointed out that Philip's conviction and death sentence were a product of Davis's perjury. He then read from Davis's statements at trial and pointed out that the state's "eyewitness" was a liar, emphasizing how "prosecutors had Davis step down from the witness stand and act out the events he saw." The pantomime demonstrated how Workman had allegedly "coolly, deliberately, pulled the trigger . . . no more than two or three feet away." But in fact Harold Davis had not been at the crime scene. Pierotti also went on to explain that he wasn't implying that prosecutors had provided Davis with information; he assured the board they were all fine men he knew personally. No, they, too, had been victims of Davis's deceit.

Jefferson Dorsey played the videotape interview of Harold Davis, which actually consisted of three interviews over time. After listening to Davis, Dorsey pointed out the problems with Davis's stating he was at the crime scene: (1) not a single eyewitness had seen an African American at the Wendy's; (2) Harold Davis's name was not on any police report; (3) there was no evidence of his car in the crime scene diagram; (4) he was not on the witness list; and (5) he was not present for the lineup. Indeed, the first contact with Harold Davis had been around noon the day after the crime when he called the precinct station.

After this review of Harold Davis's testimony, Jefferson Dorsey summoned his first witness: Vivian Porter. The hearing had been under way for thirty-one minutes when Ms. Porter took the stand. She explained that she ran a transition house for women coming out of prison and women who needed help in drug recovery. She then recounted the story she had told at the first clemency hearing about how she and Harold had been smoking marijuana; were stopped by a policeman, who left suddenly in response to a call; and how they had eventually passed by the Wendy's and saw the crime tape and lots of policemen. She concluded, "Harold was with me. It was impossible for him to have witnessed this crime."

In his opening remarks, Chairman Traughber had mentioned there would be no cross-examination, implying that counsel could not challenge testimony. However, he did not enjoin the board members from such activity. Indeed, Larry Hassell jumped in immediately, aggressively going after Vivian Porter. He asked her if she was familiar with the area, and she responded affirmatively. He then went into great detail over her directions, grilling her on street locations, pointing out that Thomas Street is not the same as Danny Thomas Place. After handing her a map and hammering her about her location, he finally blurted out, "Is anyone coaching you in your remarks?" She said no. Then he asked, "You drive right through all that police activity with drugs?" Porter explained that when you're doing drugs, the safest place to be is near policemen responding to another crisis, because they never check you.

Bill Dalton inquired, "How did you get brought into this?" Porter explained that Harold's sister had been talking to the attorneys on the phone when she was over there and told her about the situation. Dalton asked, "Did you call these people?" Porter explained again that Jackie, Harold's sister, asked her to meet with Philip's lawyers. All of this was in the 1990s long after the trial. Dalton wondered why she hadn't volunteered her information before then or at the trial. Porter explained that she had moved to Atlanta before the trial and had no idea Harold was offering such a story, nor did his family.

Then Don Dills grilled Porter about the discrepancy in time between her written affidavit, in which she said she sat in the car with Harold for "two or three minutes," and her oral testimony that it was "ten to fifteen minutes." The hostility was crackling in the room. Porter explained herself and said she meant to say ten to fifteen in the affidavit but didn't. It was a mistake and she was sorry. She meant ten to fifteen minutes.

By this point members of the clemency board were acting like sharks that smelled blood in the water. Whatever guise of objectivity they might have possessed in the beginning was long gone. They were in attack mode on Vivian Porter.

Dalton said, "You're giving Mr. Davis a lot of credit for telling the truth in the videotape but not at trial. He was a crack addict. Surely you two weren't watching the news and doing drugs that night." Porter explained that was exactly what they were doing and that was how Harold Davis learned about the police officer slaying at the Wendy's.

"Is this the only night you ever watched the news?" Dalton said with sarcasm dripping.

Chairman Traughber said to Porter, "You have characterized Mr. Davis as being a person who couldn't be believed back then because he was taking drugs."

Porter responded, "Yes, sir."

"Were you in the same category?" Traughber asked.

"Yes, sir."

"So why should I believe you now?" Traughber said.

Porter's replied, "Because I'm delivered and I've been set free and I don't have anything to gain."

Vivian Porter explained how she had changed her life and had been to Alcoholics Anonymous, and what she had learned. At this point, however, it was clear that she and the whole defense team were, in the words of Jesus of Nazareth, "casting their pearls before swine."

Philip's clemency team knew this hearing would be difficult. As noted earlier, Charles Traughber, the chairman, was married to Lois DeBerry, speaker pro tem of the Tennessee General Assembly. Both of them, African Americans, were prominent in the Memphis political establishment. Just as Judge Julia Gibbons and her district attorney husband, Bill Gibbons, their white counterparts, were part of the political establishment, Traughber and DeBerry were enmeshed in the black part of the power structure. Either way, it was an uphill journey for Philip, because his presentation challenged the police and prosecutors who upheld this political structure.

Although John Pierotti could not bring himself to say it, because he, too, had been part and parcel of this structure, the only way Philip could have been convicted was if the police and prosecutors made him the fall guy. They had manufactured Harold Davis, coached him on what to say and how to step down from the witness stand and reenact the shooting. It was a shell game from the get-go to cover up the fact that they had killed one of their own. And now the cover-up had become a conspiracy with the involvement of the clemency board, attorney general's office, and the governor's office. A lot of people wanted to bury this story with Philip Workman rather than deal with the facts of the crime scene and the autopsy. Hence the Tennessee inquisition of Vivian Porter during the clemency hearing was the most recent manifestation of the state's determination to discredit anyone who would stand up for Philip Workman.

Jefferson Dorsey intervened in Porter's questioning by saying, " Have we coached you, advised you? Are you gaining anything by testifying here today?" Porter stated she was not.

Dr. Kris Sperry, who had testified at the initial clemency hearing, could not make it to this one, so a videotape of his questioning was played. Afterward Mr. Dills asked, "I'd like to know, how did Dr. Sperry come into this process?" And Dalton added, "I'm assuming he was hired by the defense team?"

"Yes, sir," Dorsey replied.

Dalton then asked, "So it was up to him to report back to you all, not necessarily anyone else?"

"That's correct," Dorsey responded.

Dalton concluded, "So if he had found evidence to the contrary, he would never have told anybody."

Anderson then asked, "When did the film surface? The x-ray?"

Dorsey answered:

> Actually, when we applied for clemency in 2000, Dr. O. C. Smith for the State generated a one-page report. At that time we saw in the report that one of the items of evidence he had looked at was an x-ray, and frankly, we were quite surprised because the Sixth Circuit Court of Appeals specifically asked if there was an x-ray, and in 1995 a Federal subpoena was issued for an x-ray.
>
> In addition to that, there was trial discovery in 1981 and '82 that never mentioned an x-ray, and there was a Tennessee public records request made in 1990 that never mentioned an x-ray. So the first time we heard of the x-ray was in, I think it was February of 2000.

Anderson then asked Dorsey, "Do you feel comfortable with the x-ray being authentic?"

"Absolutely, sir," Dorsey replied. "I've seen the x-ray. I was the one who went down and got a copy of it."

***

Philip's lawyers then summoned Cyril Wecht as their forensics expert. He began by discussing Philip's ammunition, the .45 hollow-point Silvertips:

> In my experience this kind of ammunition will become flattened, it will mushroom, it will become deformed. Indeed, that is why hollow-point ammunition was first conceived a few decades ago: the idea was they thought it would have more stopping power. Officers

were unhappy with the traditional bullet, which they felt sometimes just went through a potential assailant and made that person then much more dangerous, as well as able to escape.

So the bullet is designed to do that. This is more so when the bullet impacts against a hard surface or object such as a bone.

And indeed, it did impact the seventh left rib in this case, producing a significant fracture. It didn't just perforate.

. . . But this bone was fractured. So the bullet fractured that bone and then it continued on through the left lung, the lining of the lung, the pleura, the diaphragm, caught the stomach, came back up, severely damaged the heart, which is really what killed Lieutenant Oliver—just lacerated the left-side ventricle, the mitral valve, and the left atrium—then continued on through a portion of the right lung and then exited somewhat more rearward and slightly higher than it had entered on the left side.

And there was one pathway and only one pathway. The x-ray reveals what is clearly depicted, or certainly implied in the x-ray in the autopsy report; namely, that no fragment of a bullet was in the body, no other bullet was in the body, and there were no other pathway to suggest any kind of collateral or additional trajectories of fragments coursing through the chest.

So what you have then is an entrance wound which is considerably, significantly larger that the exit wound. That, in my experience, is extremely atypical for this kind of ammunition. Extremely atypical for hollow-point ammunition . . . I would just like to remind the Board that this bullet went from left side to right side, and in addition to breaking the rib, went through, as I've already said, the lungs, the heart, the stomach, the diaphragm.

So you have that, and then you have a bullet, which as I understood from FBI Agent Wilkes's testimony [at trial], revealed absolutely no trace evidence of blood, tissue, or fiber. In other words, despite that bullet having done all these things, it emerged. And this very experienced and highly competent expert from the FBI, using their sophisticated equipment, was unable to identify anything of a biological nature or anything from an article of clothing. That has puzzled me. Again, I consider it to be very atypical.

Then you have a bullet, which I have seen in picture and heard described, which has retained its aluminum jacket. I find it very difficult to understand how a .45 hollow-point aluminum-jacketed soft-lead-core bullet would strike the bone and go through all those tissues, et cetera, and emerge with not a great deal of deformity, and also with the aluminum jacket still attached to the lead core of the bullet. Extremely atypical . . .

What I'm left with here is a very, very atypical scenario for a .45 aluminum-jacketed soft-lead-core hollow-point piece of ammunition inflicting this wound in Lt. Oliver.

Pierotti asked Dr. Wecht, "And the conclusion of all of this . . . what is your medical opinion whether or not that particular shell or slug that was found would have been the slug that killed Lt. Oliver?"

"In my opinion, then," Wecht replied, "based upon a reasonable degree of medical probability, that slug, that spent bullet which was found, was not the bullet that went through Lt. Oliver."

Chairman Traughber said, "Reasonable degree of medical certainty, what is a percentage?"

"For the jury it is beyond reasonable doubt," Wecht answered. "It is similar to that."

Traughber kept pressing for a percentage, but Dr. Wecht told him that *reasonable certainty* was not the language medical examiners use in testifying forensically. "I would hate to give you a number," he said.

Mr. Dills then commented, "I'm impressed with the *Who's Who in Israel, Who's Who in the United States*, you've testified in death cases many times."

"Yes, but never in a clemency," Wecht replied.

"What would be the percentage you testify for the defense?" asked Dills.

Wecht answered indirectly, "85 percent of the time I testify for the prosecution."

"Do you believe in the death penalty?" Dills asked.

Wecht replied, "I would certainly have no problem in certain cases."

Dalton then repeated, "In the last five years would you have testified 85 percent for the prosecution?" He followed that with, "Did you work on the O. J. Simpson case?"

Wecht indicated that he had consulted on the Simpson case and had also worked on President John F. Kennedy's assassination and believed the Warren Commission was wrong in its conclusion.

Dalton began asking Wecht about Q1, the so-called magic bullet that O. C. Smith had identified as the fatal bullet fired from Philip's gun.

Traughber said to Wecht, "State has said they found round (Q1). Would mutilation be on it?"

Wecht answered, "Yes. Trace evidence, not visible to the human eye, would be there."

Dr. Cyril Wecht, Dr. Kris Sperry, Dr. James Bell, and FBI agent Wilkes had all concluded that because of its pristine condition, Q1 could not have been the fatal bullet. There was no fabric, blood, tissue, no biological indication on the bullet that Dr. O. C. Smith maintained was the fatal bullet. Nor was the Silvertip jacket loosened. To every forensics expert, including O. C. Smith's "mentor," Dr. Bell, the entire bullet seemed to be the same as the bullet Philip had ejected out of his gun. Yet Dr. Smith was insistent on maintaining Q1 was the bullet that caused the mortal wound to Lieutenant Oliver.

***

Wardie Parks was the next witness called to testify. Parks had been a member of the jury in Philip's trial. Like Vivian Porter, Parks was an African American.

Parks told those assembled, "The judge charged me I should have been listening to everything that came out of the witness chair, . . . one of those witnesses perjured himself and the ballistics show Workman didn't do it . . . If these studies had been brought up, he [Workman] wouldn't be sitting here now. [The] public defender representing Mr. Workman didn't question ballistics evidence."

"You had the opportunity to ask questions at trial," Chairman Traughber said. He seemed to think that Wardie Parks somehow should have known that both Harold Davis and the Memphis police were lying. At trial the prosecutors had staged a mini-drama with Davis coming down off the witness box and reenacting the shooting, and the defense lawyers never challenged the prosecution, instead accepting the state's theory of the case. Given the level of deception present at trial, Traughber still thought Wardie Parks should have been able to penetrate the shroud of deceit.

A frustrated Parks said to the group, "I'm charging you all. I'm washing my hands of this situation . . . You all do what's right according to the law."

But Dalton continued questioning him: "How did you find out the witness changed his testimony?"

"It was Chris Minton who told me," Parks replied. "About a year ago."

Dalton asked again, "Who told you?"

"Chris Minton," Parks repeated.

"What did they tell you when they called you? The two of them and you. Didn't [they] have the benefit of cross-examination?" Dalton said. "Maybe General Summers here would challenge it and say it's not true. What would you say?"

Parks replied, "I believe it and I stand on it. We're talking about taking a man's life."

Larry Hassell then inquired, "Any other doubts about the trial besides Mr. Davis and ballistics?"

"I do not," said Parks.

Sheila Swearingen asked, "Did Mr. Workman admit he shot the weapon that killed Lt. Oliver?"

Parks replied, "I don't think so but I don't know. You have the transcript."

At this point Chairman Traughber read from the transcript the two exchanges between Philip and the prosecutors. Philip, who did not recall shooting anyone, had been instructed by defense counsel that his "one millimeter of a chance" was not to disagree with the state nor seem to antagonize the prosecutors. So in response to the two questions about if he shot Lieutenant Oliver, Philip had stated he "guessed" he did.

If any doubts remained after the shabby treatment of Vivian Porter and Wardie Parks at this hearing, the attempt to treat Cyril Wecht as biased and accentuating his Jewishness by mentioning the *Who's Who* listing in Israel, Traughber's reading of the so-called confession made it totally clear that this proceeding was a railroad train to the death house. And the state had yet to summon its first witness.

***

The afternoon session began at 12:30. The lead counsel for the state was William Gibbons, the Shelby County district attorney. His role underscored the state's determination to avoid another setback like what happened after the first clemency hearing with the stay of execution from the Sixth Circuit Court of Appeals. Gibbons, husband of the federal court judge who had ruled against Philip's habeas corpus petition, lent his considerable political presence to the process of Philip's extermination. Gibbons was assisted by ADAs John Campbell, Jerry Kitchens, and Glenn Pruden, senior counsel from the attorney general's office.

Bill Gibbons's opening statement reiterated the state's theory that Philip Workman killed Lt. Ronnie Oliver. He said, "The facts have not changed in nineteen years. He is not deserving of clemency." Then he turned the questioning of the first witness over to his associate Jerry Kitchens.

Kitchens questioned Aubrey Stoddard, the policeman who had arrived at the scene immediately after Lieutenant Oliver.

Stoddard: "[About] 10:30 I received a hold up in progress alarm. Steve Parker, my partner, was in another car. The dispatcher told me to disregard the call as a false alarm. I went anyway since it was only a block away. Parker came in behind me and stopped on the south side of the building. I was on the north side. They walked out of the restaurant and Oliver grabbed him in a bear hug from behind. I grabbed him from the front around the neck, looked down and saw the pistol between my belly and his. He shot it and hit me in the arm. I fell backwards and heard six or seven shots where Workman and Oliver were struggling. Workman ran by me and fired another shot at me and missed. He went over a fence. I was getting up and Steve Parker came over and checked on me and then he checked on Oliver."

Kitchens: "The only person you saw with a gun was the defendant?"

Stoddard: "Yes, sir."

Kitchens: "Did you pull your gun out?"

Stoddard: "Never came out of my holster."

Kitchens: "Did Officer Parker shoot his gun?"

Stoddard: "No."

Traughber: "Any doubt about who shot you?"

Stoddard: "No."

Traughber: "Is he in the room?"

Stoddard: "Yes, sir. He's right back there." (Indicating Philip Workman seated behind him).

Dalton: "He shot at Officer Parker or did he go over the fence?"

Stoddard: "Yes, about a minute after he shot at me." (Stoddard initially stated Workman went over the fence without shooting at Parker).

Stoddard was then excused and Officer Parker was called to the stand. Officer Parker was now assistant U.S. attorney in the U.S. attorney's office in Memphis.

Parker: "I ran up to Lieutenant Oliver and looked up, and he (Workman) was not fleeing and (his) pistol pointed in my direction to shoot at me. I ducked and he fired."

Traughber: "You testified you did not fire your weapon."

Parker: "Yes, sir."

Traughber: "You did not have another weapon?"

Parker: "No, sir . . . I swear to God I did not fire any weapon. I swear I didn't even have a shotgun. I saw Mr. Craig's affidavit (a citizen witness who saw Parker with a shotgun) and he was mistaken. Somehow he was mistaken . . . Officer Stoddard was running toward me and Lieutenant Oliver lying there mortally wounded."

Dalton: "You sure you didn't shoot your gun?"

Parker: "Yes, sir. [There's] no way Stoddard could have shot his weapon. [The] gun was still in the holster, was not on the pavement or in his hand."

Dalton: "Back then you said they didn't have radio attached to [their] shoulder. He would have had it in his hand."

Parker: "That technology wasn't in existence then. Not in 1981 and I don't remember it in 1984. [This statement was elicited to impugn Vivian Porter's testimony.]"

Traughber (reading from a police report of the crime): "'Suspect did exchange gunfire with Officer Parker.'"

Parker: "Whoever wrote this made a mistake. I never fired a gun."

Dalton: "Your gun [was] checked after the event?"

Parker: "Yes."

Parker then gave an elaborate story of trying to get his gun out of the holster and why he couldn't. Along with Stoddard, we now had two fully trained, competent Memphis police officers who were unable to get their weapons out of their holsters at a robbery with shots fired and an officer down.

Parker finished by saying, "Bottom line, [the] jury found him guilty, numerous courts upheld the verdict. Four people were with guns there. Three wore guns to protect people. He was the one person there to victimize people."

Parker was dismissed and Clyde Keenan was called as the next witness. ADA John Campbell questioned Keenan, who made the following statement:

> In 1981 I was Lieutenant XO [in charge] of [an] investigative squad called the Shoot Team. We handled all shootings by police officers. We followed behind the investigative unit. [On August, 5, 1981] I heard the call for help, officer down. I was there in a minute. I was first supervisor on the scene. Ronnie Oliver was a very close friend. We were drinking buddies. [I] knelt down beside him, he was gasping, couldn't find the wound, covered with blood.
>
> Officer Parker was the first person to give me information about the suspect. Ran down for me what had happened. Officers took Lieutenant Stoddard to a squad car. I checked his pistol real quick before he left. It had not been fired. I dumped all six cartridges in my hand. Gave it right back to him. 100 percent positive that handgun had not been fired.
>
> Shotguns are locked in [a] rack behind officer's head. Made sure all police weapons were accounted for. Oliver had no shotgun. Officer Stoddard and Officer Parker's locked in rack of car. Investigative shoot team checked both weapons and neither had been fired.

After Keenan completed his testimony, Keenan was asked, "Did you check the weapon before he went to the car?" Keenan replied:

> I sent my investigator, Gary Ball, to the hospital. He checked it at the hospital. Had not been fired. Lieutenant Oliver had fired all six rounds. The only person that could have shot Lieutenant Oliver was Mr. Workman.
>
> We found the [fatal] round on the scene within hours. Crime scene investigators took possession of it. Not sure about the tool box round. [This] bullet is slightly to the west of Lieutenant Oliver's body. Fourteen to twenty feet from his body. This was a lead slug. Different than a jacketed hollow-point.

Traughber raised a question about the "tool box round," but John Campbell cut him off, saying, "Dr. Smith will go into detail about that."

In follow-up questions, Keenan admitted he saw no vehicle parked near the police cars (where Harold Davis had claimed his car was located), nor did he explain why there was no photo of the bullet hole in the van, no recovery of the bullet in the van, nor any attempt to chart the path of that bullet.

***

The next witness to be called was Dr. O. C. Smith, who once again brought his Power Point presentation. It was the usual razzle-dazzle—as Shakespeare put it, "full of sound and fury and signifying nothing." But performed unchallenged before a group of laypeople, it could seem impressive. Nevertheless, it contradicted the trial record in some fundamental and irreconcilable ways.

1. Smith stated that the wounds in Philip's buttocks were not from shotgun pellets but from dog bites. Certainly Philip had suffered dog bites when he was apprehended, but the treating doctor at John Gaston Hospital in Memphis in 1981 had also identified shotgun pellets in his buttocks.

2. Smith had gone to the crime scene to reenact the shooting with Stoddard and said that they'd "also had people from the Attorney's General's office working with us." How could this be dispassionate, objective science?

3. In discussing the wound path through Oliver's body, Smith stated that it was a path "which one would expect from a nondeforming, nondefragmenting projectile. A bullet that doesn't blossom or mushroom, a bullet that doesn't break into pieces." But rather than concluding, as did Dr. Sperry and Dr. Wecht, that this evidence eliminated Philip's ammunition, Smith concluded, "The Silvertip ammunition can indeed produce the wound type of the type that was present in Lieutenant Oliver's body."

4. Smith then engaged in a description of what could only be termed poppycock to justify his conclusion by flatly contradicting Keenan's prior testimony: "Now, bullet Q1 is the bullet that was recovered from the parking lot. I believe that that is the bullet that went through Lieutenant Oliver's body without expanding, that it produced a small exit wound because again it didn't deform." Smith presented a slide that showed Oliver's wound magnified, which he described as follows: "a very clean, crisp hole here, and what seems to be a tag of tissue here. This type of wound certainly could have been produced by a hollow-point bullet. It is consistent with the shirt because the shirt has a plug of material cut from it like a flat point or a hollow point, and this bullet wound has features that suggest a hollow point as well." Of course, it was a hollow-point bullet, but it was a copper-jacketed .38 police round, which would *not* mushroom like the aluminum-jacketed .45.

5. In the discussion of the x-ray, Smith downplayed the fact that his office had withheld it for twenty years and stated that the x-ray would not have picked up the aluminum on the .45.

In the verbal gyrations to justify how Q1, the pristine bullet at trial, had become the fatal bullet, Smith truly outdid himself. His presentation showed his test of shooting into gelatin while holding Q1 in his hand. He discussed the FBI shooting into wallboard. Then he concluded with the following, showing various slides as he spoke:

Now, what I did was model the behavior of what I considered happened to Lieutenant Oliver. I took a 1980's era MPD [Memphis Police Department] polyester uniform shirt, used the rib cage of a canine, and put 10 percent ordnance gelatin—which is a recognized human tissue simulant—behind it, and I fired one round and one round only through this model, striking the rib and recovering the bullet back behind the gelatin . . .

This is what the hollow-point bullet did. It went through the cloth, through the rib, hit here and then began to tumble and exited the gelatin . . .

There is the nose with the contents removed.

There is the nose of Q1 from the parking lot.

There is the side of the test bullet. There is the side of Q1 . . .

[B]asically only two guns were fired, from the circumstances I was able to uncover. Lieutenant Oliver did not shoot himself.

Dr. Smith reported that all the tests he described had been conducted the previous year. However, in the current year,

> what I did was obtain a pig's foot and shot a Silvertip ammunition through it and then excised the wound and had it analyzed by a state of the art instrument called a scanning electron microscope with energy dispersant analysis of x-rays.
>
> And we see here that there are aluminum residues in the wound of this experimental firing . . .
>
> So in 2001, a year later, why do we know that it was a Silvertip bullet that killed Lieutenant Oliver? First, because for the same original reasons. The model certainly explains why the bullet did not expand, and now we know that the gunshot contains aluminum.

In the questions from the board, Dills stated, "What I'm hearing you say is that you're testifying without a doubt in your mind that the caliber .45 weapon took Lieutenant Oliver's life."

Smith replied, "There's not a doubt in my military mind."

Jefferson Dorsey objected to the aluminum testimony because it had not been submitted ten days before the hearing as required by the rules. Smith's report of shooting into the pig's foot and the finding of aluminum were news to Philip's lawyers in this testimony. Dorsey indicated that his experts had not had a chance to review this experiment. After a lengthy back-and-forth, the chairman ruled they would look at the hard copies of Smith's reports but would return them and not list them as exhibits. Of course, as Dorsey pointed out, "It's sort of hard to get somebody to ignore something once the cat is out of the bag" through the testimony.

***

At 6:05 P.M. Philip was voluntarily put under oath to make a statement. He said he was sorry that the parties present had to be there. He apologized to the Oliver family for "creating this situation in the beginning with armed robbery . . . I'm deeply sorry." He then recounted his version of the events, stressing he had been concussed by a blow to the head and strung out on cocaine. He also noted it wasn't until his lawyer brought him the documents discovered through the Tennessee Public Records Act that he realized he could not have shot Lieutenant Oliver.

Philip testified, "I walked out [of the Wendy's] by myself . . . [Lieutenant Oliver was outside and I asked,] 'Is there a problem or something?' . . . Another car was coming around the side of the back . . . and I bolted to the right without thinking . . . I ran across the parking lot . . . and I fell down . . . I was saying, you know, 'Don't shoot! I give up!' . . . I had no physical contact with Officer Oliver."

Chairman Traughber interrupted, saying, "You dispute Officer Stoddard as saying that when he saw you and Lieutenant Oliver and he had grabbed you, you dispute that? . . . You dispute that you shot him in the arm?"

"I don't know," Philip replied. ". . . When I received the blow to the head I discharged two [involuntary] shots . . . it seems to me the first one went straight up in the air . . . and it seems like the second shot went toward a flash . . . Yes, I dispute I shot at Officer Parker. I dispute I shot Lieutenant Oliver. I feel nobody's going to believe me."

Traughber read the statement Philip gave at trial: "'I pulled it out.' Question: 'And you shot with every bullet in there?' Response: 'I pulled the trigger. I guess it was pointed at the officer.'"

Philip explained, "At trial I said I guess it was pointed at the officer. My attorneys were telling me not to make waves and lose my one millimeter of a chance of for a life sentence if you contradict the officers. People don't believe you if you say you surrendered."

Traughber indicated that he found Philip hard to believe. "I made some notes last year," he said. "You are clear about things on your side of the table. You are specific on matters that help you but vague on what may hurt you. I have wondered: Is he trying to say things convenient for him?"

"I mean no disrespect," Philip answered. "I'm feeling in five days I will be executed. Trial attorneys left me with the impression the more I remember, the less likely the jury will remember I had a drug problem . . . I never felt at trial like I stood a chance . . . If I had known, though, that there were three [citizen] witnesses that could have testified that they saw me running, holding my head, I would have insisted on something . . ." He continued, "It's a very intimidating situation [at trial] such as this today for me also . . . I knew that such a tragedy had happened and that I had caused it because I did create armed robbery . . . I certainly already most definitely feel that you're not going to recommend me to Mr. Sundquist for clemency."

Traughber then shifted to Philip's escape attempt (see "The Fourth Circle") and grilled him with questions.

> Workman: "I was in such despair. I knew I would die fast. I'd be out of my misery."
> Traughber:"You could [have taken] your own life."
> Workman: "Many times I contemplated tying a sheet to the pipe in the back of my cell."
> Traughber: "This shows a pattern. Shoot Officer Oliver, shoot Stoddard and place two other people [correctional officers driving the car to take him to court] in danger. This is the pattern you showed in the crime. Hard for me to believe [you are innocent]."
> Workman: "If my intent was to hurt someone there was no lack of opportunity to do so."
> Traughber: "I don't believe it."

In point of fact, during the escape incident Philip had a gun pointed at the backs of the two officers in the seat in front of him. He easily could have shot them both. But he did not fire his weapon, because he did not want to hurt them—a fact Traughber chose to disregard.

At the end of a long day, the clemency board voted unanimously (6–0) to proceed with the execution. One member, Sheila Swearingen, I observed open her material and read a statement she had prepared *prior to the clemency hearing*. By the time of this clemency hearing, the chairman of the clemency board, the attorney general, the governor's legal counsel, the commissioner of corrections, and Justin Wilson had all participated in a series of meetings planning clemency. The attorney general functioned as the legal adviser to the clemency board, as the chief prosecutor of Philip

Workman, and as a legal adviser to the governor. The fact that these multiple roles created a potential conflict of interest seemed not to faze him or other parties involved.

The clemency meetings culminated in January 2001 when members planned the post-execution press statements. They would re-create the crime scene in Memphis and conduct a reenactment of what "really happened" in order to educate the people of Tennessee who had been gulled by the "liberal media" into believing Philip didn't shoot Lieutenant Oliver. Obviously, if post-execution crime re-creation had been scheduled for the press, there would be an execution. Philip's fate had been sealed weeks before he had his second clemency hearing on January 25.

The execution was scheduled for January 30, 2001. As Philip had told the clemency board in his remarks: "I'm feeling in five days I will be executed."

**

A number of facts about the case were known but ignored through Philip's two clemency hearings. Although we had known the power of the state was unrelenting against Philip, being on the brink of his execution after knowing the facts that emerged post-trial in this case left us feeling like we were trapped in a war zone with little ammunition left. The final assault was coming and all we had left were our bare hands. However, the idea of Philip's premeditating Oliver's killing made sense if one went back to the original decision that was made by police the night of the shooting: that Philip Workman was a restaurant robber, a drug addict, a scumbag, and although he didn't kill Ronnie Oliver, he *could* have. And if he was not stopped, it was just a matter of time until he would kill someone for drugs. All subsequent decisions flowed from that key decision that had been made in the Memphis Violent Crimes Unit early in the morning of August 6, 1981, with the "exchange of information" made when the autopsy photos of Oliver revealed it was not Philip's bullet that inflicted the mortal wound, as they had expected. Rather, it was "friendly fire" from another policeman.

A psychological mind-set, a personal and cultural interpenetrating, reinforcing worldview, must have existed in the Memphis criminal justice establishment to do what the authorities did to Philip. The precise description for this view can be found in the German word *untermenschen,* the literal translation being "subhuman." *Untermenschen* was the term used to describe the Jews by the German Third Reich. According to the Nazis, Jews were subhuman in their very being. Forty-some years later, in the view of the Memphis police, Philip became subhuman because of his actions of robbing a restaurant, shooting a policeman, and, as he put it regretfully in his own words, "creating the scene." The Nazis passed laws to codify their cultural perspective. Similarly, the criminal justice establishment of Memphis, and later the government of Tennessee and the federal government, codified their actions toward Philip after falsely labeling him as a cop killer. From each perspective of the majority culture, Nazi and American, the category "subhuman" applied to its victim. Once that psychological transfer was accomplished and followed with political acts, anything could be done to the victim, because the victim was less than human. The victim of the dominant culture was deserving of his fate by definition of the tyrannical culture. It mattered not that the victim was innocent, or in Philip's case innocent of the murder of a policeman. Rather, it was by definition that the victim deserved extermination because of his status as *untermenschen.* Laws were established and manipulated to accomplish the removal of the psychologically defined deserving victim due to his unworthiness of personhood.

For the victim, it was of no consequence whether one was judged inherently subhuman or subsequently subhuman because of an alleged action; either way he or she was slated for extermination by the tyranny of the majority. (Although we are examining the specific manifestation of this phenomenon in Memphis, Tennessee, it is a feature of the tyranny of the majority in the United States, which incarcerates more people per capita than anyone else in the world. According to Marc Mauer of The Sentencing Project in Washington, D.C., "The United States has an incarceration five to eight times greater than other industrialized nations.") Indeed, there is a Manichean feature to American culture, reinforced by the media, that the "worthy guys" are law enforcement and the "unworthy guys" are those who are charged with crimes. Philip's case is the logical outcome of this worldview. (For a historical analysis of how this came to be the case, see Douglas A. Blackmon's *Slavery by Another Name: The Re-Enslavement of Black Americans from the Civil War to World War II* and my own forthcoming *Slouching toward Tyranny: The Making of the Tyranny of the Majority in the United States of America*.)

Once the prosecutors and police fabricated a story, the two shooter theory; invented an eyewitness, Harold Davis; and relied on cooperative defense attorneys who did no real investigation and assumed the state's theory, even advising their client not to "make waves" or he would lose his "one millimeter of a chance" of not getting the death penalty, the trial was all set to be the sham of the century in Memphis. After a production worthy of Tony Award consideration, Philip Workman was found guilty and sentenced to death.

Really, it could not have gone any better for the state. A purported cop killer sent to death row with inept legal counsel and prosecutorial malfeasance. The embarrassment of one policeman accidentally killing another hidden by a veil of venality and deceit. And so it goes.

However, in 1990 new defense counsel came on board for Philip and did the investigation that should have been done pretrial. And there was the matter of the record the cops and prosecutors had created in devising their Philip Workman morality play. Chris Minton utilized the Tennessee Public Records Act for the first time in a death penalty case, and the initial statements by police and parties involved became available.

There were three citizen witnesses to the events at the crime scene: Garvin Null, Jeff Rickard, and Steve Craig. Null and Rickard drank beer inside Null's truck, which was parked at the Gulf gas station across from the Wendy's restaurant. Null saw a bunch of police cars pull into the Wendy's. Several cars departed the restaurant, leaving two officers talking outside. Steve Craig followed two police cars pulling into Wendy's. Craig pulled into the Holiday Auto Parts lot to watch. He exited his vehicle to walk to Wendy's and talk to his friend Stoddard and Oliver. By the time Parker pulled up, Craig saw Philip fleeing the scene. Null saw Oliver hit Philip on the head with a flashlight. Stoddard shot at Philip, and in turn Philip shot Stoddard, who shot back at Philip again but instead hit Oliver. A police report of that night notes: "M/W [Male/White] runs north thru the parking area and was caught by the officer and during the struggle . . . Stoddard was shot in the arm . . . Oliver was shot in the chest." Craig was back in his car lying down when he heard six more shots. He raised up and saw Oliver on the ground.

Despite the two shooter theory advanced at trial, a lot of bullets were fired that night at the Wendy's. Philip fired three and ejected one: one went up in the air when he was struck on the head with a flashlight; the second was fired at a "flash," which was Stoddard shooting at him, and Philip's return bullet struck Stoddard in the arm; the third one was ejected when Philip forgot he had a semiautomatic; and the fourth shot was fired up in the air as Philip climbed over the fence. Memphis policeman Stewart heard three gunshots, a volley of six rounds, then a couple of more shots. Memphis policeman Geil heard two shots, which he mistook for a car backfiring, then another shot, then seven to eight shots. Memphis policeman T. L. Cobb heard eight to twelve shots. Null heard about nine shots in five seconds, Jeff Rickard heard nine to twelve shots. This is much more gunfire than the six rounds Lieutenant Oliver fired and the three that Philip fired. Who was doing all the shooting?

Steve Craig saw Officer Parker shoot his shotgun two or three times at Philip as he fled. Stewart arrived at 10:35 and saw Parker "going around the Northeast corner of Holiday building with a shotgun." Officer Stoddard fired several times trying to hit Philip after Philip was struck on the head. None of this information had been brought before the jury, because the defense lawyers accepted the state's two shooter theory.

Null, Rickard, and Craig all saw Philip holding his head as he fled the scene. At the hospital he received seven stitches and was treated for shotgun pellets in the buttocks as well as dog bites. Again, this information had been available for the defense counsel but was not effectively mounted into a coherent defense.

Then there was the matter of the x-ray that was withheld for almost twenty years until its unexpected presence became known to the defense just before the first clemency hearing. It established the presence of a "through and through" bullet with no fragmentation and rendered the Sixth Circuit Court of Appeals panel decision in tatters.

Dr. O. C. Smith had created unscientific experiments and reached unwarranted conclusions in defiance of experts in the field. Indeed, in the wake of Philip's second clemency hearing, with the testimony of the aluminum in the pig's foot, a Memphis lawyer, Robert Hutton, checked with the two people who worked with Smith on the test. A Mr. Koontz and a female associate analyzed the samples, observed the results of the test, and gave statements that there was no aluminum found in the first test sample. The second test sample was conducted on an aluminum slide, so any aluminum would have been conveyed by the slide "through the state of the art instrument called a scanning electron microscope with energy dispersant analysis of x-rays."

After the second clemency hearing, Dr. Werner Spitz, the leading expert in the field, gave an affidavit that a bullet does not leave traces in soft tissue, despite O. C. Smith's elaborate experiment. Nor was there any trace of aluminum in Lieutenant Oliver's body. As in the first clemency, Smith was demonstrated to be a liar and a fraud in his presentation to the clemency board. Nonetheless, Philip Workman hurtled toward a January 30 execution.

After being on death row since the spring of 1982, Philip had been moved to the death house for the first time for an April 6, 2000, execution. However, he had obtained a stay of execution from the Sixth Circuit Court of Appeals in light of the discovery of the x-ray. The en banc court, all fourteen judges, issued a 7–7 decision on September 13, 2000, thus dissolving the stay. In a tie vote the case reverts to the panel decision, which was 3–0 against Philip. In an article in the *Memphis Commercial Appeal* titled "State Wants Workman Dead Soon, Says No Cause for Delay," attorney general Paul Summers expressed the feelings of the state: "Workman has provided this court with no good reason to defer the federal courts at this late stage. A date for execution of his lawful sentence should be promptly set" (*Memphis Commercial Appeal*, September 19, 2000). Summers had made this statement even though seven federal appellate judges found in favor of Philip.

On January 24, 2001, Philip again occupied the death house despite the fact that he had a stay of execution in effect as the U.S. Supreme Court considered his case. He had been moved to deathwatch in contradiction of a Department of Corrections policy that prohibited a prisoner being taken to deathwatch with an intact stay of execution. Once the Supreme Court turned him down, the Tennessee Supreme Court had set a second execution date: January 30, 2001. Philip was in his cell preparing to watch the Super Bowl on January 28 when the death squad suddenly appeared and ordered him to pack his possessions. He was being moved to the death house despite a stay of execution, because the state was seeking to have the stay lifted. Fortunately, the stay held, and Philip returned to his regular cell seventy-two hours later. The Tennessee Supreme Court, however, set yet another execution date—Philip's third—for March 30, 2001.

No one in Tennessee had been moved to deathwatch three times and lived to tell the tale, but Philip would now make his third trip to the killing ground. The second clemency hearing, like the previous one, proved to be a futile effort since Tennessee officials had already made up their minds to execute Philip before the hearing even began. In fact, the chairman of the clemency board, the state's attorney general, the governor's legal counsel, the commissioner of corrections, and the governor's senior policy adviser had already planned the state's post-execution press reenactment of the crime to demonstrate what truly happened. So, obviously, Philip Workman's fate was sealed weeks before his second clemency hearing on January 25th.

At 10:00 a.m. on Thursday, March 29, 2001, chancellor Ellen Hobbs Lyle presided over a hearing in Workman v. Bell. Chancellor Lyle, attorneys from the attorney general's office, and Philip's lawyers gathered to decide who would serve as his spiritual adviser prior to his 1:00 a.m. execution on March 30, some thirteen hours from the commencement of the hearing. Philip had requested that his pastor accompany him for the final three hours of his life. The state of Tennessee, through its representative, Riverbend warden Ricky Bell, wished to replace Philip's personal pastor (me) with an institutional chaplain at 10:00 P.M.

Philip's case had moved from court to court, always managing to lose—and usually by one vote, in one case a tie vote—and he feared his third trip to deathwatch augured the final journey to Building 8. He wanted me to be with him until the end, but in this situation the state's argument was all too familiar: security. According to the state, they would be better able to maintain their security procedures with an in-house chaplain. We argued that the state statute specifically grants the presence of the minister "preparing the condemned prisoner for death." As Philip's minister and an ordained minister in good standing in the United Church of Christ, I was the pastor preparing him for his extinction. I had worked closely with Philip for two years and known him for an additional ten. I should be the minister with him until the end of his life.

Chancellor Lyle listened carefully to each side's arguments and asked the assistant attorney general, "In the course of Rev. Ingle's twenty-five years of ministering to death row in Tennessee, has he been a security threat in any institution?"

"No, your honor," came the reply.

At 2:35 P.M. Chancellor Lyle faxed her decision to the parties involved. I would be allowed to spend the last three hours of Philip's life with him as his pastor.

***

During the late afternoon of March 29, Philip had his final visits with his brother Terry, the only member of his family who could bear to go through the ordeal, and friends. At the conclusion of those visits, he was offered a traditional final meal. He chose a vegetarian pizza but asked that it be given to the homeless in Nashville. When his request was denied, he said he would go without a final meal.

At 7:30 P.M. I arrived at deathwatch within Riverbend prison. The area is located in Building 8 behind the large visiting room for the general population. Deathwatch consists of four holding cells, a darkened control booth, a noncontact visiting booth, the witness room, and the death chamber that houses the electric chair and the lethal injection paraphernalia, complete with gurney.

After signing the logbook, the third book I had signed after initially clearing the prison's first checkpoint, I walked toward Philip. He was saying farewell to his lawyers through the glass of the noncontact visiting booth. As I awaited their departure, a guard informed me we would visit in the foyer where I was standing and then move to a noncontact area. I pointed out to the guard that I had obtained a court order that enabled me to visit just outside Philip's cell. The guard replied, "I have my orders from the warden." I stopped Philip's legal team as they emerged from the visiting booth. As I explained the situation, they nodded and told me Philip had informed them about the warden restricting my visit despite a court order. I gave them Chancellor Lyle's home telephone number, and they agreed to check into the matter.

The guards brought Philip into the foyer. He was shackled at the waist. We awkwardly embraced and sat down in the molded plastic chairs. After talking about how his family was doing, I sighed and said, "Philip, I know all this is real. But it seems so surreal. I can't believe it's happening."

"Me either, Joe," he replied. "I just can't believe it's come to this. After all the evidence we've found. But it's real all right."

As Philip and I sat in the deathwatch foyer, we recalled his long-held belief that he was "not innocent enough." "Surreal" seemed to be a mild description of where we found ourselves in the bowels of Riverbend, less than five hours from Philip's being strapped to a gurney and poisoned to death by lethal injection.

Our hour together was soon completed. Philip needed to make some final phone calls to his family, and I needed to find the defense lawyer stationed in the prison to see if Chancellor Lyle's court order would be enforced. We hugged good-bye, and I left deathwatch as Philip returned to his cell.

At 9:30 P.M. I signed back in to the deathwatch log. The lawyers had clarified matters with the warden, and I could go back to Philip's cell and remain there until they came to take him at 12:55 A.M. As I signed back in, I wrote "minister" under the category "role." In the space above my signature, I noted someone had written "observe the minister." The name next to this was that of the Catholic deacon who ministers to death row prisoners. I was certain that there were two reasons for this note: (1) I was not the in-house chaplain, and (2) I was a longtime opponent of the death penalty. As I proceeded back to Philip's cell, Jerry Welborn, the institutional chaplain, stopped me to talk. At that point I had been fighting to be with Philip since 10:00 A.M., and I really didn't want to tarry and visit with Jerry—or anyone else for that matter. After speaking a few words of condolence and concern, Jerry asked to see my communion kit, which already had been inspected. I opened the portable kit and showed him the wine and wafers. He gave the okay sign to the guards behind the darkened glass, and I walked on to Philip's cell.

Philip was in the holding cell at the end of the tier farthest from the death chamber. After passing through the larger cage door, I pulled up a chair outside his cell. As I settled into the chair, I noticed how bare the cell was. His leather-bound Bible was his primary companion. I brought Philip up to date on Chancellor Lyle's order on personal pastoral visits. Philip mentioned that the Catholic chaplain wanted to come and say good-bye. I told him that was fine and observed that it shouldn't be difficult for him since the chaplain was already in a chair about twelve feet behind me. We then talked about Philip's children and grandchildren. He was concerned about his brother Terry, who was determined to be strong and to shoulder this burden alone for his family. Then we discussed the funeral service, where Philip wished to be buried, and the final details of a healthy man preparing for his imminent demise.

At 10:30 P.M. we heard that the U.S. Supreme Court declined to accept Philip's appeal on the clemency hearing. Once again, Philip had fallen just one vote short, this time with Justice John Paul Stevens writing a dissent. Philip and I decided to share communion. I opened my communion kit, spread the linen cloth over a small table, and set up the wine and wafers. We prayed together, and then after blessing the elements we partook of the bread and wine. When the service concluded, we prayed for God's blessing to strengthen us through the ordeal.

The Catholic chaplain came over to visit Philip. I scooted my chair away and waited for them to finish. When they said good-bye, the chaplain returned to his chair behind me. Philip and I discussed his odyssey through the courts and, as Jerry Garcia of the Grateful Dead put it, "What a long, strange trip it's been."

At midnight Philip said he wanted to pray by himself. I nodded and concurred. He retreated to the rear of his cell, dropped to his knees with folded hands, and looked through the narrow vertical window as he offered his prayers to God. The sight of Philip with his head uplifted in prayer and focused on the night sky almost unhinged me. A man prostrate before his God, sweating the proverbial blood of Jesus in Gethsemane, resembled a specter in his hospital-white attire. I prayed for strength for us to endure this madness.

As I read the 139th Psalm to myself, time slipped by, and it was now March 30. Philip remained on his knees, lost in prayer. At 12:10 A.M. I gazed up at the television. A local reporter narrated the scene outside the prison, and a bulletin flashed across the bottom of the screen: "THE TENNESSEE SUPREME COURT HAS GRANTED A STAY OF EXECUTION TO PHILIP WORKMAN." Transfixed, I heard the reporter reiterate the bulletin, and it scrolled across the screen again. Then I shuddered. "Oh, my God," I thought. "They're going to delay this temporarily, maybe for an hour or so, and then do it."

I strained to listen to the reporter and read the bulletin a third time. I glanced at Philip. He was still praying, oblivious of the news, whatever it meant. I waited for the phone to ring with news from the lawyers. Time passed. No phone call. No clarifying reports.

At 12:20 A.M. Philip stood and brushed off his pants. He turned and walked toward me. As he approached the cell door, I informed him, "Philip, you have a stay of execution from the Tennessee Supreme Court. I don't know what the grounds are or how long it will last. But you have a stay."

Philip staggered in mid-stride and took a step back. My words had the effect of a punch delivered to the solar plexus. Bewilderment, consternation, and confusion flashed across his face. He had prepared himself, steeled his will to deal with his slaughter, and this sudden turn of events was unnerving. He steadied himself and walked toward me. "What does this mean?" he said. "Do I have my evidentiary hearing?" He grasped my shoulders through the bars, and I grabbed his shoulders in return.

"I don't know. All we know is the Tennessee Supreme Court granted a stay. I don't know why or for how long." I nodded in the direction of the television. Philip asked the guard to turn it up. The news was the same from the reporter outside the prison, and the bulletin at the bottom of the screen remained unchanged.

"Philip, let me get a hold of the lawyers," I said. The guard dialed the number of defense lawyer Jefferson Dorsey, with whom I had earlier discussed the pastoral visit. "Jefferson, what's going on? Philip is on an emotional roller coaster here. Do we have a stay? How long?" The words rushed from me. "Do we have an evidentiary hearing?"

Jefferson responded, "We have a stay. The Tennessee Supreme Court clerk is on the other line. They're faxing the order. Let me check on the evidentiary hearing." A pause, then Jefferson returned. "We have an evidentiary hearing."

Incredulous, I shouted, "We have an evidentiary hearing!"

Philip stood on his tiptoes, elation flushing his face. He addressed the deathwatch guard: "That's all I've wanted for ten years! A chance to put on the evidence to show I didn't kill Officer Oliver."

I hung up the telephone, and Philip and I embraced through the bars. Then he began talking about who we could put on under oath and what we could prove now that had been unknown at the time of the 1982 trial. His words cascaded over me with the enthusiasm of a rushing waterfall. Through the joy, the television blurted, "The evidentiary hearing will be held in Memphis later today." Philip and I were stunned into silence. As we looked up at the television, the reporter was saying that the evidentiary hearing would go forward almost immediately.

Philip and I looked at each other in horror. He grabbed my shoulders in a strong grip. Looking directly into my eyes, he delivered a plea. "Joe, you've got to tell them to go ahead and kill me. I can't take any more. A hearing later today will be a joke, and they'll move me back here again. I can't go through this anymore."

I looked into those pained brown eyes and said, "Philip, hang on, man. This is just a news report. Let me check with the lawyers. It can't be right."

Philip was deflated, wounded. The immense pressure of the state machinery of death had driven him to his wit's end. I motioned the guard to dial Jefferson Dorsey's number again. "Jefferson, you have to read me the court order. The news is reporting the hearing will be in Memphis in a few hours. What's going on?"

"Joe, look, that can't be right. Let me check." In a few minutes, he came back. "The news media are wrong. The order will be transmitted to Memphis today, but the hearing is not set."

I thanked Jefferson and told Philip the news. We embraced and decided to pray. Holding hands through the bars, we offered a prayer of thanksgiving. We praised God, gratefully mentioning names of those who had helped, and then began to realize the imminent danger had passed.

After we finished, the guards wanted to hustle me out. Philip was going back to his cell in Unit 2, and I teased him, "Man, you're going back to a clean cell." (Philip had meticulously cleaned his cell before his removal to deathwatch so that the next man would have a freshly scrubbed "home" to move into and enjoy.)

Philip laughed and said, "Yeah, it will be good to get back there." We hugged each other good-bye, and I exited.

Before leaving the prison, I sought to confirm the accuracy of our latest information about the evidentiary hearing. As I passed several prison administrators, who appeared quite glum, I received all the confirmation I needed. I walked out of the stale air of Building 8 into the welcome fresh air of spring, and a guard greeted me with an extended hand. We shook hands, and he said, "Tell Philip I'm so glad. God is good." I shook his hand and replied, "I'll let him know. God is good."

***

As I signed out at the main checkpoint in the administration building, I bid good night to the guard with whom I'd shared friendly repartee about life the last few days. Then I walked out into the parking lot, where the press gathered and requested a statement. I described the sequence of events Philip had endured.

The paramilitary disassembling of an execution was under way as I drove out of the parking lot. The state troopers, who had searched all cars and frisked everyone entering the lot, were now down to a lone car pulled off to the side of the road. The helicopter that had buzzed overhead for security purposes had flown back to base. The crowd of three hundred protesters of the execution and four celebrants of it had returned to their homes.

As I eased my car into a parking space at the motel where Philip's friends and family awaited my return, I gripped the steering wheel as hard as I could and breathed deeply. The tension in my body was palpable. I recalled the somber scene I'd left earlier in the evening inside this motel. Philip's loved ones were girding their loins for the worst. We had read scripture and prayed, and we created a scenario we all planned to enact at 12:55 A.M. Philip and I would read the apostle Paul's letter to the Romans 8:31–37. Then he and I would join hands in prayer, each of us extending a hand toward those in the hotel room so that they could join us spiritually, if not physically, in completing the prayer circle. The loved ones in the hotel room would be holding hands and extending a hand to unite with us.

I knocked on the door and heard the reply from within. "It's Joe! Open it up!" There were hugs all around, shouts, laughter, and unmitigated joy. I exclaimed, "Jesus kicked butt tonight! He may have had on lawyers' shoes, but he kicked butt!" As the energy release of the pandemonium eased down, we exchanged our stories of what had transpired during the evening. I munched on some leftover Chinese food, finally feeling hungry. My adrenaline and exhaustion were intermingled, and I could not shut down to relax. At 3:00 A.M. we had a final prayer.

I drove home through the early morning spring darkness with my window down. When I reached the long, winding gravel driveway, I turned off the headlights and drove in the moonlight. The spring peepers were going strong. A barred owl hooted from across the way. The stars shone brilliantly. The eighth Psalm came to mind: "O Lord, when I consider the beauty of our creation, what are we humans that you are mindful of us?"

I entered my house through the basement, and as I arrived at the top of the stairs I saw my wife, Becca, waiting for me. She seemed sad and worried.

"Are you okay?" she asked.

I realized she hadn't heard about Philip's stay of execution. I grinned. "Philip got a stay from the Tennessee Supreme Court. He's alive."

Becca's face transformed into disbelieving joy. "What? How?" she asked, eager for information.

We hugged each other, and I sat down and relayed the entire evening's events to her. She then shared what she and our thirteen-year-old daughter, Amelia, had experienced while I was at the prison with Philip.

Earlier in the evening they had attended Christ Church Cathedral, our family's place of worship, which hosted a service for Philip. Terry, Philip's older brother, spoke at the service, and Amelia, who had grown close to Philip through his phone calls to our house, was an acolyte. After the service Becca and Amelia joined the throng protesting the execution. In the crowd assembled outside the prison, they saw a woman lying on the ground, wailing with grief. It was Susan Groves, Philip's former girlfriend, who had been our houseguest last spring when Philip had come within thirty-four hours of execution.

"I want my daddy, I want my daddy," Amelia began to sob after seeing Susan.

"Daddy needs to be with Philip right now," Becca said as she held Amelia. "Philip needs him. He'll be out as soon as he can."

"I want my daddy," Amelia continued to cry. Becca caressed her, loved her, and comforted her. Then two guards approached them.

"Are you all right?" one of the correctional officers asked.

"Yes, we're fine, thank you," Becca replied.

"Just wanted to be sure you're okay," said the officer.

As the guards walked off, Amelia burst out, "Boo-ya!" Although the officers did not hear the remark, Becca and Amelia laughed at Amelia's teenage audacity and determination.

Later that night Amelia went to sleep crying, worried about Philip. Shortly after 1:00 A.M. the phone rang, and Becca answered. It was a hate call. Then at 2:20 A.M. an elderly African American lady telephoned and asked that I pray for her vision. Amelia slept as Becca fielded the phone calls.

After Becca and I told each other of the night's events, I moved Amelia over in our bed to make room for my wife to sleep beside her. Awakened, Amelia whispered, with her bottom lip trembling, "Did they kill him, Daddy?" I pulled her to me and whispered in her ear, "Philip is alive and well, honey. He got a stay of execution." Before my second sentence was completed, she showered my face with kisses. And together the three of us laughed and tumbled on the bed.

It was 4:00 A.M., and for the third time in a year Philip had survived the state of Tennessee's effort to kill him. Now, three hours past the appointed killing time, we laughed and celebrated life. As the guard at the prison put it, "God is good."

THE FIFTEENTH CIRCLE

On the ground that newly discovered evidence exonerated Philip, Memphis defense lawyer Robert Hutton had filed an *error coram nobis* petition on Philip's behalf in the state trial court a week before his scheduled execution on March 30, 2001. The petition reviewed all the evidence unearthed post-trial and asked the court to stop the execution and set an evidentiary hearing. The petition was denied and appealed until it came to the Tennessee Supreme Court. The court, with Justice Frank Drowota writing for the majority, issued the unexpected stay of execution less than forty-five minutes before the scheduled killing and sent the case back for an evidentiary hearing in Memphis. The order stated in part, "At the hearing, Workman will have the opportunity to establish that newly discovered evidence may have resulted in a different judgment if the evidence had been admitted at the previous trial." The court took this action after a two-year public education campaign about Philip's case through television, radio, and newspapers had persuaded a majority of Tennesseans that Philip Workman did not kill Lieutenant Oliver. So, although it was surprising, the action resonated positively with most Tennesseans.

On Friday, March 30, Robert Hutton appeared as a guest on the radio show of Mike Fleming in Memphis. As a devout Catholic, Hutton's main purpose was to explain the scriptures and how the death penalty was contrary to Christian teaching, but Fleming pressed him about the Workman case. Dr. O. C. Smith had appeared on Fleming's show the week before as part of the state's attempt to counteract the "liberal media," and Fleming now asked Hutton to evaluate Smith's two clemency performances. Hutton minced no words and stated that Smith was "a liar."

Three days after Hutton's radio appearance, he received a letter threatening O. C. Smith. It stated, in part, "A greater task you have given me to destroy the LIAR who would bear false witness." Hutton turned the letter over to state and local authorities, and it was determined that some right-wing religious nut case who perceived himself as a defender of Philip was threatening Smith.

Judge John Colton Jr., who would hold the evidentiary hearing, had been on the bench since 1990. He was part and parcel of the Memphis criminal justice establishment, and that did not bode well for Philip. He was the judge who had determined Robert Coe competent for execution despite Coe's taking seventeen different drugs (anti-psychotics, anti-depressants, and anti-anxiety medications) for his mental illness. As a result of Judge Colton's decision, Coe was executed.

The first indication of how bad things would become was when Judge Colton, *sua sponte*, or on the court's own initiative, entered a gag order in Philip's case on April 6, 2001. The state had been taken apart in the press by the exculpatory evidence that appeared on Philip's behalf during the past two years. Judge Colton would have no more of that from the lawyers representing Philip. The order encompassed the Memphis and Nashville lawyers.

On April 9, 2001, a scheduling conference took place in Memphis before Judge Colton. Robert Hutton arrived, representing Philip, and the state handed him a motion requesting production of Harold Davis's statements forty-eight hours before Davis was to testify. Judge Colton ordered Hutton to respond immediately.

Hutton pointed out that Judge Colton did not have jurisdiction of the case, because the mandate had not issued from the Tennessee Supreme Court. He also indicated that he would be filing a rehearing petition, which would further delay the issuance of the mandate.

Judge Colton responded, "Now, the court's going to find that it has jurisdiction to rule on matters before it at this time. Also, the court is going to grant the motion of the state directing the defendant to produce any audio or written tapes or statements of Harold Davis and an order of protection. I'll need an order from the state."

Hutton replied, "I just got it this morning. I haven't even had an opportunity to read it. I haven't had an opportunity to research the law. I'm entitled to at least ten days to file a response to that and I'm requesting a Rule 9 interlocutory appeal immediately, your honor."

But Colton was determined, saying, "I'm going to deny that at this time. Mr. Hutton, I'm going to require you to file with the clerk of this court all of the articles or documents that have been asked for by the state. We'll hold them under seal and this court will examine them *in camera* [in private or in the judge's chambers] prior to our hearing and we can make a ruling at that time on whether or not the properly should be admitted." Then the court agreed to grant Hutton a Rule 9 appeal.

John Campbell of the Memphis DA's office made sure that Judge Colton kept the gag order in place for *all* lawyers representing Philip, not just Hutton. Colton volunteered that the lawyers would be "in a heap of trouble" if they violated the gag order.

When Campbell asked about a date, Colton looked at his calendar and suggested April 23. Hutton informed the court why he could not be prepared on that date, and then Campbell endorsed the April 23 date, saying, "What the state would just ask for is a soon date so this doesn't drag on." Disregarding Hutton's statement, Judge Colton set the hearing for April 23.

The whistle that could be heard in the distance at the conclusion of this hearing was the train whistle on the engine of the locomotive gearing up to take Philip back to the death house. The Memphis cabal was ginning up to take care of Philip Workman once again with a railroad to the gurney and the deadly drugs.

***

The following sequence of events unspooled and revealed Judge Colton reversing himself to comply with the district attorney's requests at each and every juncture, thus converting an August 13 motion hearing with no proof scheduled to be entered into a full-blown evidentiary hearing:

On April 17, 2001, the Tennessee Court of Criminal Appeals stayed the proceedings in Colton's court. Then on May 2 the appellate court vacated all orders entered in the *error coram nobis* proceeding for lack of jurisdiction and remanded the case to the trial court for a hearing.

May 14, 2001, featured a hearing to recuse Judge Colton. ADA Campbell argued against the recusal because he had seen Judge Colton rule in his favor in almost every instance. To no one's surprise, Judge Colton denied the recusal motion and reinstated the gag order.

An ex parte (on behalf of only one party) motion hearing was held on June 27, 2001. Hutton informed the court of investigator Ron Lax's attempts to locate Harold Davis. "Most recently we know he called his son in Fresno, California, on May 31st," Hutton said. "I'm going to ask the court for permission to start [the] process to try to get a subpoena for the telephone records."

On July 31, 2001, the state obtained a telephone number for Harold Davis from his mother. Campbell reached Davis at a motel in the 404 area code. Davis promised Campbell he would come back to Memphis around August 11 to testify at the August 13 hearing.

Judge Colton issued a letter on August 1, 2001, informing the state and defense that no proof would be taken at the hearing scheduled for August 13. Meanwhile, unbeknownst to the defense, the state was in the process of arranging Harold Davis's travel to Memphis for the hearing on August 13. As they explained to Judge Colton after receiving his August 1 letter, "We were afraid that we wouldn't be able to get him [Davis] and wouldn't be able to find him. So that was why we wanted to come in here and get the judge to reconsider."

The state received a fax from Judge Colton on August 2 stating that the hearing set for the thirteenth would be continued. The state requested that the court reconsider continuing the August 13 hearing.

On August 3, 2001, Harold Davis committed a theft at a Belk's Department Store in Jacksonville, Florida. He was taken to the Clay County, Florida, jail. Campbell was notified and stated, "Once he was arrested, he did not want people to know where he was and we honored that request. We didn't tell you [the defense] where he was. We told you he'd be here."

At a 2:00P.M. hearing on August 3, Judge Colton reversed himself. Now that the state had Davis in custody, Colton was ready to allow proof in the hearing on August 13 after all and stated that he would do so.

At 4:15 a hearing was held on the state's motion to reconsider. Judge Colton said, "I don't know why y'all are here, but, I think I know why you're here, but tell me why you're here." ADA Jerry Kitchens told him that he should reconsider the court's prior order and reset the hearing for August 13. Colton granted the motion and instructed the lawyers to present proof on August 13. This meant that within ten days the defense must have witnesses and experts and be fully prepared for a hearing that they had previously assumed would be held probably months in the future. Kitchens noted that although Dr. Cyril Wecht may have become unavailable because Hutton had canceled subpoenas in light of the court's previous order continuing the hearing, "other issues," meaning Harold Davis, should be ready to go. Then, disingenuously, Judge Colton stated, despite knowing Harold Davis was available to testify, "Well, the Court has absolutely no idea what's going to be presented to it."

On August 6, 2001, Kitchens and Campbell were aware that Harold Davis was in Jacksonville, Florida. Two days later Philip's lawyers filed a motion for a continuance because they had not yet found Davis nor had the state made them aware of his whereabouts.

On Saturday, August 11, 2001, the headline in the *Memphis Commercial Appeal* Metro section read:"Where is Harold Davis? Wanted: Workman case witness." Defense lawyer John Pierotti told the *Commercial Appeal*, "I would be astounded if Harold Davis appeared in court Monday morning." Again, unbeknownst to the defense, prosecutors had located Harold Davis in the Clay County Jail in Jacksonville, Florida. He was locked up for shoplifting. Indeed, they had contacted him a week earlier and he agreed to testify for the state. None of this information was shared with the defense. But the prosecutors and Judge Colton knew Harold Davis was in hand.

Harold Davis was booked in the Germantown jail at 9:25 A.M. on Sunday, August 12, 2001. Incarcerating him in Germantown, a suburb of Memphis, would make it more likely he would not be discovered by the defense. If he were booked in the Shelby County jail in downtown Memphis, the defense would surely find out. The prosecutors had withheld the fact they had Davis and were incarcerating him in the Germantown jail rather than the Shelby County jail so that he would be hidden from the defense. Thwarting a subpoena is a federal offense, but apparently that's just the way they do business in Memphis.

What prosecutors didn't know, however, was that a minister who had known Davis since childhood spotted him at the Memphis airport when he had arrived. After speaking with Harold and learning he was in town to testify at the Workman hearing and was being held at the Germantown jail, the minister called Davis's sister to let her know where her brother was being detained. In turn, she contacted Philip's defense team.

Later that Sunday afternoon Kitchens and Campbell met with Davis in the Germantown jail. Kitchens called Hutton from Campbell's home telephone after the visit. Meanwhile, Davis's family had already contacted Robert Hutton to let him know Davis was in the Germantown jail.

Harold Davis's sister came to see Harold in the jail after the district attorneys, the investigator Ron Lax, and clemency lawyer Pierotti had spoken with him. When she visited her brother, she read him the riot act, telling him in no uncertain terms that he needed to tell the truth at the hearing the next day. He was the son of a minister, his family's name was on the line, and he needed to let everyone know the truth: he did not see Philip Workman kill the police officer.

***

The *error coram nobis* hearing on Monday, August 13, began with fireworks. Robert Hutton moved for the recusal of the prosecutors for misleading him and lying about the whereabouts of Harold Davis. One of the prosecutors allowed, "He agreed a week ago to come here and to tell the truth about this case, and that is what we expect him to do." Judge Colton denied the recusal motion, and Harold Davis took the stand for the prosecution. However, when Davis stated he was no longer clear about what happened that night, it became clear that Harold Davis was not the witness the prosecution had expected. In response to a direct question by defense lawyer Robert Hutton, Davis stated he had not seen Philip Workman shoot the police officer on August 5, 1981.

Prosecutor Jerry Kitchens went after Davis with a hostile, vindictive manner. For several hours he harassed, pressed, and harangued Davis. Despite defense objections, Judge Colton allowed the aggressive questioning to continue. Davis grew weary and weak under the verbal assault. He weaved and wavered in his testimony. He indicated that drugs, the loss of his father, and living on the streets for the last twenty years made it difficult to remember. "I remember being behind a police car and a police car turned into the Wendy's," he said, "but after that I'm not sure." Davis was emotional, sometimes crying under the pressure from the prosecutor. "A man's life is at stake and it's not right for me to say what's true or not because my mind is not fully there. I've lived on the street twenty years where it's easy to lie. It's self-preservation." Davis also stated that after his testimony at trial, two white guys came to the hotel and insinuated that if I changed my testimony, people I know might be harmed. He indicated he thought those men were policemen.

At the end of the day, an exhausted Harold Davis was taken back to the Germantown jail. It was clear this man could not be a reliable witness for the prosecution if Philip were granted a new trial.

Davis was summoned to the stand once again Tuesday morning. Under further questioning from Kitchens, Davis said defense lawyers had scared him two years ago. Chris Minton and Jefferson Dorsey had talked to him in Phoenix. "I told them what they wanted to hear," Davis said. "I was coming down off of drugs, and I would have said anything to keep my freedom. I took it that otherwise they were going to drag me back to Tennessee and put me in jail." This statement defied belief in that the two defense lawyers had clearly identified themselves and had made it known that they just wanted Davis to testify to the truth. Also, they had no power to take him anywhere, and he knew that was the case. He reiterated that he did not remember what happened after the pulled into the Wendy's parking lot.

Robert Hutton then led Davis through his testimony in the 1982 trial of Philip Workman. Hutton read a series of answers Davis had given at trial, including his reenactment when he came down off the witness stand and demonstrated how Philip allegedly shot Oliver. After reading that testimony along with other parts of Davis's "eyewitness testimony," Hutton asked, "True or not true, Mr. Davis?" Davis responded without hesitation to each question, including the reenactment of the murder: "Not true." He concluded, "I'm coming forward with the truth today."

After returning to jail, Davis suffered severe headaches. He was taken to a hospital and his brain was scanned. The stress of prosecution's relentless attack had a profound physical and emotional impact upon his well-being.

On Wednesday morning, Davis took the stand at 8:30. After telling defense lawyers that he did not see Philip shoot Lieutenant Oliver, he told prosecutors that he remembered turning into the Wendy's behind a police car and remembered leaving, but beyond that he could not "distinguish fact from fiction. I just don't know."

At 8:45 A.M. testimony was interrupted and the court was informed by medical personnel who had examined Davis in the Germantown Methodist Hospital after his testimony the day before that a brain scan indicated he had swelling of the brain and should be returned to the hospital. (Evidently, the result of the brain scan had just now become available.) Davis was removed from the courtroom on a gurney and returned to the hospital. He received treatment for high blood pressure and swelling of the brain.

Davis returned on Thursday, August 16, for a final day of testimony. There was little added to his testimony, and the prosecution and defense battled to ask the last question in hopes of his definitively landing on one side. Davis stated that his poor memory was the result of drug use, personal problems, and possibly a series of small strokes. Even the prosecutor admitted that Davis had a history of strokes.

Vivian Porter took the stand then and testified that Harold Davis had been with her on the night of the Wendy's robbery and Lieutenant Oliver's slaying. She said they had driven past the crime scene but did not drive onto the lot. She also told how she and Davis learned of the police killing on television back at her dwelling.

The hearing concluded with another hearing for scheduling further witnesses on August 24, 2001.

Dr. O. C. Smith, the star prosecution witness at Philip's two clemency hearings, did not testify in the evidentiary hearing. The reason was simple: prosecutors did not want him subject to cross-examination. It was clear to both the defense and the prosecution that if Smith were subject to examination by Philip's lawyers, his stories and experiments would fall apart like wet tissue paper. So the state had no witnesses to support their position. All they had to stand on was record of the case created at trial.

After this bizarre week of testimony, including a witness being wheeled out of the courtroom on a gurney driven to stroke-like symptoms resulting from prosecutorial harassment and the judicial laxity that allowed it to occur, one needed to recall the standard set forth by the Tennessee Supreme Court: "At the hearing, Workman will have the opportunity to establish that newly discovered evidence may have resulted in a different judgment if the evidence had been admitted at the previous trial." No objective person who listened to Harold Davis, the "sole eyewitness," in that Memphis courtroom would believe him or take his word in order to convict another human being of murder and then sentence him to death.

Then again, this was not an objective setting. It was a Memphis courtroom presided over by a judge who prior to and throughout the evidentiary hearing consistently favored the prosecution—a prosecution that had placed so much pressure on a witness that he had to be treated at a hospital for stroke-like symptoms Tuesday night after his testimony. Then, after a mere fifteen minutes of testimony on Wednesday morning, he was removed from the stand and placed on a gurney to be taken back to the hospital. His high blood pressure had resulted in swelling of the brain. There was simply no limit to what the Memphis police, prosecutors, and judges would do to maintain a twenty-year cover-up of the fact that one of their own police officers had accidentally killed another one in friendly fire trying to apprehend Philip Workman after a robbery.

***

The *error coram nobis* hearing continued on October 16, 2001, with the testimony of forensic pathologist Dr. Cyril Wecht, who had testified at Philip's second clemency hearing. Dr. Wecht reiterated his testimony from that hearing, explaining that Philip's bullet could not have killed Lieutenant Oliver. It would have been a "very atypical scenario" in his experience. He clearly informed Judge Colton that he was sure "to a reasonable degree of medical certainty" that it was not Philip Workman's bullet that had taken Lieutenant Oliver's life.

In cross-examination, Dr. Wecht stated he couldn't be absolutely sure that the fatal gunshot did not from Philip's gun, but that was not the scientific standard. The standard was "to a reasonable degree of medical certainty," and the evidence made the case that met that standard. Wecht also denied prosecutors' insistence that defense attorneys had shaped his opinion by giving him only information that was favorable to Philip. Wecht responded forcefully, "I have no bias in this case. I have no cudgel to bear, no axe to grind and no flag to wave." He was simply providing his medical and scientific opinion.

Prosecutors were very hostile to Wecht and kept up persistent questioning for the entire afternoon. Wecht clearly stated that he did not agree with the prosecution's assertion that the bullet was found the day after the shooting in a parking lot 104 feet from where Lieutenant Oliver was shot. Wecht was adamant that the prosecution's magic bullet showed very little of the damage that would have occurred if it had hit Lieutenant Oliver, striking his rib and passing through his body: "A soft jacketed hollow point bullet would be expected to deform or fragment when it hit a bone and it's not designed to exit the body." So much for O. C. Smith's experiments and the prosecution theory.

If any doubt remained as to the result of evidentiary hearing before Judge Colton, the final scene of this tragedy, on November 5, 2001, made clear what was to come. Wardie Parks, the juror on Philip's trial who testified at the clemency hearing, took the stand. Parks testified and strongly believed that if the jury had known the scientific evidence that demonstrated it was not Philip's bullet that killed Lieutenant Oliver, and that the "sole eyewitness," Harold Davis, was not at the crime scene, the jury would not have voted to convict Philip of murder, much less sentence him to death. Amazingly, Judge Colton ruled Parks's testimony "not relevant," although he preserved it on the record for the appellate courts.

Again, the standard set by the Tennessee Supreme Court for the evidentiary hearing was clear: "At the hearing, Workman will have the opportunity to establish that newly discovered evidence may have resulted in a different judgment if the evidence had been admitted at the previous trial." Yet by his ruling Judge Colton was completely disregarding how the new evidence affected an original trial juror and how it most certainly would have resulted in a different verdict had the truth been known. This is the information at the heart of the Tennessee Supreme Court ruling and, along with the five affidavits from other jurors at the trial indicating they too would have voted differently, it left no doubt that "newly discovered evidence may have resulted in a different judgment." But for Judge Colton that information was "not relevant."

**

If the information was considered irrelevant, one wonders *why*? The record of events leading up to the evidentiary hearing and the manner in which it was conducted reveals why Wardie Parks's statements were not considered pertinent. Just like at the clemency hearings, the evidence that was probative for Philip was dismissed and the state consistently favored the prosecution. Judge Colton had initially tried to hurry the case along, seizing control before the mandate had even issued from the Tennessee Supreme Court. A series of his decisions, including the gag order of the lawyers, were reversed by the Tennessee Court of Appeals because Colton acted without authority. Despite that hand slap, as soon as the case came back he put it on the fast track: he denied the defense effort to recuse him; he converted a default hearing on August 13 into an evidentiary hearing once he learned from prosecutors that they had Harold Davis in hand; he and the prosecutors colluded in keeping the information from the defense that Davis was going to testify on August 13, despite a defense subpoena for Davis. The defense was so misled that they filed a continuance motion on Friday before the hearing on Monday because of their inability to find Davis. But the fortunate accident of Davis's minister seeing him at the Memphis airport and learning from him that he was in town to testify the next day let the proverbial cat out of the bag.

Harold Davis was supposed to be the state's key witness. Prosecutors offered no other proof beyond the trial court record. On the defense side, however, Vivian Porter, Cyril Wecht, and Wardie Parks provided compelling testimony as to how the scientific forensic knowledge and the fact that Harold Davis was not at the Wendy's when the crime occurred would have given the jury "newly discovered evidence [that] may have resulted in a different judgment if the evidence had been admitted at the previous trial."

Judge Colton indicated he would rule within thirty days. He did so and denied Philip a new trial. He ignored the two African Americans who had testified cogently and compellingly at the evidentiary hearing: Vivian Porter and Wardie Parks. This was consistent with their treatment by the Board of Probation and Parole, an all-white body except for its pro-prosecution chairman, Charles Traughber. The inference was clear: black people were not believable when contradicting the police and prosecution. And science was not important either, as Dr. Wecht's testimony was ignored.

A twenty-year-old Memphis cover-up that had started in August 1981 continued with Judge Colton's decision. Once again, the good old boys of Memphis were ginning up the killing machinery for Philip Workman. And so it goes.

Joe Ingle displays cover of Philip's book.

THE SIXTEENTH CIRCLE

On March 13, 2002, a janitor found a bomb and two smaller explosive devices in the stairwell outside of the Shelby County Regional Forensic Center. Dr. O. C. Smith was asked to examine the devices and confirmed they were explosives. He then called the police. There was a suspicion that the bomb was the work of a writer of a series of threatening letters who seemed to be a Philip Workman supporter and signed his letters "STEEL in the hand of the KING OF KINGS." Here are some examples of those letters.

From a letter to Lawrence Buser, writer for the *Memphis Commercial Appeal*:

> GOD BLESS YOU for your articles about the fearful conspiracy of deceit and LIARS trying to CRUCIFY and INNOCENT man, a LAMB OF GOD beloved of our LORD and SAVIOUR.
>
> I received HOLY ORDERS from a MESSANGER OF GOD on Friday in the FORM of Robert Hutton, son of the ONE TRUE CHURCH speaking to me through the MIke Fleming show. He told me the LIAR, O.C.SMITH, a DOCTOR-KILLER committing two MORAL SINS. He is BEARING FALSE WITNESS with his lies decit and untruths in an effort to MURDER PHILLIP R. WORKMAN.
>
> Long have I waited for my HOLY ORDER to fight against the DOCTOR-KILLER abortionists but now I know OUR LORD was saving me for something larger.
>
> Through your help I understand better the "Little General" commands of DEMONS doing the work of SATAN in CESAR's WORLD.
>
> GOD BLESS YOU A THOUSAND TIMES.
>
> John 15:13
>
> Steel in the hand of the KING OF KINGS

A similar letter to a private citizen on April 3, 2001, read:

> BLESSED Mr. [_____] Your words today came to me through the Mike Fleming show as the VOICE of the slain LAMB OF GOD. Truly you have been sent as HIS MESSENGER to me his TOOL in the HAND OF CLEANSING.
>
> Your armored breast thrust through the many arrows of lies deceit and conspiracy has brought you beyond the turmoil and into the battle's respite to utter the WORD OF GOD into mine ears.
>
> Long have I awaited the SACRAMENT OF HOLY ORDERS to fight against the DOCTOR-KILLER abortionists but now the path is clear before my eyes. A greater task you have given me to destroy the LIAR who would bear false witness and the DOCTOR-KILLER who would murder the INNOCENT child of the HOLY FAMILY, PHILLIP R. WORKMAN. The EVIL ONE is in the body of O.C. SMITH soulless PAWN OF HE DEVIL, guilty of TWO MORTAL SINS. SATAN was given DOMINION over the

WORLD, but now that CESAR'S WORLD is the underworld the ONE TRUE CHURCH must ACT.

These two MORTAL SINS will condemn him into HELL forever. No ACT OF CONTRITION can turn him, no penance can REDEEM his DAMANATION. But his EVIL actions on EARTH must END.

DOCTOR-KILLERS killing the INNOCENT and UNBORN offend GOD and the CHRISTIANS of the ONE TRUE CHURCH. God is calling upon US TO ACT and DESTROY the EVIL DOERS, pawns of SATAN with souls lost and SPAWNED in HELL. He cannot have the DEMONS cast from him. Only by DEATH is GOD's WORLD RECLAIMED.

I will not fail, by YOUR FAITH am I led. Let your HOLY MISSION proceed shortly unopposed, for the greater GLORY OF JESUS CHRIST AND HIS CHURCH.

John 15: 13

STEEL in the hand of the KING OF KINGS

Yet another strange letter was sent to William Gibbons, the district attorney, but ended thusly:

Do not use this beyond redemption SPAWN OF SATAN. He must be returned to HELL for no PURGATURY can cleanse a soulless DEMON inhabiting a body made by THE EVIL ONE. My HOLY ORDERS are clear, my preparations are complete, my aim is TRUE and SURE, my strokes are POWERFUL and QUICK, my heart is RESOLVED and my SALVATION is assured through the HOLINESS of my GOOD WORKS. Your case pivots about his LIES, abandon him to THE LORD'S VENGENCE, he will not have time to be of use to you.

John 15:13

STEEL in the hand of the KING OF KINGS

***

On June 1, 2002, Philip's birthday, a bizarre incident occurred involving O. C. Smith. After leaving work earlier in the day, Smith returned to the Regional Forensic Center at 9:00 P.M. and informed the only employee on duty that he had returned. A little after 10:00, as Smith once again left the building, he was headed to the parking lot when someone threw an acid-like substance in his face to subdue him and then wrapped him in barbed wire, head to toe, with a bomb strapped to his chest.

Smith was found by a security guard at 12:30 A.M. on June 2. He had been locked to the security bars of a window. It was reported that his arms were outstretched in the form of a crucifixion.

In a June 3, 2002, press conference, Jim Cavanaugh, an agent of the federal ATF (Division of Alcohol, Tobacco and Firearms) stated:

There is a good chance that the man who wrote the letters is the bomber . . . This person is someone in this area who has strong religious beliefs, and we are asking for the public's help to find him because he is dangerous. The explosives make him a danger to a personal level toward Dr. Smith.

The attacker is described as a white man, 20–30 years old, 5'8 to 6', and pale complexioned . . . Authorities say he attacked the medical examiner because Smith was a prosecution witness in the long-running case of convicted cop killer Philip Workman (*Memphis Commercial Appeal,* June 4, 2002).

Memphis police investigators and bomb-squad officers were interviewed for an episode of the nationally syndicated television show *America's Most Wanted.* Agents later said the program produced some "very interesting" tips.

On July 26 O. C. Smith stated to ATF agents that he had been attacked. ATF agent Gene Marquez stated, "We're confident we can solve the case," claiming it was "our priority investigation right now." The ATF said it had evidence linking the attack to previous bombings and threatening letters.

In a November 8, 2002, interview ATF agent Cavanaugh told the *Memphis Flyer* that the bomber may have gone underground like the Unabomber. He believed the attacker was a lone, fleshy-faced white man, thirty to forty years old. He wore gloves, punched Smith in the stomach, and jumped on him, did not carry a gun or knife, and chained Smith to a window grate in a "semi-crucified" position. Asked if he thought the attack might have been staged, Cavanaugh responded, "I've been a cop too long to not think that there might be something else. I'm open to any angles."

Philip Workman reflected in the glass of the visitor's booth.

The Seventeenth Circle

On June 2, 2003, the day after Philip's forty-ninth birthday, the Tennessee Supreme Court set a fourth execution date for him of September 24, 2003. Dr. George Woods, an internationally respected neuropsychiatrist who has extensive experience with trauma patients, interviewed Philip on September 9. Woods spent three hours with Philip and thoroughly reviewed the record of his case. He noted that Philip had been on deathwatch three times and was expecting a fourth trip in the near future due to his September 24 scheduled execution date. The following are excerpts from the evaluation of Philip Workman by Dr. Woods.

CLINICAL ISSUES

Mr. Workman has been exposed to the Execution Procedures of the Riverbend Maximum Security Facility 3 times. This will be the fourth occasion that he has undergone the Execution Procedures. This is the 4th visit to the Death Watch section of Riverbend for Mr. Workman. Each time has been occasioned by the understanding that he was giving his life for a life he took. In Mr. Workman's situation, he claims factual innocence of the crime, so this understanding is more complex to interpret clinically.

Mr. Workman described his first exposure to the Death Watch protocol on April 3, 2000. "My heart started to explode." He talked about the level of self-denial he had experienced, which included not packing his belongings until the last possible moment.

As he was discussing the counter rituals that condemned inmates develop to deal with the protocols put in place by the prison, the steps described are very similar [to] those of someone who is dying from a terminal disease or attempting to commit suicide. He gives his possessions away to those that he has come to believe would appreciate them, his pencils, extra clothing, his caps.

Mr. Workman had made contact with his daughter, Michelle, and had become close to his grandchildren. His daughter decided that she wanted to be with him during these last days, and, along with his brother, Terry Workman, stayed close by in a motel with her children.

Mr. Workman couldn't sleep the night before he assumed he would be taken. Understanding that there was someone waiting to take his cell as soon as he was executed, he cleaned the cell, out of courtesy. About 3 A.M. Philip took a shower and got dressed. It seemed but a few minutes, and "There they were . . . come in numbers." The team that comes for Death Watch inmates are dressed completely in black, and are volunteers that, because of their size, responsibility, and willingness, are even more intimidating.

After being strip searched, Mr. Workman was shackled, and walked to the Death Watch cell. None of the other Death Row inmates said anything to him as he walked by their cells. It was his sense that every inmate was glad this time wasn't their time, and couldn't find much to say. He could see their faces in the openings of their cells.

Mr. Workman described an ". . . almost dreamlike state . . . You're there, but you're not there . . . It's not you.

Mr. Workman received a stay on April 4, 2000, a day and a half before he was to be executed. He remembers feeling a "... rush of energy ..." and feeling elated. However, returning to his cell on Death Row, he knew that his life had changed.

"I didn't know whether to unpack," Mr. Workman recalled. Since that first exposure, he has never unpacked immediately.

In September, 2000, a fellow inmate woke him up to tell him that his stay had been lifted. When the extraction team, the similar assemblage of large men dressed all in black, came the second time, on January 28, 2001: "My breath was taken away."

In spite of clearly recognizing the circumstances he was facing, again, experiencing the execution ritual, Mr. Workman had developed a pathological denial, an inability to face the execution ritual as straightforwardly as he had the first time. He had not packed, although he had been, again, giving things away since Christmas.

In the interim between Mr. Workman's first exposure to the execution protocol and his second exposure, Mr. Workman started experiencing dreams of being executed. He also had nightmares of being in the Death Chamber, 20 to [30] feet from the electric chair, and it is malfunctioning. He dreamed of watching others being executed, and being in an electric chair that is being driven through a mall.

Mr. Workman noted that one of the experiences that imprinted the execution procedures most on him was the number of strip searches. He would take off all his clothes, sometimes his upper garments first, at other times his pants and underwear. He would be told to squat, in the event something had been secreted in his anus. He was strip searched upon each visit, even though they were all non-contact. On certain days, this would mean being strip searched 16 times.

On the second Death Watch to which he has been exposed, Mr. Workman received a stay, and was returned to Death Row from Death Watch 11 hours before he was to be executed. His relief was tempered. Mr. Workman recognized this experience was not over. "You're on pins and needles."

Mr. Workman hardly unpacked anything after his second exposure to the execution procedures. He found himself continually anxious. His concentration was becoming impaired. He found himself unable to focus on those things that had occupied [him] the last 22 years, his Seventh Day Adventist ministry, his daughter and grandchildren, his belief that he was factually innocent.

The third time the extraction team came to take Mr. Workman to Death Watch was, according to Mr. Workman, round 11 A.M. on a Tuesday, within a few months of his previous exposure. He saw them coming through the aperture in his cell. The five guys, dressed in all black, made him, again, "... anxiety ridden."

Mr. Workman remembered those few administrative persons responsible for carrying out the execution procedures that were also willing to talk to him, including the Warden, saying the same thing, "Workman, it's that time again." Truer words couldn't have been spoken.

He received the denial of clemency. The night before he was facing execution, for the third time, his attorneys came to visit him. He said that he could tell by their faces that the news was not good for him. As it turned out, his attorneys had received misinformation concerning the litigation, believing that all appeals had been exhausted.

Mr. Workman called his daughter. She had not been able to bring herself to come to the third Death Watch. The time was about 12 o'clock. Mr. Workman remembers specifically not asking the Lord if this was his final one.

He describes himself as, " . . . not really there." With 40 minutes before being executed, Mr. Workman received a stay.

RELEVANT FAMILY HISTORY

Philip Workman was born into a family of abuse and neglect. Mr. Workman was running away from home early in life, attempting to escape physical beatings. The trauma-derived coping skills continued throughout his adolescent years.

He was abandoned by his mother at an early age, and subjected to an alcoholic, abusive father. After 22 years on Death Row, he understands the impact of his nuclear family on his own emotional growth, and has done well for 22 years, until now.

MENTAL STATUS EXAMINATION

Philip Workman is a white male who looks his chronological age. He was dressed in prison garb. I introduced myself, after his attorney initially introduced me. I explained to him that this was not a clinical doctor-patient relationship, therefore what he said to me could be shared with other members of his defense team, and those with whom they chose to share it.

His mood was anxious, and he started tearing, then crying immediately. Mr. Workman said, "This is going to be very hard for me . . . it's one of those things you don't want to show."

He denied perceptual disorders, hallucinations, delusions, etc. He was certainly oriented to person, place, time, and circumstances. He acknowledged nightmares during the periods he has been to Death Watch, and in the interims between.

Mr. Workman's affect was occasionally tearful. His speech was normal in rate, although there were a number of pauses. Thought processes were ruminative. This ruminative thought process was impairing his concentration, in his estimation.

Mr. Workman found himself hypervigilant, even taking into consideration the proscribed circumstances he found himself. He had found his responses increasingly impaired from his first execution procedure to this, his fourth.

Thought contents were mildly paranoid, anxiety-ridden. He denies suicidal ideation.

DIAGNOSES
Axis I: Post Traumatic Stress Disorder, acute
Axis II: Deferred
Axis III: Deferred
Axis IV: Legal Problems
Axis V: Current-55, Year-65

ANALYSIS

Mr. Workman fits the criteria outlined in the Diagnostic and Statistical Manual-IVTR (DSM-IVTR) for Post Traumatic Stress Disorder. Those criteria are:

A. The person has been exposed to a traumatic event in which both of the following were present:

1. the person experienced, witnessed, or was confronted with an event or events that involved actual or threatened death or serious injury, or a threat to the physical integrity of self or others

2. the person's response involved intense fear, helplessness, or horror.

Note: In children, this may be expressed instead by disorganized or agitated behavior

B. The traumatic event is persistently reexperienced in one (or more) of the following ways:

1. recurrent and intrusive distressing recollections of the event, including images, thoughts, or perceptions. Note: In young children, repetitive play may occur in which themes or aspects of the trauma are expressed.

2. recurrent distressing dreams of the event. Note: In children, there may be frightening dreams without recognizable content.

3. acting or feeling as if the traumatic event were recurring (includes a sense of reliving the experience, illusions, hallucinations, and dissociative flashback episodes, including those that occur on awakening or when intoxicated). Note: In young children, trauma-specific reenactment may occur.

4. intense psychological distress at exposure to internal or external cures that symbolize or resemble an aspect of the traumatic event

5. physiological reactivity on exposure to internal or external cues that symbolize or resemble an aspect of the traumatic event

C. Persistent avoidance of stimuli associated with the trauma and numbing of general responsiveness (not present before the trauma), as indicated by three (or more) of the following:

1. efforts to avoid thoughts, feelings, or conversations associated with the trauma

2. efforts to avoid activities, places, or people that arouse recollections of the trauma

3. inability to recall an important aspect of the trauma

4. markedly diminished interest or participation in significant activities

5. feeling of detachment or estrangement from others

6. restricted range of affect (e.g., unable to have loving feelings)

7. sense of a foreshortened future (e.g., does not expect to have a career, marriage, children or a normal life span)

D. Persistent symptoms of increased arousal (not present before the trauma), as indicated by two (or more) of the following:

1. difficulty falling or staying asleep

2. irritability or outbursts of anger

3. difficulty concentrating

4. hypervigilance.

5. exaggerated startle response

E. Duration of the disturbance (symptoms in Criteria B, C, and D) is more than 1 month.

F. The disturbance causes clinically significant distress or impairment in social, occupational, or other important areas of functioning.

There is no question that Mr. Workman has experienced repeated stressors that would qualify for Criteria A. The causative factors don't speak to the quality of the stressor, especially when there have been multiple exposures. That Mr. Workman's defense team has filed repeated motions to save his life, in the face of allegations of factual innocence, cannot be held culpable for the repeated stressors. One would assume that all possible remedies available under the United States Constitution would be available. These exposures to the execution procedure have increased the severity of symptoms which, limited by significant denial, were minimal initially.

Mr. Workman dreamed—and says he continues to dream—distressing nightmares of the execution procedure he has described in detail. Intrusive thoughts, particularly of the multiple strip searches, are discussed by Mr. Workman. Starting this interview was difficult for him, and he specifically noted that discussing these previous exposures would be difficult for him. He began to cry. He was able to continue, after some less emotionally-charged discussion. These symptoms meet Criteria B.

Meeting Criterion C is somewhat problematic. The last symptoms in Criterion C, a sense of a foreshortened future, is imposed on Mr. Workman legally, so it can't be a part of the symptomatology required to meet Criterion C.

Mr. Workman describes an inability to organize himself, giving his things away later and later, closer to the time he would possibly go to Death Watch; an increasing difficulty unpacking his possessions each time he came back from Death Watch. He believes this impairment in organization is secondary to problems with concentration, not memory. "I can't get this stuff out of my mind." Mr. Workman feels there has been an escalating degree of anxiety related to each Death Watch, with its attendant execution procedures.

The rituals that have worked for Mr. Workman for the 22 years he has been on Death Row have started to deteriorate, not in the face of his execution, but, he believes, due to the repeated, acute, exposures to dying. He describes a decrease of activity, which he attributes to his paralyzing anxiety and concomitant hyperarousal, an oxymoron if there ever was one. The first and second time Mr. Workman was escorted from Death Watch to Death Row, he told the members of the Extraction Team that he hoped he didn't have to see them again. He didn't say anything to them on the third Death Watch.

Mr. Workman believes that he is innocent of the crime of capital murder. [He] states that his attorneys uncovered new evidence proving his innocence shortly before his first exposure to the death watch procedures. This evidence includes a recantation by the eyewitness at trial, and scientific evidence, which, allegedly, proves that Mr. Workman could not have been the person who shot the victim, Lt. Ronald Oliver.

Although problems sleeping may have occurred prior to Mr. Workman's first exposure to the execution procedures, these problems were certainly magnified during his multiple exposures to the execution procedures. There are Criterion D symptoms Mr. Workman suffered from specific to the time that Mr. Workman was exposed to the execution procedures.

Mr. Workman experiences significant problems with his concentration, due primarily to his ruminative thoughts. Repeated exposures to highly regimented execution procedures have heightened his vigilance. A constant expectation, rooted in reality, but augmented by repetition of such a costly, definitive protocol.

Mr. Workman has been under Death Watch three times in a 12 month period. He was symptomatic, with distressing dreams, ruminative thinking, hypervigilance, intrusive thoughts, and impaired concentration; since his first exposure to the execution procedures. The course of his symptoms, therefore, meets Criterion E.

What are the ways in which these symptoms impair Mr. Workman's functioning? A difficult question, given the physical and emotional limitations of his circumstances. An increased isolation from his family, though, is one way in which Mr. Workman is cutting off his social relationships. His daughter has not been to the last two Death Watches. He has not been able to prepare for his death in the same rigorous manner with which he did initially.

The repeated exposures of Mr. Workman to the execution procedures are consistent with Complex Post Traumatic Stress Disorder, which occurs more commonly with repeated exposure to stressors. The stressor of sure death is the ultimate stressor, and there have been medical protocols developed to insure interrater reliability when evaluating multiple exposures to execution. The Physicians for Human Rights, in collaboration with the United Nations, have developed both medical and psychological protocols that may be relevant.

At the time I saw Mr. Workman, he was less than ten days from being placed on death watch a fourth time. There is no reason to assume that a fourth trip to Death Watch would not, to a reasonable degree of medical certainty, retrigger the symptoms of Mr. Workman's post-traumatic stress disorder.

SUMMARY

Philip Workman has undergone 3 certified encounters with being killed. That he hasn't been killed is a matter of law. The fact that he believes himself factually innocent must be added to the weight of his culpability in the exposures to death he has experienced. The causative factors of his exposure are, clinically, less important than the fact that he has been exposed. Mr. Workman's recent exposures are, inextricably linked, to his belief that he is factually innocent.

Thank you for allowing me to examine Mr. Workman.

George Woods, MD

THE EIGHTEENTH CIRCLE

After the denouement shortly before the scheduled March 30, 2001, execution date, Philip and I had resumed the routine of weekly visits, usually on Thursday evenings. We would sit in a small visiting room designated for lawyers and ministers in Unit 2 of the Riverbend Maximum Security Institution. In the larger visitation room for death row, religious services were held during the time Philip and I visited. Our conversation was often accompanied by a background of enthusiastic, somewhat off-key hymn singing along with prayers and a sermon.

Philip had experienced a genuine religious conversion some years earlier resulting in his immersion into the Bible. Although I was his official spiritual adviser, Philip could locate scriptures faster than I could. His leather-bound Bible was filled with passages underscored in various colors of highlighting. Often we would discuss passages of scriptures. I gladly anticipated our time together each week. Philip's humor, love of family and life, and his grappling with Christian discipleship were a framework for our life together. It was a routine we maintained through the *error coram nobis* hearing and into 2003.

Philip was not surprised at the result of the hearing before Judge Colton. He had predicted the negative outcome even as he studied Judge Colton's pretrial maneuvers. As he put it, it was all too typical of Memphis justice and quite predictable.

What flummoxed Philip and all of us were the unusual events involving Shelby County medical examiner O. C. Smith. First were the threatening letters cloaked in religious language, then the bomb in the stairwell outside Smith's office, and finally the bizarre attack made on him on June 1, 2002. The image of Smith wrapped in barbed wire in a cruciform position with a bomb affixed to his chest was mind-boggling. Philip and I discussed it, but neither of us had a clue as to what it was all about. Philip suggested Smith had done it to himself, but that seemed a stretch even for the Memphis gang. Our visits rocked along pleasantly on a weekly basis.

A year after all of these strange goings-on, on June 2, 2003, the Tennessee Supreme Court set Philip's fourth execution date for September 24, 2003. Shortly thereafter the Workman clemency team set a meeting for June 24, 2003.

Although a new governor had been elected, Phil Bredesen, a Democrat, it was difficult to harbor much hope that he would be helpful on the death penalty front. Bredesen's wife, Andrea Conte, had founded what became the largest victims' rights organization in Tennessee in the wake of being kidnapped outside of her Nashville retail shop in December 1988. The organization was called You Have the Power, and the group was outspoken in its support of the death penalty. The governor was also strongly in favor of capital punishment.

On June 17 I awoke at 4:00 A.M. after having a clear vision of Philip. In the dream, we were discussing his fourth death warrant. The case had so many bizarre and unexpected twists and turns, it had invaded my dream world. I arose from bed and made some coffee.

On Thursday, June 19, I visited Philip at Riverbend prison. We greeted each other with a hug and sat down to visit. There was much to discuss regarding clemency, his family, and life. However, a death row guard had informed Philip that his visit with me should be limited to "religious matters," since according to the prison our visit was intended to be a religious visit. Philip and I shook our heads over the guard's remarks and then laughed. As I pointed out to Philip, this was an interesting position not only regarding the right to free speech but also regarding what one considers "religious." It is very clear in the Bible that the warp and woof of life is *all* of God's creation, as we the people of God have been summoned to be participants through discipleship as partners in the world. There is no biblical separation of religion and life. Religion is not lived apart from the world but *in* the world, or as the apostle Paul put it, "in the world but not of the world."

The perspective of the guard was only one of many petty realities prisoners and visitors endure. Once I brought a legal pad to take notes about scriptures and write down family members' telephone numbers. The visitation officer at checkpoint would not let me take the legal pad back to death row, because I was making a religious visit. Somehow the presence of my legal pad broke some imaginary boundary that separated a religious visit from a legal one. Scenes like these could seamlessly fit into Joseph Heller's novel *Catch 22*. But unfortunately here they were real and not fiction.

During our June 19 visit, Philip was more upbeat than he had been in our previous visit. I was worried that in the face of what was now his fourth death warrant—and no prisoner in Tennessee besides Philip had survived more than two death warrants—he would withdraw and begin steeling himself for execution once again. At our last visit he had seemed depressed. This evening, however, he was full of energy. We discussed clemency ideas, the legal work, getting his brother Terry down to Nashville from Kentucky for press interviews, and we were animated, having fun. Philip's humor was keen. He also did not put much hope in newly elected Governor Bredesen, saying, "Joe, I'm the first one out of the box he has to make a decision on. He was just elected. I can't see him giving clemency to the first person, especially with the FOP [Fraternal Order of Police] bringing pressure to bear because I supposedly killed a cop."

I argued with him a bit about the governor, but I saw his point. Then he said something that chilled my soul: "If I go back over to deathwatch, I have to know what the deal is. I can't go through another final appeal and wondering what will happen. I want to know when I go over there what is going to happen." Implicitly, he was referring to the agony, the emotional tumult of his last trip to deathwatch, when I had informed him that the Tennessee Supreme Court had unexpectedly granted a stay of execution forty-five minutes before he was to be killed. That news had come after a final communion service, prayers, and completion of a lengthy solitary prayer by Philip on his knees at the rear of the deathwatch cell. Although the stay of execution had been a welcome relief, it was also an emotionally wrenching ordeal. Now Philip was saying he could not go through that experience again.

While Philip and I visited, a half dozen prisoners gathered with volunteer clergy for a worship service in the adjacent room. As we talked, the sermon was clearly audible. It was about enmity and ill will, and the volunteer preacher boomed out his words for the men. As I sat listening to Philip, the preacher's references to enmity in the background were eerily appropriate. Philip knew about enmity. For more than twenty years he had been suffering from official enmity and political calculation designed to exterminate him.

I truly admired Philip's honesty. He was so clear about what he could and could not do. It was a trait that led Chris Minton to refer to him as the "captain of the ship." Philip knew his case in the minutest detail and wanted to be sure it was presented correctly down to the last fact. Indeed, he would be visiting with Chris Minton the next day to go over the contradictions made in the testimony of the police officers and medical examiner O. C. Smith during the two clemency hearings.

Philip inquired about my wife, Becca, and our soccer-enthused daughter, Amelia. I told him the results of her latest tournament. The visit wound down and we closed with prayer. I prayed that God would deliver Philip from "the valley of the shadow of death."

***

On July 3 I went out to the prison at 6:00 P.M. to visit Philip. I was exhausted from work and really didn't want to go in such a frazzled state. I was looking forward to resting on the three-day holiday weekend. My multiple sclerosis was flaring up with resultant numbing in my left leg, and I needed to slow down. But I also really wanted to see Philip, and he was expecting me. He had enough disappointment in life without my not coming to visit as promised.

I made the ten-minute drive from my house to the prison and proceeded through checkpoint. After walking back to Unit 2, I entered the sally port, a series of locked gates, and went into the foyer where visitors sign in. The guard had just finished signing me in when Philip strode into the small visiting room ten feet from me. We embraced, our respective Bibles banging on each other's back, and settled down to visit. The religious volunteers had already begun their service in the large visiting room next door. As Philip and I began to talk, the sermon penetrated the wall that separated us.

Philip was in a buoyant mood. Once again I thought to myself, the reality of prison ministry is that often it is the prisoner who does the ministering, not the clergy. We covered the gamut of issues in his case and talked about our families. When it was time to conclude the visit, we held hands in prayer. I asked Philip to lead the prayer since I felt spent. He prayed for "a hedge of protection around my brother and his family" and thanked God for sending me out to see him. He closed by saying, "We trust you Father, praise your name, and ask for your blessing. Your will be done." Philip never prayed for himself in our prayers together.

We parted with an embrace and I went back outside. As I moved down the sidewalk, I heard a knocking on a vertical window of one of the death row cells. Two ebony fingers extended in a peace sign. I flashed the peace sign back to my brother. Despite concrete and reinforced glass, shackles and chains, the threat of official killing looming over everyone on death row, the human spirit triumphed. Although we couldn't always see or feel it, "seeing through a glass darkly" as the apostle Paul put it, we would be surprised by grace. A peace sign flashed in a death row window, a prayer of sustaining strength for me from a man the state of Tennessee decreed had just seventy-nine days left to live, and now a rabbit nibbling grass in the twilight outside the death chamber as I walked by. Inevitably, it is the little things that sustain us. And they often come from those who Jesus termed "the least of these by brothers and sisters."

***

I was sleeping soundly during the early morning hours of July 4. In a dream, I suddenly found myself in an old football stadium. It seemed to be Dudley Field at Vanderbilt University. There were hundreds of people milling about. As I moved through them beneath the stands, I realized I was marching with a purpose. I was trying to find Philip. There were tunnels connecting underneath the stadium, and I marched through them desperately seeking Philip. He was about to be executed somewhere down the darkened pathways. I couldn't find him, and the dread of getting there and seeing him killed conflicted with the haste to be there for him.

Finally, a guard appeared: "Are you Workman's minister?" he asked. I replied, "Yes." He gestured and began walking. "Follow me." We were going through a dark tunnel full of people.

Suddenly we emerged in the death chamber. I went over to the gurney where Philip was strapped down, one leather belt tightened across his chest with his arms and legs extended and also fastened to the gurney. His posture resembled a crucifixion. He was not moving. I realized he was already dead. I wheeled the gurney out of the killing chamber. Everyone moved out of the way as I rolled him down a tunnel. Suddenly I saw his toes twitch. I thought he might not be dead. I recalled that one of the drugs in the lethal injection protocol cocktail freezes all muscles. Maybe somehow his heart temporarily froze while they put the stethoscope to his chest to confirm his death. The drug had worn off and now maybe he was reviving. After all, this was the Department of Corrections that had once hired a crop duster to be its medical director, so stranger things have happened than failing to kill a prisoner. I looked at Philip's face. His eyes opened and he gazed at me. Oh, my God! He was alive! I ran down the tunnel, pushing the gurney as fast as I could go.

I knew I couldn't take him to a hospital, because the authorities would find him. I remembered that in the 1930s, a fifteen-year-old African American boy, Willie Francis, was electrocuted in the Louisiana electric chair. Although it was an excruciatingly painful experience, it didn't kill him, because the chair malfunctioned and he was able to survive. The case was subsequently litigated to the U.S. Supreme Court, which allowed the state to electrocute him again. Evidently, the Eighth Amendment to the U.S. Constitution prohibiting "cruel and unusual punishment" did not apply to black children facing electrocution twice.

I began thinking of my friends who were medical doctors, and I began calling them on a cell phone as I pushed the gurney down the winding tunnels. Finally I emerged into open air in the middle of the football field. Gathering my bearings, I pushed the gurney down the field and out through the end zone to the parking lot where my pickup truck was parked. As I was lifting Philip off the gurney, struggling to put him in the passenger side of the truck, his six-foot frame feeling like dead weight, I prayed that he wasn't literally dead weight. Then I awoke.

I sat upright in bed. I glanced at the clock and saw it was 4:00 A.M. I was sweating, my heart racing. I propped myself up and recalled the dream, shuddering as the details rolled back through my mind. I kept seeing Philip on the gurney looking too peaceful. Then I arose and wrote down the dream. There would be no more sleep that morning.

***

When I visited Philip on July 24, after our welcoming hug Philip opened his Bible with its detailed leather cover. A piece of paper fell to the floor. It was his ten-year-old son's handwriting. He mused, "I sure would love to see that boy again." We both knew that was unlikely, since the child's mother had moved out of state three years earlier and kept him away from Philip.

Another sheet of paper tumbled out of the Bible, this one inscribed with three words in Philip's writing: "Death, grave, forever." Philip picked it up and began an exegesis of the concept of eternal fire, thumbing through his Bible and locating the passages that he felt spoke about it. As he flipped from one biblical book to another, the heavily annotated margins and underlined passages in various colors revealed a man who had spent many hours studying the scripture. Indeed, as we now spent forty-five minutes examining scriptures, I chuckled to myself: here I was the theologically trained minister, and I couldn't keep pace with Philip's speed and knowledge of various verses as he located them in the Bible.

We talked about his case for a while. Philip looked me in the eyes and said, "Sixty-two more days," referring to the fact that his execution date was just a little more than two months hence.

I responded, "Yeah. Two months and two days. A lot can happen with that much time."

When I left the prison that evening, the long summer twilight was upon us. It was stunning to try to comprehend that the man I had just visited was slated to be exterminated by the state of Tennessee. I had no doubt that Philip knew the scripture better than anyone involved in the process of determining his fate. Indeed, his life of Christian discipleship was a witness to the power of the love of God. Although he was not evangelical, as were many of the prisoners who attended the Thursday services while we visited, Philip made a quiet and powerful Christian witness. I had known Philip for almost twenty years and seen the transformation in him that had resulted from his spiritual experience. He was not the same person who had come to death row in 1982. But I knew from bitter, personal experience with other death row prisoners across the South dating back to 1975, becoming a spiritual person in prison doesn't mean the state won't kill you.

As the door opened into Unit 2 for my next Thursday evening visit with Philip, an enthusiastic refrain of "Glory, glory, Alleluia" greeted me. The Thursday worship group had commenced with singing in the larger visitation room. Philip greeted me with a hug in our small room, singing the chorus of a hymn, "Jesus Loves Me, This I Know." We settled in for the visit.

The good news I shared with Philip was that Larry Marshall, from the Northwestern Center for Wrongful Conviction, was willing to once again become involved in his case. I had telephoned Larry and learned that he had read of Philip's latest execution date. He was heading off on vacation but agreed to take whatever papers we forwarded to him and work on them during his holiday. Philip was pleased at the news and pointed out which documentation Larry would need to get up to speed on the case again. As usual, Philip was in total command of his case, knowing every document and indicating the best ones to forward to Larry Marshall.

One of the things preying on Philip's mind was concern for his son. He wanted the boy to be taken care of if the execution wasn't stopped. The boy was with his mother out west, and there wasn't any hope for a visit. She had broken off her and her son's relationship with Philip after she had visited with him before his near execution in the spring of 2001.

However, I had located a private investigator who had helped find the boy. Philip wanted me to talk to the investigator again and have him check on his son. I agreed to call him and see if we could obtain an update on the boy just to be sure he was okay. Philip looked at me and said, "That would really give me some peace of mind. Just to know he was all right." I recalled that Terry, Philip's older brother, had agreed to help the lad until he turned eighteen, so we needed to stay in touch with the child if possible.

We closed with prayer and I prayed this time. As we held hands, I asked God to lead us out of this madness, to protect and sustain Philip in his time of need. We then hugged good-bye and I left.

There were certain moments in Philip's case when the incongruity of what was happening was overwhelming. Philip gave voice to this perspective during our August 7 visit: "This whole thing is so crazy, Joe. Here I am, the supposed bad guy. But I'm the only one telling the truth. We have police lying, prosecutors manufacturing witnesses, the attorney general bending over backwards in violation of the law to have me killed. Then there is the FOP and this 'thin blue line' stuff who are stepping forward because they don't want to admit one of their own is lying and accidentally killed a fellow police officer. It's just too crazy."

As usual, Philip had hit the nail on the head. All of the forces of societal "good" in the crime-fighting arena—police, prosecutors, and their respective organizations—were lining up to falsely accuse, convict, and cold-bloodedly murder a restaurant robber with the state's killing machinery. Although they had assumed the mantle of legitimacy from their roles in law enforcement, they were actually in violation of the law on several levels, not the least being that a robber was not eligible for the death penalty unless he killed or conspired to kill someone in the commission of the felony. Clearly Philip had done no such thing.

But law enforcement and law upholders no longer wished to discuss the evidence, since the ballistics report and Harold Davis's recantation had demolished the rationale for the death penalty. It did not matter to the forces of "good" that the law (according to *State v. Severs*) prohibited the death penalty in Philip's case. Nor did they care that five trial jurors had stated post-trial that they would not have voted for a murder conviction, much less the death penalty, without Davis's testimony. The situation had deteriorated beyond rational discussion to an exercise of pure power politics. It had become the politics of killing in its rawest form.

Returning home from my visit with Philip, I found a poem I recalled reading that bespoke my mood.

In Distrust of Merits

The world's an orphans' home. Shall
We never have peace without sorrow?
Without pleas of the dying for
Help that won't come? O
Quiet form upon the dust, I cannot
Look and yet I must. If these great patient
Dyings—all these agonies
And wonderings and bloodshed—
Can teach us how to live, these
Dyings were not wasted.
     —Marianne Moore

***

As I considered the time winding down to Philip's scheduled September 24 execution date, I was moved by a Vietnam memoir by John Laurence, *The Cat from Hué: A Vietnam War Story*. Laurence, a journalist who spent considerable time in the field, including the Tet offensive of 1968, wrenched this story out of his gut some thirty years after leaving Vietnam. It was a compelling and chilling look at a misbegotten war.

Laurence described his feeling of going into a battle zone: "My physical perceptions were ultra alert. Colors looked brighter, sounds sharper, my reflexes quicker. Everything appeared with precise clarity. And yet the speeding, fast-moving fight unfolded in slow motion, like a macabre ballet . . . the sights and sounds [. . . were] holding me in the grip of overwhelming powerlessness, a feeling of being on the border of madness myself, not knowing nor being able to change or caring what might happen next."

The feelings Laurence detailed were similar to those I have experienced under deathwatch with the condemned. The heightened perceptions, the adrenaline racing, the clarity of everything accompanied with unbelievable tenseness. As acutely attuned and focused as I was in those situations, the time passed "in slow motion, like a macabre ballet." And, of course, the powerlessness felt outside the cell of the condemned as they awaited slaughter did place me "on the border of madness myself." This riptide of feeling had to be dammed by the strictest emotional control, because my role was to be the comforter, the channel for the love of God to be brought to people under intense suffering.

Elsewhere Laurence talked about "the addiction" of battle. The adrenaline rush, the camaraderie, the intense reality of everything; he found himself addicted to it. It seemed to be powerful even as it was destructive. As I reflected on those emotions, I recognized the similarities in my work against the death penalty. The close friendships, the power of being in a fight to the death, the energy generated by being in the fight, and the exhaustion of it all after the battle was won or lost. This was a cold-blooded killing machinery we were struggling against. As Walt Kelley, the author of the comic strip *Pogo*, said, "We have met the enemy and he is us." It is our calling to root out this evil from our national soul, because it is us at our worst. When it is banished and the death penalty is no more than the historical relic it should already be, I will have no desire to return to this madness.

***

On the night of August 12, 2003, the Workman clemency team met. Earlier in the day, after the filing of clemency papers, a press conference announced the results of Harold Davis's taking a polygraph test. The test, administered by a veteran FBI agent, revealed that Davis did not see Philip Workman shoot Lt. Ronald Oliver. The only "eyewitness" didn't eyeball anything, because he wasn't there.

Members of the press then adjourned to a press conference that Governor Bredesen was holding on another matter. When a reporter surprised him with a question about Davis's passing the polygraph test and the filing of clemency for Philip, Bredesen indicated he would send the information to the parole board for an advisory opinion and reminded the press that there was a reason why lie detector tests were not admissible in court.

This seemingly innocuous response was quite chilling to those of us who knew the history of mishandling in Philip's case: (1) the parole board had been the subject of litigation from the kangaroo format and abuse of Philip and his witnesses in the two earlier clemency hearings; (2) I had observed one member of the clemency board had written her decision in advance; (3) the former Memphis policeman who recused himself had proceeded to lobby the other members to vote against Philip; (4) Officer Clyde Keenan had testified about checking the various guns and holding the dying Lt. Oliver in his arms when the police log of the crime scene arrival noted he appeared three minutes after Oliver was transported to the hospital; (5) the Shelby County medical examiner had provided outlandish testimony about a scientific test he conducted that supposedly proved Philip's bullet shot Lieutenant Oliver. All of this, along with much more, was orchestrated by the Shelby County district attorney and the attorney general of Tennessee—the same attorney general who purported to be an impartial adviser to the parole board and the governor. Certainly if

Governor Bredesen wished to be viewed as objective and above reproach, he would not crawl into bed with a "criminal justice" establishment with no regard for the truth.

**

At 2:15 on the morning of August 13, I awoke in a cold sweat. The nightmare I had been experiencing was vividly clear. I was in the death house with Philip awaiting his execution. Just as it had been in January 2001, I was outside his cell as we awaited the death squad to come and take him to the killing chamber. But in the dream nobody came, and the time passed for the execution. There had been no word from the courts or the governor. The deathwatch guard didn't know what was going on either. I decided to find someone with information.

I walked out of the holding area and through a steel door. Suddenly I was in a room bathed in light with a gorgeous view of what seemed to be the Smoky Mountains. A huge plate-glass window provided a spectacular vista. I walked across the blond oak floor to gaze out the window. Coming to my senses, I looked for someone in charge who could tell me what was going on with the execution. There was no one to be found.

Hours became days. The entire clemency team was with me in the death house, and we knew nothing. Philip was anxious, but we were in an information vacuum. The stress was building because we feared that any moment the death squad would appear to take Philip.

Suddenly we were transported farther south to Georgia. Will Campbell, who set up Southern Prison Ministry in 1972, and who along with Tony Dunbar helped me begin my work in Southern prisons, was somewhere in south Georgia. We had to find Will to get a read on the situation we were dealing with regarding Philip.

We were in a swampy area in south Georgia. It was almost tropical with lush vegetation and Spanish moss. Will was supposedly in the swamp. We arrived at an abandoned multicolored school bus where he was located. Beautiful tropical birds flew out the windows and through an open roof, startled by our approach. We wandered out of the swamp into a building.

I recognized where I was now. It was my neighbor Dr. Tom John's kitchen. I was perched on the counter looking out the window down the driveway. Will was on his way. A car arrived with two women, who came to the door. A member of the clemency team opened the door. The women had no news about Philip or Will. They had just heard we were there and had come to offer support. I felt like Philip's killing was imminent and no one was telling us. The authorities wanted us out of the way so that they could do it with dispatch and with no concern for another last-minute stay of execution. The pressure was building in my chest, and I awoke from my dream.

The house was still. My heart was racing. After glancing at the clock, I got up and went out to the study. There I wrote the nightmare down on a sheet of paper. After writing all I could recall, I turned out the light and sat in the darkness. The dread of going back to deathwatch with Philip coursed through me. I prayed for God to deliver Philip from this ordeal. Then I sat in the dark. There would be no more sleep this night.

I crawled back into bed at 5:30 A.M. to be near Becca. She put her arms around me. I told her I'd had a bad dream about Philip, and she pulled me to her. I rested my head on her chest, listening to her heartbeat. There was strength in that beating heart. As I lay quietly and listened to her heart, I thought how blessed I was to have this woman as my wife. Through her ovarian cancer, my multiple sclerosis, all the state killings I have endured, the vicissitudes of daily life, Becca has been there for me. Her beating heart seemed to tell me everything would be all right. Somehow, some way, it would be all right.

***

My next visit with Philip occurred a few days later. We discussed the legal situation of his case. He was in good spirits. Then he turned to the matter of his son. He really wanted to hear about him, and I told him I would check back with the private investigator to see if he had found the boy. When I called the investigator later, I learned he had been able to obtain a picture of the boy from the mother. However, she wanted no further contact from us. He would forward the picture to me.

The clemency hearing with the parole board was set for September 11, 2003. In order to imagine the inquisitional nature of the last two clemency hearings for Philip, picture a hearing before a commissar in the Soviet Union. Despite witnesses presented—a recanting eyewitness, one of the foremost forensic experts in the country testifying that the bullet that killed Lieutenant Oliver did not come from Philip's gun—the fix was in from the beginning. Indeed, the tenor of the meeting was such that everyone knew early on that clemency would be denied. It was a political sham, and that is all one could expect from Philip's next hearing. A request to the governor to consider clemency independently of the parole board was denied.

On September 4 I received a postal notice of an attempt to deliver a certified letter. Becca wondered what it could be. Quickly realizing the date and calculating we were three weeks from Philip's execution, I knew what the notice meant. It was the official invitation from the warden and the State of Tennessee, sent by certified letter, telling me I was authorized to witness Philip's execution as his spiritual adviser. I told Becca I would pick it up at the post office the next day.

Judge Bernice Donald, a federal district judge in Memphis, scheduled a hearing for September 15 on Philip's case. She indicated that she would consider whether or not she should grant a stay of execution. There would be no consideration of the merits of the petition. Given her lateness in scheduling the hearing, this could mean a battle in the Sixth Circuit Court of Appeals with a decision coming down after Philip had been moved to deathwatch for the fourth time.

The night of September 10 Philip called me at home. His voice was somber. He told me he was packing his possessions and preparing to wash down his cell for its next occupant as he had done in March 2001. The process of dividing up his property and preparing to leave his "house" was a sad one.

In a telephone conversation I had with Terry Workman we discussed the cruelty of the death warrant process. Terry was on the mark with his description: "It's like forcing Philip to play Russian roulette. We can't appreciate or understand what that does to his mind. This is the fourth time." I agreed with Terry and told him that was precisely why Dr. George Woods had diagnosed Philip with post-traumatic stress disorder.

My next visit with Philip began with a hug. I was exhausted, working long days and devoting time to raise money for his defense, clemency team meetings, public speaking, utilizing all the energy I had to fight an execution and becoming totally drained of strength. He looked at me and asked, "Will you bury me?" For a man expecting to move to deathwatch in a mere nine days, it was a natural question. But it caught me by surprise. All of my actions had been invested in keeping Philip alive. I had neglected the obvious: the state of Tennessee planned to kill him in twelve days. I told him, yes, I would bury him.

111

We moved into a painful discussion of what it was like for him to experience his fourth death warrant. As the visit progressed, I realized Philip was attenuated emotionally. He was in a place very similar to his last hours on deathwatch in 2001. His somber, painful tone reflected the cruelty of the last three deathwatches and the toll exacted upon him yet again. My God, I thought, this whole process was obscene! Even if they failed to kill the prisoner, the torture inflicted upon a human being in carrying out his premeditated murder was simply cruel and unusual punishment.

We finished the visit after almost two and a half hours, closing with a prayer. I had arranged for Philip's brother Terry and his adult daughter, Michelle, to be interviewed Sunday by a local reporter. Philip was looking forward to their visits on Sunday and Monday. I hoped their presence would impart some renewed strength to him. After I finished speaking at the Vanderbilt Divinity School on Friday, two churches on Sunday, and the interview late Sunday afternoon, I would turn to making funeral arrangements on Monday, September 15.

I was on overdrive doing everything humanly possible to keep Philip alive. But I also knew that Psalm 116 was correct. It was God who "rescues from death, my eyes from tears, and my feet from stumbling." Both Philip and I were caught in a powerful tide of death that sucked us into the vortex of the state's killing. "The cords of death entangled me; the grip of the grave took hold of me; I came to grief and sorrow." The challenge was to maintain our faith, as the psalter put it, "Then I called upon the Name of the Lord: 'O Lord, I pray you, save my life.'"

***

At 10:15 A.M. on September 15, I received a telephone call in my office. The voice on the phone was instantly recognizable: "Joe, this is Dave Cooley." I replied to the deputy governor, whom I knew, "Hello, Dave, how are you?" He said he was fine and moved to the business at hand. "The governor wanted me to let you know that at 10:30 he is holding a press conference to announce a 120-day reprieve for Philip Workman pending the outcome of a federal criminal investigation." I was stunned. "Well, Dave, thank you for letting me know, and thank the governor." We exchanged cordial good-byes.

Great God Almighty! Just when you think, as Ecclesiastes 1:9 states, there is "nothing new under the sun," this happens! In thirty years of working against the death penalty, I had never seen or heard of an execution being stopped pending a federal criminal investigation. I immediately called Terry Workman in Kentucky and Michelle, who was still in town. They were also shocked. I told them all I knew and urged them to watch the press conference.

The press conference was televised live. Governor Phil Bredesen and attorney general Paul Summers spoke. The ironies wrinkled the television screen as Summers read the following statement:

> Based upon information that I recently received regarding the pendency of an investigation that indirectly relates to the Philip Workman case, I recommended to the governor that he issue a temporary reprieve of the execution of Mr. Workman's death sentence. At the risk of compromising the investigation, I cannot at this time be specific with regard to the nature and subject of it. I must emphasize this investigation does not involve the facts of the Workman case; nor does it directly affect the validity of his conviction for felony murder in the 1981 death of Memphis Police Lieutenant Ronald

Oliver. Nonetheless, given the nature and subject of this investigation, there is sufficient connection such that, in the interest of fairness and justice, the execution of Mr. Workman's death sentence did not need to proceed as scheduled.

Attorney General Summers had been deeply involved in the two clemency hearings that had tried to kill Philip. In the spring of 2001 he had vetted himself to news media as a possible prime candidate for governor largely on the basis of getting Philip executed. Now he was announcing a reprieve. I knew that Summers must be choking on every word of his statement, and the expression on his face revealed that this was the last thing in the world he wished to be doing in conjunction with the Workman case.

Governor Bredesen then spoke:

> The attorney general recently informed me of a federal criminal investigation under way that may be related to this case. As a result, today I am issuing a postponement of Philip Workman's execution until this investigation is completed and we can assess its relevance to the case.
>
> So long as there are outstanding issues that may be related to this case, the only proper thing to do is wait until those questions have been answered. I am a supporter of the death penalty, but committed that it be carried out in a judicious manner.

In Memphis that same day, federal district court judge Bernice Donald held a hearing on whether or not to grant a stay of execution for Philip Workman. Given the news from the state capital, Judge Donald ruled she would hold matters in abeyance until the results of the criminal investigation were obtained. Then she went a step further: she indicated she would also hold the case pending a decision in the Sixth Circuit Court of Appeals on another Tennessee death penalty case that involved the same issue Philip was raising in his petition. This action, along with Governor Bredesen's reprieve, meant Philip would be in safe harbor legally until the spring of 2004.

Philip's clemency team met on Tuesday night. It was a relaxed group with champagne and lemonade in full supply. We discussed what these events meant and toasted Philip, the lawyers, the governor, and one another. Although we could only speculate, the key piece of the puzzle seemed to be the attorney general's reference to an ongoing "criminal investigation." The only federal criminal investigation we knew that had been ongoing in conjunction with the Workman case was that of O. C. Smith, the Shelby County medical examiner.

Joe Ingle leaves home to visit Philip on death row.

THE NINETEENTH CIRCLE

As mentioned earlier, on June 1, 2002 (Philip's birthday), O. C. Smith had been discovered wrapped in barbed wire outside his office. This is the man who had provided outlandish testimony in two clemency hearings and who stated with 100 percent of his "military mind" that despite the FBI's definitively ruling out the bullet at trial as the fatal bullet because of no trace of cloth, human tissue, or blood on it, the bullet designated Q1 was fired from Philip's gun and had killed Lieutenant Oliver. In addition to the barbed wire, a crude bomb was attached to Smith. Smith blamed Philip's supporters for his plight and also claimed that an acid-like fluid had been thrown on his face. The ATF investigated the incident under the Patriot Act, since a bomb was involved that threatened first responders.

Various Workman supporters, folks against the death penalty, were interviewed by ATF agents. After the initial shock of Philip's reprieve and announcement of the criminal investigation, a consensus emerged among those familiar with Philip's case that Smith must have placed the bomb on himself. He had been flustered by the criticism in the wake of his clemency testimony, especially Robert Hutton's calling him a liar on a Memphis radio talk show. The act of strapping a bomb to himself and wrapping himself with barbed wire, as crazy as it seemed, could be seen as logical when one considered how the event directed a feeling of sympathy toward Smith. For those of us involved in Philip's case, it was just the latest bizarre chapter in the Memphis charade directed at Philip Workman.

It was tempting to believe this was the initial card falling in the house of cards that had been built to send Philip to death row. But this feeling had appeared before. As Chris Minton stated, "When Harold Davis recanted I thought it was the end of the death penalty case. The only eyewitness changes his testimony, so that should be it." We had all experienced those feelings at critical junctures in the case only to be thwarted by another shenanigan from either the political establishment or the courts. We had come to realize that the authorities would go to any lengths to kill Philip no matter what came to light. The only wildcard in the equation at this point was Governor Phil Bredesen.

When I saw Philip on Wednesday night after the press conference given by the governor announcing the reprieve, we had a good long visit. He was decompressing from the tension of coming within nine days of being killed. For the fourth time, he had packed his worldly possessions in boxes and scrubbed his cell. Clearly, he was being tortured by this process just as surely as if he had been placed on the rack. He was frayed, his nerves attenuated, the ordeal of it all had taken its toll.

Soon we were into the Bible, discussing various scriptures. We had a lively discussion about Constantine and his influence on the early Christian church. I promised to mail him a copy of *Constantine's Sword* by James Carroll, the excellent history of anti-Semitism in the Christian church. Two hours sped by and we held hands for a final prayer. I prayed Philip's "hedge of protection" prayer, asking God to put the hedge of protection around Philip. Then I left and ventured out into the dark autumn evening to go home.

On September 24, the day Philip had been scheduled to be executed, I went back to see him. We greeted each other with a hug, and I exclaimed, "Happy September twenty-fourth!" He chuckled and said, "Yeah, let's see. They would have me dead by now and about to be buried." We both smiled. There was much to talk about, but we were both exhausted, so it took us awhile to begin unpacking the emotional toll this most recent ordeal had taken on Philip. He relived the scrubbing of his cell and the packing of his possessions. He then moved into the latest developments of the O. C. Smith case.

Smith had appeared before a grand jury in Memphis. A special prosecutor, from Arkansas, had been appointed to the case. It appeared Smith's wrapping himself in barbed wire and planting a bomb on his chest might prove to be the spur needed to reverse the death penalty gears in Philip's case. Smith had been trained to make explosives in the military and had them on his farm. Given the questions about his behavior, he was asked to take a leave of absence from his job as Shelby County medical examiner. When he refused, the Memphis district attorney vouched for him. This was no surprise, given the official mischief these two had created over the years.

Philip and I shared a sermon I had preached and read the 116th Psalm. We discussed scripture stories of God's being on the side of the widow, the poor, the orphan, and the prisoner. He then came back to the pain of the death penalty process in which he was enmeshed. He was a deeply wounded man. Then we closed with prayer.

The ironies in Philip's case were always striking. The latest, however, that O. C. Smith actually attached an "explosive device" and wrapped himself in barbed wire, was the most fantastic event in a case that had morphed from a case against Philip Workman for a murder he did not commit into an effort by the "criminal justice" establishment trying to execute Philip Workman regardless of the facts. This cast of characters had acted with impunity for so long, it probably seemed quite normal for Smith to wrap himself in barbed wire and plant a bomb on his chest. It never dawned on any of them that the world beyond Memphis might have an idea of justice that didn't involve, as the Red Queen said to Alice, "Convict[ion] first. Facts later."

***

I dreamed of Philip again. We were in a prison, but it was an open area inside the prison, and people were freely walking about, like at the old Tennessee State Prison. A question arose as to whether or not Philip was married. I had performed the service, so I was certain he was married, but one of the guards said he was not married. Another guard said Philip was married but to a different woman. The entire discussion became humorous, and in the dream I realized how pleasant it was to be concerned about relatively normal issues like to whom Philip was married, if at all. Perhaps my subconscious was realizing that Philip was free of packing his possessions before deathwatch and final family visits, and that I was no longer planning for a funeral.

***

As autumn became vibrant with the coloring of leaves in October 2003, Philip called me at home one night. "I'm just waiting for the who, what, when, where, and if to come out of Memphis," he said. It was a succinct description of the feelings experienced by everyone involved in his case. We were awaiting the conclusion of the investigation against O. C. Smith. Grand juries moved deliberately in determining when to issue an indictment, but surely after a fifteen-month investigation a decision would come soon.

On Thursday, November 6, I went out to see Philip. We had a good visit; he caught up on Amelia's soccer team going to the state tournament in Chattanooga, and we discussed his case. Our background music from the worship service next door was "Were You There When They Crucified My Lord." Philip read Hebrews 11:6 ff. and Isaiah 43:11 and 25. I opened my Bible and it revealed Isaiah 61 and I shared it, along with its New Testament appearance in Jesus's inaugural sermon in Nazareth, Luke 4:18. Philip revisited his deathwatch Psalms 27 and 31:1–4, songs of succor provided by God to those under attack. I shared Psalm 146:4–9, a song proclaiming God as one "who executes justice for the oppressed, who gives food to the hungry. The Lord sets the prisoners free; the Lord opens the eyes of the blind. The Lord lifts up those who are bowed down; the Lord loves the righteous. The Lord watches over the sojourners, he upholds the widow and the fatherless; but the way of the wicked he brings to ruin."

These times when Philip and I discussed scripture, what it meant, and how it aided us in navigating our lives, I found very helpful. Indeed, I don't consider it unusual at all that the most moving Bible study I experienced was on death row. It seems appropriate for someone on the path of discipleship whose savior suffered the death penalty himself through crucifixion. I prayed when Philip and I concluded our visit. I remembered that after our last visit Philip had prayed for a "hedge of protection" around our respective families. I reminded God that Isaiah and Jesus had both proclaimed "release to the captives," and I prayed for help in gaining Philip's freedom.

***

Perhaps I have imbued too deeply the Bible's proclamation of liberty to the captives. I dreamed Philip was at the Walls, the old Tennessee State Prison where he arrived in 1982, which is now often utilized as a movie set. He was under deathwatch, and I could smell the dried urine–soaked environment in Unit 6, the old death row. In my dream, he seemed lighthearted. As I moved from one row of cells to the next, I became aware that Philip was no longer in the prison. Indeed, he had escaped and was in a country, either Canada or Sweden, that did not have the death penalty and refused to extradite him back to the United States.

He was happy and safe. I welcomed the investigation as to how he escaped, because I had no idea how the escape had been carried out. He had kept his secret from all his friends and had just done it. I received a white mesh cloth from Philip with instructions and money. I filled the mesh sack with athletic equipment—basketballs, handballs, and so on—for the guys on death row that I purchased according to Philip's instructions and with his money. I then took them out and delivered them to the prisoners. It was Philip's farewell gift to his friends on death row.

***

Visiting Philip in the winter meant arriving and departing in darkness. A killdeer often accompanied me as I made my way through the sliding gates and down the sidewalk to Unit 2, death row. The bird's keening sound in the night seemed to make her my companion. Sometimes I glimpsed her as she flitted over the razor wire that sparkled with the glare from the prison security lights.

My next visit with Philip found him in a buoyant mood. He wanted me to be sure to read the legal briefs his lawyers had filed before Judge Donald in Memphis. He thought they gave the best recounting of the contradictions in the state's position from trial through the two clemency hearings.

As we talked, the hymn singing by the worship group seeped through the wall, "Were You There When They Crucified My Lord." Then the preacher took off with his sermon. Philip smiled and said, "Preach it, brother."

As in every visit, Philip sat and talked with his baseball cap perched upon his head (no baseball caps were allowed on deathwatch, however). The cap was emblazoned in white letters with Job 13:15 printed on the black cap: "Though He slay me yet will I trust in him." The purple band underneath the cross had WWJD (What Would Jesus Do?) running across the band. The cap summed up Philip's theological perspective.

He was in pain from his arthritic right knee. I could only think of how insane this process was in which he was ensnared. He couldn't get decent medical care in the prison. There really was no reason I shouldn't be able to walk him out of the prison with me, get him the medical care he needed, and let him be a productive member of society. He had more than served his time for robbing the Wendy's restaurant in Memphis. I would welcome the opportunity to walk him out from prison, drive him to my home, and let him settle in my guest bedroom. We closed the visit with prayer.

On December 4, I arrived at Riverbend prison to visit Philip. The windy, rainy evening was accompanied by temperatures in the forties and dropping. The killdeer again cried in the night as I walked from checkpoint to Unit 2. I saw her winging beneath the arc lights that kept the compound lit. When I arrived outside Unit 2, all the canna lilies and impatiens were gone. The hard, cold earth was all that remained of their presence last week. Winter had come to middle Tennessee.

The strains of "O, Come All Ye Faithful" and "Silent Night" could be heard from the larger visiting room. The heartfelt Christmas singing underscored the power of God to move people, even in the heart of the killing machinery.

I told Philip that I had recently viewed Dixie Gamble's excellent short film *Beyond Right and Wrong*, which premiered at the Belcourt Theater in Nashville. Dixie had been moved by Robert Coe's story of mental illness and ultimate execution on April 6, 2000. She had a mentally ill son, and it was easy for her to imagine her son confessing to something if he were off his medications, whether or not he actually did it. In just nine minutes of questioning, and without benefit of a defense lawyer, Coe had confessed to the rape and murder of a young girl. He was profoundly mentally ill, and there was no physical evidence to connect him to the murder. Indeed, another suspect in the case had fresh scratch marks on his neck, his tire tracks matched those found at the scene, and he was spot on for the physical description of the assailant of the little girl. However, Robert Coe had grown up poor and isolated in rural western Tennessee. He had a history of mental illness and had been recently released from a Florida mental hospital and returned home. He had exposed himself in public, thus alienating numerous people in the community. Although the movie was not about Coe's guilt or innocence, after seeing the problems of an impoverished, mentally ill man caught in the machinery of state killing, one couldn't help but wonder if the right man had been executed.

Philip recalled that he had been on deathwatch with Coe in early April 2000. At 4:00 A.M. on April 3, he and Coe had been marched over to deathwatch together from Unit 2. The squad escorts "looked like linemen on a professional football team" to Philip. On the way over to Building 8 from Unit 2, Philip and Coe did not talk. Robert was placed in deathwatch cell one, with his personal possessions in cell two, and Philip was placed in cell four with his personal items in cell three. They both obtained stays of execution and were brought back together at 11:00 A.M. on Tuesday. There was no doubt in Philip's mind that Robert Coe was profoundly mentally ill and that he was capable of true compassion.

Philip shared the story of the last time he saw Robert. It was a short time after their return from deathwatch and just prior to Coe's move back to deathwatch for a final time. Robert looked at Philip through the narrow glass window of his cell, clasped his hands together in a gesture of prayer, and nodded at Philip. Robert Glen Coe, on the verge of his own extermination, indicated he was praying for Philip Workman.

As Philip described the scenes of the story with Robert, I thought of how cruel this entire process must be for Philip. Four serious execution dates had been set for him. He had been to deathwatch three times—coming within forty-five minutes of execution on his third trip—prepared to make the final trip four times by packing his gear and scrubbing his cell, and had his neighbor on deathwatch removed from his cell and exterminated by the state of Tennessee. It was a miracle that Philip was able to sit and discuss all of this with me after everything he had experienced. *May God keep him from returning to deathwatch* was my prayer. I didn't know if it was humanly possible for Philip to withstand that process yet again.

A tired Philip Workman wipes his eyes.

THE TWENTIETH CIRCLE

On December 9 Philip and I were discussing the Christmas holidays. He pointed out that December 25 wasn't really the birthday of Jesus but the adaptation of a pagan holiday by the early Christian church. Philip thought that if Jesus came back and saw the Christmas hubbub, he would probably say, "Well, all of this is all right if it helps people out. But the main thing you need to be doing is following my teachings."

My last visit with Philip in 2003 took place on December 30. We discussed how the Sixth Circuit Court of Appeals had considered the appeal of the railroading of his case through two farcical clemency hearings. We shared the feeling that it seemed his criminal case was in suspended animation. The lack of news from Memphis about the grand jury proceedings deliberating about an indictment for O. C. Smith left us out on a limb. Philip thanked me for sending him *Constantine's Sword* and for the picture of his son that the private investigator had obtained. Referring to the book, he exclaimed, "It's a big one!" I nodded and added, "A lot of church history is packed in there." As we held hands, he prayed and concluded with asking for "the hedge of protection for my brother and his family." We parted looking forward to 2004 together.

On January 9, 2004, Governor Bredesen issued the following statement:

> After conferring with the attorney general, I have decided to extend Mr. Workman's reprieve until the federal investigation is completed and its relevance to the case is determined. As a result, I am extending the temporary reprieve until April 15.
>
> I believe the death penalty should be carried out judiciously. As long as there continue to be outstanding questions related to this case, the proper thing to do is wait until those questions have been answered.

As Philip and I visited on a bitterly cold night in mid-January of 2004, he talked about his feeling of "being on a ledge":

> Since my first deathwatch in 2000, I feel like I'm just hanging on a ledge. We keep finding more facts, but I'm still here. To sit here and know they're doing all in their power to cover up for O. C. Smith . . . I mean, think about it. Sergeant Parker, who shot my butt full of shotgun pellets and then denied he did it, is now in the U.S. attorney's office in Memphis. And that other Memphis guy, Kitchens, he is in the U.S. attorney's office too. I'd sure like to know what is going on with that grand jury.

Given all that had transpired in the Workman case, the description of one of my neighbors seemed apt: "It just gets curiouser and curiouser." I ceased speculating about it and decided to just take one day at a time. There are too many events over which we have no control. To dwell on the possibilities would drive one to distraction.

When I arrived at the prison on February 3 to see Philip, the checkpoint officer called back to Unit 2 to inform them I was coming. Sergeant Rushton, whom I have known since the Walls, broadcast back over the intercom, "Send him on down, because we're getting a cell ready for Ingle too." I think that was Rushton's sense of humor, but with Rushton you could never be sure.

Philip was concerned about his daughter, Michelle, now a mother of three who lived in Georgia. She was getting a divorce from her husband, so the up-and-down relationship seemed to be bottoming out. But it was hard to tell from afar, and there was nothing Philip could do except be supportive of Michelle. We shared scripture and had an easygoing visit.

On February 10, 2004, O. C. Smith was indicted by the grand jury in Memphis. There were two counts on the indictment: (1) illegal possession of a destructive device and (2) lying to federal investigators. In response, Smith submitted a resignation letter of sorts. The Shelby County district attorney, Bill Gibbons, who had earlier written Governor Bredesen urging him not to extend Philip's reprieve, issued a statement indicating they would continue to utilize Dr. Smith in their murder cases.

It was clear that the district attorney and his cohorts in the Memphis criminal justice establishment had had things their way for so long in the Workman case that their arrogance enabled them to continue in a manner inimical to their own self-interest. The Shelby County authorities had pushed for Philip's execution since 1981 and subsequently worked with the Attorney General of Tennessee, the Governor's office and the clemency board to ensure his extinction. The fact that they believed O. C. Smith could perjure himself under oath in clemency hearings, wrap himself in barbed wire with a "destructive device" on his chest, as well as lie to federal investigators, yet could also continue as legitimate medical examiner demonstrates how far in cloud cuckoo land the criminal justice establishment in Memphis truly was.

The entire scenario had the quality of what historian Barbara Tuchman described as "wooden-headedness." In her book *The March of Folly: From Troy to Vietnam*, Ms. Tuchman identified examples of people throughout history who acted contrary to their own self-interest by maintaining policies that actually damaged them. Two classic examples of "wooden-headedness" were King George III of England versus the colonies and the Renaissance popes.

This was the quality that exuded from the actions of Shelby County officials for twenty-three years in Philip's case. They were so blinded by their increasingly manic desire to execute Philip that they appeared willing to do anything: manufacture witnesses, perjure themselves, withhold exculpatory evidence, collude with the attorney general—the list seems endless. All of this because they insisted on holding to the figment of an idea they had created: that Philip Workman killed a police officer after robbing a Wendy's restaurant. Ever since the return of the photos of the wounds of Lieutenant Oliver's body hours after the crime, they had known Philip did not kill the policeman but that it was a case of friendly fire. Nonetheless, the wooden-headedness began, and it was still going more than twenty years later. I had not seen this level of deceit and corruption of justice in more than thirty years of working against the death penalty in the South.

In response to O. C. Smith's indictment, Governor Bredesen appointed Dr. Bruce Levy to investigate Smith's clemency testimony. Levy, the Tennessee state medical examiner, had been appointed by Governor Bredesen to his current job, and when Bredesen was mayor of Nashville, he had appointed Levy as the medical examiner for metro Nashville. Levy was to report back to the governor by the time of the expiration of the reprieve, April 15, 2004. This move was either political cunning to place a fig leaf over Smith's bald-face lying or an answer to a prayer.

All that those working for Philip had sought through the courts, the public, and the governor was for someone to examine Smith's sworn testimony at the two clemency hearings. An objective review would find that the doctor had perjured himself. There were statements from two reputable medical examiners—Dr. Kris Sperry and Dr. Cyril Wecht—along with the FBI trial testimony that eliminated the bullet Smith had identified as the fatal bullet, Q1, as creating the mortal wound. Also, the leading expert in the field of gunshots and author of the definitive textbook, Dr. Werner Spitz, declared that the test Smith had carried out by shooting into a pig's feet was bogus and that the tests could not possibly reveal what Smith's results purportedly demonstrated.

As mentioned, the district attorney of Shelby County, William Gibbons, issued a statement of support for O. C. Smith and indicated he would continue to utilize his services. Indeed, the day after the indictment had been rendered, Smith was testifying in a case. When informed of the indictment, Dr. Cyril Wecht, president of the American Board of Legal Medicine, succinctly appraised for the *New York Times* his thoughts on the doings in Memphis: "If he could fabricate a story like this that a Hollywood screenwriter on LSD would have difficulty coming up with, who could believe him in a courtroom?" Evidently, Wecht was not familiar with the manner in which justice was administered in Memphis.

James Cavanaugh, an agent with ATF who was in charge of the case against Smith stated: "When a prominent figure in law enforcement such as the medical examiner is charged with a crime, it strikes at the heart of the criminal justice system. But our responsibilities here are clear, to follow the facts and to enforce the law without fear or favor." This was a foreign notion to those who had pursued the killing of Philip Workman for more than two decades.

As the press stories continued to filter out of Memphis, it became clear why the district attorney's office remained wed to having O.C. Smith testify in cases. An objective review would find that the doctor had provided testimony that strained credulity. All the Memphis actors in this drama wanted Smith to feel supported in the face of the indictment. (Ultimately, Smith would be saved by a hung jury). If Smith felt abandoned by his cohorts in the effort to get Workman executed, he might discuss the role he and others had played in putting together the charade directed at Workman. The sham clemency hearings would be revealed, and another investigation would be under way of officials engaged in manufacturing a witness and arranging witness testimony. If the price of avoiding exposure and prosecution was allowing Smith to continue to testify, it was a small sacrifice made for this masquerade of justice.

***

When I visited Philip in mid-February, he was agitated. Although the sermon from the room next door percolated through the wall, he did not comment upon it as he usually did. I was focused totally on Philip. He was feeling pain in the left side of his chest. He thought it was stress, but he was obviously concerned. Focusing on the tissue samples O. C. Smith had testified about during clemency, Philip was convinced Smith might have altered the samples to place aluminum in them in an attempt to convince Dr. Levy that they were the remains from Philip's aluminum-jacketed bullets. Philip believed that if the altered tissue had fooled Levy, Governor Bredesen would ignore everything else and execute him.

As I listened to Philip, I realized that in this case anything was possible. After two clemency hearings with Smith making preposterous statements under oath, complete with misleading medical tests and demonstrations, why couldn't there be another attempt to stage things to ensure Philip's execution? The logic of the killing machinery dictated they weren't about to stop at this point, indictment be damned.

The most alarming element in Philip's demeanor was the tone of his conversation. It was almost as if he felt doomed. He was saying that no matter the justice or truth of the situation, he was going to be killed. That is what really concerned me. An almost fatalistic feeling came through in the weariness of his soul. He was convinced his lawyers were not taking the Shelby County situation seriously enough. He felt they were almost assuming they were going to win since O. C. Smith had been indicted. But Philip wanted another forensics expert to analyze the tissue from Lieutenant Oliver's wound to rebut Smith. Despite affidavits from the two people who performed the tests contradicting Smith, Philip felt he still needed another expert.

As the visit progressed, I realized I just needed to be there for Philip. It was not a question of a rational discussion; he was emotionally strung out and in physical discomfort. Four death warrants, three trips to the death house, twenty-three years in prison for a murder he did not commit—no wonder his nerves were frayed.

I listened, we talked and finally closed with a prayer. I prayed for God to console, comfort, and strengthen Philip. I prayed for guidance for all of us—lawyers, family, friends, and Philip—to lead us on a path of justice and righteousness. Finally, I prayed we would see the day when Philip finally walked out of prison an exonerated man.

On the night of Monday, February 23, Philip telephoned. We discussed what we could over the phone, given the reality of the prison personnel taping his phone calls. As he talked, I could hear the anxiety in his voice. He wanted to be sure I was coming out to visit, and I told him I would be there Thursday evening. His worry was palpable through the telephone lines. He was convinced that the Shelby County diehards would manipulate the samples given to Dr. Levy and that Levy would in turn determine that it was Philip's bullet that killed Lieutenant Oliver. Given what had happened thus far in this case, courtesy of Shelby County authorities, further chicanery could not be ruled out.

I had a restless night after talking to Philip. I lay in bed thinking of him. More than anything, I could feel his dread and fear. No matter how much I sought to shake it, I could not. Finally, I just lay back staring up in the darkness. At every turn Shelby County police and prosecutors, along with the attorney general's office, had done all in their power to kill Philip, and it had exacted a terrible emotional toll on him. Dr. George Woods had diagnosed him with PTSD some months ago, and his condition had worsened. I was beginning to worry that even if we won, Philip would be so damaged by the ordeal that he would have a hard time returning to what we call "normal." For the first time I feared that we might win but at a cost so high as to render the win meaningless. *God have mercy on us all.*

When I next saw Philip he was in a different state of mind. He was deeply concerned that his lawyers were willing to accept any clemency offer the governor may provide. He felt strongly that he should not have to do any time for shooting Lieutenant Oliver, since he *didn't* shoot him. He looked directly at me and said: "The lawyers don't understand. They don't know what it's like in here. They think life without parole is a victory. I'd rather die than do that. I've done twenty-three years. I'm tired. I can't go on like this indefinitely. My body is letting me know it's breaking down. I can feel some things aren't right. I did some dumb things to myself when I was young that are costing me. I won't take a life sentence. I have to see some light. They've had me on the ledge for too long. I have to see some light."

After listening to Philip for a good while, I said to him: "You are in a totally different frame of mind. When we last talked, you were worried about being killed. Now you're talking about what kind of clemency you might get. What accounts for the change?" He indicated that it was the lawyers' visit he'd received the day after our last visit. They obviously were hopeful about clemency and seemed to have some inside information about it. I was relieved to hear the change in his tone of voice. Maybe we had finally reached the turn in the road in this case, but, frankly, I would believe it only when I saw it.

***

My next visit with Philip was on a glorious 70-degree day in March. We fell into a discussion about religion. We both agreed that if Jesus came back today, society would put him on death row. The gospel of Jesus of Nazareth was a scandal at the time, and it is no less a scandal today. Human beings are no better or worse than Jesus's contemporaries and would react accordingly. Now, that would be worth a movie (unlike Mel Gibson's *Passion of the Christ*), but I don't expect to see it.

We dwell in a society that was aptly described by Pope John Paul II as "the culture of death." Our death rows are merely the tip of the proverbial cultural iceberg. When Mother Teresa visited death row at San Quentin, she reminded the guards that the prisoners were "children of God." Indeed, you can see Jesus in each one. Yet there are more than three thousand people confined for extermination in the country. All of this and more Philip and I discussed in our visits.

On March 25 I went out to see Philip again. The men in the worship service were singing "How Great Thou Art" followed by "Traveling Home." Their enthusiasm provided a pleasant backdrop to our conversation. We talked about how there was interest in Philip's case from national media, and we reviewed what the possibilities were for his speaking with them at this point. This was the latest in what had been a long and winding road with Philip and the national media, so we would just have to wait and see what transpired.

Philip was deeply concerned about Greg Thompson, who had an August 27 execution date. Greg was profoundly delusional. Among his delusions were that he had won a Grammy award, which he had buried in his backyard. Philip had some ideas for Greg's lawyers, and I agreed to convey them to the legal team. Philip prayed his "hedge of protection" prayer in closing. As I walked out of the unit and back toward the administration building, the killdeer, my companion on these visits during the winter, was nowhere to be found. I guessed she must have spring fever.

When Governor Bredesen had assigned Dr. Bruce Levy to evaluate O. C. Smith's clemency testimony, I was conflicted. I hoped for the best, but I feared the worst. My fear was rooted in political reality. Levy owed his appointment to mayor and then governor Bredesen. If the governor wanted the report to angle a certain direction, I felt sure Levy would accommodate him. The report would reveal as much about Governor Bredesen as it would Dr. Levy.

When Levy's report was released in April, I immediately thought of the line from T. S. Eliot: "April is the cruelest month." The report concluded that it was Philip's bullet that had struck down Lieutenant Oliver.

When I went out to visit Philip at the prison, we sat down together and reviewed the Levy report. Its utter reliance on the prosecution's record at trial was breathtaking. Levy had swallowed the prosecution's theory of there being only two shooters: Philip and Oliver. In a television interview about his report, Levy termed all the evidence debunking the two shooter theory as the "grassy knoll theory" of the crime. This disparaging reference sounded like a statement made by the prosecutors rather than by an objective forensic scientist. Among the points Levy ignored were the following:

1. The treating physician's report at the hospital documenting Philip's injuries after the crime, which included dog bites and gunshot wounds on his buttocks.

2. The police records that indicated the police weapons at the crime scene were not properly checked for firing, despite sworn testimony to the contrary.

3. The FBI testimony at trial that Q1—the bullet O. C. Smith swore with 100 percent certainty of his "military mind" was the fatal bullet—could not have been the mortal bullet, because it bore no trace of blood, bone, tissue, or fabric.

4. Finally, the fact that O. C. Smith, who had lied through two clemency hearings—Levy did admit Smith's tests were "demonstrative" rather than conclusive—was now under indictment for lying to federal investigators and placing a bomb on his chest that endangered first responders.

Dr. Levy actually had the gall to write the following: "I believe that the high regard and respect that he has for Dr. Bell [Smith's predecessor] motivated him the breath [*sic*] and depth of his re-investigation." How about the likelihood that O. C. Smith was in cahoots with the prosecutors and police to manufacture some kind of "evidence" to confirm their illicit shenanigans in framing Workman because the public exposure of their case would cost them all credibility? The latter was a much more probable scenario than any wishful dreaming about Smith's motivation. The entire report rested on no scientific proof, literally no consideration or analysis of the forensics evidence. Rather, it was a rehash of the trial prosecutor's efforts.

The real problem was that Levy's report revealed Governor Bredesen's position on the question of clemency, as the report would not have been issued without the governor's blessing. It chilled me to the bone despite the lovely spring.

In May 2004 Philip and I continued our Thursday evening routine. We read some psalms together, especially the 38th Psalm. He reminded me how much that psalm meant to him on deathwatch. We also focused on the First Letter of John. It is one of my favorite epistles, and we discussed the meaning of love the writer shared.

Philip had been approached about having his story told on *48 Hours*, the hour-long documentary series on CBS. Although the show's producers seemed mostly interested in the antics of O. C. Smith, Philip hoped the coverage might generate some renewed focus on his own case. There appeared to be little to lose at this point.

On April 29 Philip and I had a relaxed and enjoyable visit. We swapped stories, read the Bible, and shared a few laughs. I reminded him of the warning in the 38th Psalm: "Put not your trust in princes."

It was an apt admonition from the psalmist in light of the Levy report, a report that featured politics, not science or evidence, as its theme. Philip was in good spirits and we closed with prayer. As I drove away from the prison in my pickup truck, I wished I had invoked the "hedge of protection" in my final prayer. Increasingly, it seemed the need for that hedge of protection grew.

THE TWENTY-FIRST CIRCLE

The Tennessee Supreme Court set an execution date for Philip Workman of September 22, 2004. It was his fifth execution date and likely meant yet another trip to deathwatch. *Sweet Jesus, have mercy on us all.*

When I went out to see Philip after the setting of the execution date, he almost charged into the room. We hugged and he was fired up about something. His thoughts were on the treatment of the Iraqi prisoners by the United States military personnel in Abu Graib prison: "When they put a bag over your head, they don't have to look at you. It makes it easier for them to do whatever they want. That picture of the woman soldier dragging that Iraqi like a dog with a chain just makes me sick. If we let George Bush and this group get away with all they are doing, this country is in real trouble."

I concurred with Philip's perspective and opined: "The Bush administration doesn't want you to look at the facts. No matter what the issue, they do all they can to disguise the facts and focus your gaze on patriotism. They want you to believe what they believe. It's a group of true believers who try to make reality cohere to their dogma."

After a thorough discussion of the goings-on in Iraq, Philip looked at me and said, "I can't believe they set another date. But I called it." Indeed, after the attorney general had filed requesting an execution date from the Tennessee Supreme Court, Philip had predicted September as the likely month. The setting of the date for September 22 revealed once again that he had an uncanny ability to forecast the next move in the case.

As we sifted through the chronology of his case, the four prior execution dates and his multiple trips to deathwatch, all we could do was shake our heads. Each instance where had he won a stay of execution was ultimately circumvented. The first stay had resulted from the location of Harold Davis, the state's "sole" eyewitness to the shooting, who turned out not to have been there at all. The second stay stemmed from the x-ray of Lieutenant Oliver's bullet wound, which the medical examiner's office in Memphis had "misplaced" for twenty years until its presence was accidentally made known in preparation for the clemency hearing. The Sixth Circuit Court of Appeals ordered a stay of execution upon discovery of the x-ray, and Philip later lost on a 7–7 vote by the en banc court. This despite the x-ray revealing what the defense maintained: that the bullet was a "through and through" wound, not fragmented as the state and some judges on the panel argued. Then came the last-minute stay of execution, Philip's third stay, from the Tennessee Supreme Court mandating the evidentiary hearing in Memphis to determine if post-trial evidence "may" have affected the jury's decision. The Colton kangaroo court disposed of that possibility in early 2002.

Then the fourth stay came after the bizarre case of O. C. Smith, the Shelby County medical examiner who wrapped himself in barbed wire, arms extended in the shape of a cruciform, and attached a bomb to his chest. This action was a means of diverting attention from his absurd testimony at clemency and his misleading tests in the name of science. His indictment resulted in two reprieves from Governor Bredesen. And now there was the hatchet job of the Levy report. Sometimes one had to shake one's head and repeat, "You couldn't make this stuff up. No one would believe it."

Philip felt frustrated. And I felt like I had fallen down the rabbit hole in *Alice in Wonderland.* Everything was upside down. The officials whose duty was to obtain justice—police, prosecutors, attorneys general, judges, governors—had subverted justice for twenty-three years in this case. They had created and clung to the initial cover-up by local Memphis police and prosecutors because it was a policeman who had been shot. Instead of admitting that a mistake had been made by "friendly fire," a strung-out robber was chosen to take the fall since he was considered a worthless scumbag anyway. Then came the lies, deceit, perjury, falsified reports, evidence withheld, manufactured witness—anything and everything to get people to believe what the city of Memphis and the state of Tennessee maintained about the Workman case. It was the George W. Bush school of thought: ignore the facts and believe what we tell you to believe, because we're the good guys. In this case, the police are the thin blue line, and they can do no wrong and we must support them. The facts are an inconvenience, so we will proceed with our murderous ways. Torture in an Iraqi prison and extermination in a Tennessee prison. It matters not whether it is Republican or Democrat. It's all about politics and not the truth. And so it goes.

***

The latest filing in the case had been Dr. George Woods's report on his examination of Philip as he was facing his fourth deathwatch experience in September 2003. It revealed the emotional trauma of the pressure of the killing machinery (see "The Seventeenth Circle").

Now Philip was under his fifth death warrant. Each day that passed drew him closer to deathwatch. He had been up and down emotionally since the setting of this execution date. I didn't know how he would survive emotionally from the repeated stress of this situation, even if he survived physically. It was a slow and steady torture for him to see his days wind down to a fixed killing date and his nights haunted by execution nightmares. The situation had been compounded this time by the fact that Philip was anticipating clemency as a result of the O. C. Smith imbroglio in Memphis. However, this prospect had been snatched away by the governor through the Levy report.

For the president of the United States to spout Boy Scout platitudes about human rights in light of what was happening to Philip Workman and more than three thousand people on death row in this country was enough to make one retch. America's barbaric system with its killing machinery is as disgusting as any in the world. The bottom line is that once a person is demonized, whether at Riverbend prison or Abu Graib in Iraq, anything imaginable can be perpetrated upon them. They are, as the Nazis put it, the *untermensch*. Legal systems and treaties become fictive devices to maneuver around in order to torture and destroy human beings. It is a fact of life in the United States as surely as it is in Iraq, and Philip's case was a prime example. To pretend otherwise and believe we are somehow better is hypocritical and ensures the scorn of those who are truly concerned for justice and human rights. Jesus of Nazareth put it best: "What you have done to the least of these, my brothers and sisters, you have done unto me."

For the first time while under his fifth death warrant, Philip brought up the difficulty he was experiencing in trying to cope with this latest execution date. Although he anticipated it, he described his feelings as "being in a storm. The sea is overwhelming you. You are sinking and there is nothing you can do." He felt Dr. Woods had misestimated when difficulties start emotionally. "It's not when you get to deathwatch. It starts right after you get the execution date. The guys don't know how to relate to you. You don't want to be glum, you want to carry on and try to be normal, but the emotions are stirred inside you. You try to maintain a normal way of doing things, but it's hard. Of course, it's worse with each execution date you get."

"How do you deal with it?" I asked.

"Prayer," he said. "Yeah, prayer and watching too much television. Working out, trying to keep my mind blank about it."

"Does it affect your dreams?" I asked.

Philip replied, "No, not yet. I just don't sleep much. The most I can get is six hours. My mind is always racing."

As Philip and I conversed about the mental anguish the killing machinery exerted on those trapped in its maw, the canna lilies were in full, glorious red bloom outside the door leading into death row. The roses had opened as well, next to the lilies. The multicolored impatiens radiated their beauty beneath the larger flowers. Inside the unit we were breathing stale, recycled air. And while the beauty of creation unfurled beyond the door to Unit 2, I sat and listened to a man describe his attempt to maintain his sanity in the wake of his fifth death warrant.

It's hard for my visitors. Sometimes they don't know what to say. The execution date just brings pressure into everything. I can't write letters. [He showed me some he had received.] Here is one from a guy who wants to write a book about my case. I appreciate it but I can't deal with it now. I can't concentrate on everything that has gone on to get this far. It's just too much. I can't even write him to tell him that. I haven't even responded to my young French friend. She has sent me three letters and I want to help her, give her some advice about how to get along with her mother. But I just can't bring myself to do it. [This was a sign of deep unease on Philip's part. He had faithfully corresponded with this sixteen-year-old French girl who came across the story of his case. They had been exchanging letters for over a year. He was filling the void of the absent father in her life. For him to receive three letters without responding demonstrated a mental enervation that was alarming.]

Clemency. I don't think I can go through that again with the parole board. [I shuddered as I recalled how demeaning they had been to him and his witnesses in what was a rigged proceeding.] Then I think maybe I just need to represent myself before them. I know the case better than anyone. Of course, they say it is a fool of a lawyer that represents himself. But I could just lay it all out to them. I don't know. I just don't know what to do.

Philip looked at me and asked, "What do you think is going to happen?"

I replied, "I don't know, Philip. But I think there is a good chance the U.S. Supreme Court will take the 60(b) issue which is also in Abu's case.[Abu-Ali, a fellow death row prisoner also on appeal, was litigating claims dismissed for supposed procedural default but which the U.S. Supreme Court had expressed a desire to review in a Florida case.] So everything should halt if the Supreme Court decides to consider the matter. The 11th Circuit Court of Appeals ruled one way on it, and the Second Circuit went the other way. Whatever the Sixth Circuit does will be a closely divided decision. When there is a split in the circuit courts of appeal, it can lead to the Supremes taking the case. And there is the fact they took it once before, so there are members of the Court interested in the issue."

All of which may be true, I thought as I spoke the words, but if my brother before me was a mental wreck by the time we obtained a stay of execution, it would definitely be a mixed blessing. The lawyers were waiting for a ruling in Abu's case so that they could seek a stay of execution for Philip being sure to frame their request in light of the Sixth Circuit's decision. So we would wait and try to maintain until a stay of execution was forthcoming.

When I entered death row for my next visit with Philip, the guys in the religious service in the visiting room were in a circle singing their hearts out. It was a rocking gospel song about Jesus rising on the third day, the Holy Spirit coming down, and hope from God. I swayed back and forth listening to them after I waved to them upon entering the foyer of Unit 2. There were quite a few verses, and I just kept moving to the beat, caught up in the hope that these men—both black and white, holding hands in a circle—lustily sang. When they finished, I stuck my head through the door and thanked them. One of them quickly offered, "You can join next time." I smiled and responded, "I wouldn't want to ruin a good thing." Then Philip came out from the back of the unit and we walked to the small visiting room.

Philip and I embraced. We discussed the illness of a mutual friend. I updated him on the progress in sending Ellen, the French teenager, a visitation form so that she could visit Philip. Philip saw himself as her surrogate father: "I feel I can say some things to her that will help her. She's having problems with her mom, but she listens to me. She is a bright Hebrew girl with a good future if she doesn't mess up."

The *48 Hours* producer had been to see him. Philip told me he had shared several documents with the producer that accentuated what a crazy scenario had unfolded around him. "I was talking to him, Joe. And I heard myself explaining my case to him. You know, if I was on the street and someone explained it to me, I would think they were crazy! Police corruption, prosecutorial misconduct, conspiracy with the attorney general—it strains the mind! But he seemed interested, and we'll see. Some of my lawyers want me to stay clear of him, and one wants me to work with him. I think we have to take a shot with him and give him our documentation." Philip requested I forward several documents to the producer. After a leisurely working visit, we closed with prayer. Philip once again prayed for "a hedge of protection around my brother and his family."

***

As we rolled into the hottest part of the summer, my multiple sclerosis flared up and I had to take to bed. Philip called me one Saturday afternoon to check on me after hearing about the flare-up. He talked about how well his visit with Ellen had gone. He had tried to give her money to help defray the cost of the trip from France, but she refused it. He chuckled as he described the visit, and I could tell it meant a lot to him.

The looming September 22 execution date for Philip did not seem to have him depressed during our late July visit. He was frustrated with his lawyers but quite determined about his course of action. He wanted to file a legal brief documenting the political nature of the case, to address the following:

> 1. Federal district court judge Julia Gibbons, a Republican appointee, denying his request for a hearing on his habeas corpus shortly before swearing her husband in as district attorney general of Shelby County. This action, dubious on its face, was taken despite Philip's case meeting the standard of having a "colorable claim" of innocence that entitled him to a hearing.

2. The three-judge panel in the Sixth Circuit Court of Appeals, all Republicans, going off the record and then misinterpreting Colonel Fackler's published work about the fragmentation rate of a hollow-point bullet from a handgun and a rifle. Then the same group reissuing the opinion months later when the error was pointed out. In the reissued opinion, the judges marked through their description of Colonel Fackler's study, but in doing so the decision no longer cohered to logic.

3. The entire Sixth Circuit Court of Appeals voting 7–7 on Philip's case, split along party lines. The split meant it reverted back to the illogical panel decision, which was 3–0 against Philip. Three Republicans voted against him.

4. The role of the attorney general of Tennessee in influencing the clemency board to deny Philip, and the orchestration of witnesses in the clemency hearing along with the district attorney of Shelby County(Bill Gibbons) and his cohorts. At the same time, the attorney general, Paul Summers, was vetting himself to various media people as a potential gubernatorial candidate with a prime reason for his candidacy his death penalty actions against Coe and Philip.

5. O. C. Smith's over-the-top testimony in two clemency hearings and strapping a bomb to his chest to illicit sympathy.

6. Dr. Bruce Levy's report, which read like the prosecutors' record at trial without regard to compelling forensic evidence that Philip did not shoot Lieutenant Oliver. It was a report of belief statements rather than a review of the evidence.

7. The fraud upon the state and federal courts through the introduction of an "eyewitness," the sole eyewitness, who was not, in fact, at the crime scene.

8. Police lying under oath, at trial and in the clemency hearings, about what happened at the crime scene.

9. The withheld x-ray that exculpated Philip by showing it was a "through and through" bullet whereas the state, and some judges, argued it was a fragmented bullet.

10. The symphony of oppression performed by the district attorney's office of Shelby County and the attorney general's office.

One might title the foregoing list, borrowing from the musical *The Sound of Music*, "These Are a Few of My Favorite Things," about the Workman case. Of course, no court would acknowledge the merit of any of these transgressions, due to procedural rules and embarrassment, but that was beside the point. If he was going to be killed, Philip wanted a complete record of the many legal malfeasances that had been perpetrated upon him. If he was going down, he did not want to go quietly into the night. He wanted the miscarriage of justice that was his case shouted to the heavens. As we parted, I was heartened that he was in a fighting mood.

My next weekly visit was shocking because it was the polar opposite of our previous encounter. The weariness in Philip's voice, the lines around his eyes, his fatigue with the fight—it was clear that this fifth death warrant was exacting an enormous toll on his emotions after all. I was filled with deep sadness. We talked for a good hour and a half. Basically, Philip wanted to be left alone. He just wanted to lie in his bunk to pray and to think. He would call me over the weekend if he wanted me to come back. He didn't want me to call his lawyer. He would talk with him personally. We closed with prayer, hugged, and I walked out of the unit into the summer twilight.

Philip called me on the night of the blue moon, July 30. He sounded somewhat better and wanted me to come back to see him the following Thursday. He didn't know if he could tell his lawyer the depth of his despair. I encouraged Philip to talk to Chris Minton. He had done heroic work on this case for fifteen years and was absolutely dedicated to Philip. I told Philip I was sure he could handle whatever he wished to share.

The first Thursday in August 2004 found me back at Riverbend visiting Philip, some six weeks from his execution date. He was composed, even laughing on occasion, and it just goes to show what a difference a week could make. We had an in-depth discussion of the scriptures. We discussed faith and how the church has often been controlling, conniving, and generally power-mad once it assumed the mantle of the official state religion from Constantine in 325 (Council of Nicea). In spite of the church, the Christian faith survived in genuine manifestations. I encountered it through people on death row like Philip Workman. Grace abounded for those whom Jesus called "the least of these my brothers and sisters." For the rest of us, encumbered in the way of the world, the life of faith was a bit of a scrap. We closed with prayer, and I left feeling much better about Philip's state of mind.

When I saw Philip in mid-August his spirits were good. He had been interviewed the previous day by the people of *48 Hours*. They were most fascinated by O. C. Smith's strange actions and his subsequent trial. When I asked him how it went, he shrugged. He had done so many interviews over the years, he didn't get too excited even if it was for a national audience. He told me he had spoken strongly against Smith as well as against the Memphis police and prosecutors.

Philip laughed as he discussed what he would do once he obtained a trial before his peers. "Here I am about a month from being executed and I'm worried about a new trial." His high spirits reflected his belief that right would triumph over might. Frankly, I was glad to see him feeling so good. I thought the TV interview was responsible for his mood even though he had downplayed it. We closed with a prayer, once again asking for a "hedge of protection," and I left in the summer evening light. The canna lilies were still blooming a brilliant red outside Unit 2 despite the heat. I had thought they would have bloomed out by now. The day was full of surprises.

Our next visit found Philip full of legal news. Chris Minton was filing a stay-of-execution request before Judge Donald in Memphis. If nothing happened by September 19, the lawyers would file directly to the governor requesting a reprieve pending the outcome of the O. C. Smith case, which should come to trial before Judge Donald before the end of the year. I thanked God that Philip had such an excellent legal team.

Out of the blue, Philip blurted out, "Could we raise some money to fly Ellen in?"

I'm sure I looked perplexed at the sudden change of subject. "Ellen?" I inquired.

"Ellen, you know, my French Hebrew friend. She wants to be here for the funeral."

Regaining my mental equilibrium, I countered, "Philip, there are a lot of things to discuss before we get to flying Ellen in."

He responded, "I know. Where I'm going to be buried. It doesn't really matter—just put me in a ditch." And he smiled.

We chuckled. I told him I had been reading the psalms, and he wanted me to read one to him. I opened my Bible to Psalm 64. "Philip, this psalm has your name written all over it." And I read him the 64th Psalm:

Hear my voice, O God, in my complaint; preserve my life from dread of the enemy, hide me from the secret plots of the wicked, from the scheming of evildoers, who whet their tongues like swords, who aim bitter words like arrows, shooting them from ambush at the blameless, shooting at him suddenly and without fear. They hold fast to their evil purpose; they talk of laying snares secretly, thinking, "Who can see us? Who can search out our crimes? We have thought out a cunningly conceived plot." For the inward mind and heart of a man are deep!

The parallels between Philip's case and the 64th Psalm made it seem like the psalmist had written it with Philip in mind some three thousand years ago. The Shelby County police, prosecutors, and judges had hatched "secret plots of the wicked" to frame Philip at trial. "The scheming evildoers" would include the attorney general of Tennessee and his staff, the clemency board, and O. C. Smith, as well as former governor Don Sundquist and his advisers. They all "whet their tongues like swords and aim[ed] bitter words like arrows."

Even with the change in gubernatorial administrations, Dr. Bruce Levy's whitewash of a report could indicate that the new administration was pursuing the same path. Given the record of e-mails from the attorney general's office working with the clemency board to execute Philip and communications from government officials to the attorney general, the psalmist was prescient: "They hold fast to their evil purpose; They talk of laying snares secretly. Thinking, 'Who can see us? Who can search out our crimes?' We have thought out a cunningly conceived plot." All of the actions the psalmist describes were taken then, as now, by people acting in their official capacities. Whether King Saul was pursuing David or attorney general Paul Summers was plotting against Philip Workman, their homicidal purpose was clear.

Philip and I closed with a prayer. "May the God of David, credited with writing the 64th Psalm, deliver Philip Workman from his enemies. Or as the psalmist put it: 'Hear my voice, O God, in my complaint; preserve my life from the dread of the enemy, hide me from the secret plots of the wicked.'"

***

In mid-September federal district judge Bernice Donald granted Philip a stay of execution so that she could consider the 60(b) petition. This effectively halted the gears of the killing machinery that were grinding under Philip's fifth death warrant. But I remained worried. Although she was a federal judge, she was still a Memphis judge. And all levels of the judiciary and law enforcement in Memphis had proven unrelenting in their hostility toward Philip since 1981.

On the evening of October 18 I received a telephone call from Philip. I had been outside enjoying the cool October air and observing the changing colors of the leaves. When I reached the phone and answered, the tone of Philip's words informed me that something was terribly wrong. In a subdued monotone, Philip informed me that Judge Donald had denied his 60(b) petition. "Joe, I'm tired of all this," he said. "These people are never going to give me a new trial." The cumulative effect of five death warrants and twenty-five years on death row emanated through the telephone lines. We both knew this decision could bring a sixth death warrant in the spring. He was also worried about his good friend Don Johnson, who was set for execution in four days. We talked for some time, and I told him I would be back to see him the next day.

Upon reading Judge Donald's opinion, I was reminded of the basic reality of the death penalty in Memphis. The parties involved in the killing machinery—prosecutors, defense lawyers, judges, police—were too close to one another. Apparently Judge Donald could not bring herself to acknowledge the malfeasance of the actors in the system in which she, even as a federal judge, also participated. So she constructed an opinion that denied relief to Philip on procedural grounds without going to the merits of the case.

The decision was exemplary of the state of the death penalty law in the United States today. No one wishes to face the deceit, the racism, the corruption that permeates the killing machinery. Judges continually side with the state on pernicious grounds because of their failure to come to grips with the unconstitutionality of the death penalty.

U.S. Supreme Court Justice Lewis Powell, who later regretted casting the deciding vote against my friend Warren McCleskey in *McCleskey v. Kemp* in April 1987, wondered if he was expected to find the death penalty unconstitutional in the face of the documented racism in the application of the death penalty in Georgia. *Yes, Justice Powell, we citizens do expect justices to rule according to the uncontroverted data that has determined that the death penalty is racially discriminatory, especially by race of victim. How else can we redress the grievous wrongs of the segment of the society untouched by the civil rights movement?* But all we received were Justice Powell's regrets while in retirement. It was a bit too late for Warren McCleskey, who was as fine a person as I have ever met anywhere, and for all the others killed by the state of Tennessee and elsewhere as result of Justice Powell's fateful vote in the 5–4 decision. Hence we have been left with judges like Judge Donald who refuse to acknowledge and rebuke a system so corrupt that its actors can lie, commit perjury, manufacture witnesses, and cover up the accidental slaying of one policeman by another by blaming the killing on a restaurant robber.

When I visited Philip in the autumn darkness of October 19, 2004, he was in a good mood. Don Johnson had received a stay of execution, and Philip was happy for his friend. In referring to Don, he said, "He's more refined than I am. I did a lot of dumb stuff, although I didn't kill anybody. I think the Lord has put me through what I've gone through as a way of purging me for my foolishness. My soul needed a lot more work than Don's. Don is more refined." Philip was acknowledging the misdeeds of his youth, and in comparing himself to his good friend, he believed Don was purer in a spiritual sense.

In the many years I had visited Philip, he had always been an honest evaluator of himself. He inventoried his spiritual state and was all too aware of his shortcomings. I found this to be a rare quality, not just among death row prisoners but among most people. It was an honor to be his spiritual adviser.

We closed with a prayer and I again utilized Philip's "hedge of protection" prayer for our families and those in danger. We gave each other a parting hug and I was out the door of Unit 2 into the chilly autumn night.

***

When I visited Philip on November 9, 2006, it was in the wake of the midterm elections. The Democrats had swept into control of both houses of Congress, breaking six years of Republican dominance. Philip was very pleased that the "Pharisees" (his term for Republicans) went down. He lamented the racist advertisements in the U.S. Senate campaign in Tennessee. He thought Bob Corker, whom he had met several years ago when I brought him out to death row, had run some racist ads against his African American opponent, Harold Ford. I agreed the ads were appealing to the worst in people and added there was probably a 5–7 percent racist vote in Tennessee that turned the election against Ford. We concluded our leisurely discussion of politics with a prayer and I headed home.

From then until the end of 2006, litigation proceeded on the 60(b) issue in several cases throughout the country and was ultimately resolved by the U.S. Supreme Court. During the same period, lethal injection issues were litigated in California, North Carolina, and Ohio; Florida halted executions pending review of lethal injection problems; and in Tennessee the prosecution of O. C. Smith continued.

On October 31, 2006, Philip's lawyers filed a "Motion to Alter or Amend" in Judge Donald's court in Memphis. They pointed out that she had used the wrong standard—*Fierro v. Johnson*, a Fifth Circuit Court of Appeals case—when the controlling standard should have been *Demjanjuk v. Petrovsky*, a Sixth Circuit Court of Appeals case.

The Demjanjuk case involved the deportation and extradition of John Demjanjuk after finding him to be the Nazi war criminal known as Ivan the Terrible. There was only one problem: Demjanjuk was *not* Ivan the Terrible, and the U.S. government had withheld exculpatory evidence revealing that fact. The Sixth Circuit Court of Appeals reversed itself upon confronting its mistake, and Demjanjuk was spared an Israeli gallows.

Philip Workman had a similar claim of fraud upon the court, since the government of the state of Tennessee and officials of the city of Memphis had withheld evidence, manufactured a witness, and engaged in a pattern of deceit and conspiracy from the trial through two clemency hearings. Now that this had been determined to be the case, Philip was entitled to the same relief as Demjanjuk.

Although the lawyers were on point legally, the political reality was that they were dealing with a Memphis judge. It is difficult to imagine any judicial official granting relief in an establishment that for twenty-five years had dedicated itself to Philip's official murder. Nor did the Sixth Circuit Court of Appeals hold much hope, for it was now dominated by Republican appointees, who rarely granted relief in death penalty cases and had never voted for relief for Philip Workman.

In December, Judge Donald denied Philip's motion to reconsider. Her view bifurcated Philip's claim of fraud upon the court. She found there was no fraud in federal court and only possibly in the state courts. Of course, everything in federal court was based upon the egregious constitutional violations that took place in state court. The entire case against Philip rested on the fraud perpetrated by the state in framing him for a murder he did not commit. To pretend such systemic fraud in state court had no effect in the subsequent appeal in federal court ignored the interlocking relationship of the courts in capital cases.

The attorney general's office of Tennessee requested the Tennessee Supreme Court set a sixth execution date for Philip Workman.

DECLARATION

Declarant, Matthew Ian John swears as follows:

1. I am an adult resident citizen of Shelby County, Tennessee.

2. I am a member in good standing of the Bar of the Tennessee Supreme Court.

3. From approximately June 1995 to November 1995, I attended the Memphis Police Academy.

4. As part of the training at the academy, we studied the topic Officer Safety. Officer Safety was a consistent theme throughout my training.

5. One of the concerns expressed during Officer Safety Training was the potential of injury occurring to a police officer from friendly fire.

6. When the topic of Friendly Fire arose, the training officers discussed the shooting of Memphis Police Lieutenant Ronald Oliver. Those Officers explained the Oliver shooting as a situation where friendly fire could have resulted in the death of Lieutenant Oliver.

7. I declare under penalty of perjury under the laws of the United States of America that the foregoing is true and correct.

Executed: _____ 10/5/05

_____
Matthew Ian John

The Encompassing Circle

As we rocked along through 2005 and 2006, my visits with Philip continued on a weekly basis and the case wound through the courts. The only new addition to the mountain of information revealing that Philip did not shoot Lieutenant Oliver came couched in irony. Matthew Ian John, of Memphis, had been in the Memphis Police Academy training to be a policeman from June 1995 to November 1995. During the course of his instruction, the topic of officer safety was addressed. One aspect discussed was the risk of injury occurring to a policeman from "friendly fire." According to Matthew Ian John, in his training the officers discussed the shooting of Memphis police lieutenant Ronald Oliver: "Those Officers explained the Oliver shooting as a situation where friendly fire could have resulted in the death of Lieutenant Oliver." So by 1995 even the Memphis Police Academy was using the Oliver killing as an example of an instance of death by possible friendly fire. And so it goes.

The respite from immediate crisis gave me time to consider Philip's case in the context of other governments that killed their citizens. I spent a good deal of time reading Holocaust literature; reviewing my trip to Auschwitz and Majdanek some ten years earlier; thinking about my 1991 conversations with Holocaust survivor and political activist Elie Wiesel; and contemplating the similarities and differences of the government of the United States as well as the state of Tennessee and the Third Reich. The results of my reflections were not encouraging. I continued working on my history of the United States informed by these considerations(*Slouching toward Tyranny: The Making of the Tyranny of the Majority in the United States of America*, forthcoming).

Hannah Arendt, in her work on Adolf Eichmann in Jerusalem, coined the term the "banality of evil." It concisely described Eichmann's efforts in making the trains run on time as he systematically planned the deportation for extermination of six million Jews and five million enemies of the state.

Dr. O. C. Smith's actions in two clemency hearings against Philip demonstrated a similar mind-set. All of his "scientific" experiments and bogus forensic analysis was with one purpose in mind: to ensure the killing of Philip Workman by the state of Tennessee. Whether it involves one person or millions of people, the mind-set that is established to facilitate their doom reveals the banality of evil.

The notes O. C. Smith recorded that were subsequently obtained under the Tennessee Public Records Act chronicle the systematic development of the "medical" justification for executing Philip. He, like everyone else involved in the twenty-five-year campaign to exterminate Philip, was just doing his job: ensuring the killing of a person at the behest of the state. O. C. Smith and Adolf Eichmann "catch the thread of all sorrows and you see the size of the cloth" (Naomi Shihab Nye, "Kindness").

The following excerpts from Dr. O. C. Smith's notes in preparation for his Power Point presentation at the clemency hearings demonstrate the efforts he went to in order to distort the truth.

October 29, 1999   modified for final time X-ray of Lt. Oliver's wounds.

October 30, 1999   used a ruler to put the finishing touches on pattern of bullets.

December 2, 1999   final work on autopsy protocol, bullets and diagram of entry/exit wounds.

February 2, 2000   modified tissue sample pictures for the last time.

February 20, 2000   final modification to pictures of a magnified gunshot wound and .45 shot into ordinance gel. Provided report to assistant district attorney John Campbell. Report states one of Workman's bullets killed Oliver and the injury to Workman's buttocks was from dog bites.(Letter obtained in the district attorney's file)

February 23, 2000   final modification of pictures of the cross-section of bullets completed.

February 25, 2000   modified picture of the magnified gunshot wound.

February 26, 2000   pictures of the magnified gunshot wound were again modified.

March 2, 2000   modified pictures of bullet hole in Oliver's shirt, the evidence envelope and vial for Q1, bullets and X-ray.

March 3, 2000   last modified picture of the bullet, jacket fragment, .45 shell casing, shirt bullet hole and gunshot sounds. The F.B.I. folder last modified.

March 5, 2000   last modified pictures of magnified gunshot wounds, Workman naked, entry/exit wounds, X-ray, Silvertip expansion, and Silvertip fail.

March 6, 2000   last modified pictures of Stoddard, Smith, Campbell and a cast of a dog jowl.

March 7, 2000   last modified pictures of bullets in picture and page 2 of medical examiner's report.

March 8, 2000   Picture of a dark cross-section of a bullet next to a white square last modified.

March 13, 2000   last modified picture of .45 vs. .38 bullets.

March 14, 2000   modified pictures of bullet holes in cloth.

March 29, 2000   last modified pictures of gun/bullet/cartridge, bullet/cloth hole, bullets, skin wounds . . . ordinance gel, plugged/Silvertips, fiber plugs, etc.

April 1, 2000   pictures of cloth holes, .45 vs. .00 buck cloth holes last modified.

April 3, 2000   8:30 A.M. Summary of testimony last modified.

THE TWENTY-SECOND CIRCLE

Shortly before Christmas 2006, California and Florida, the states with the largest death rows in the country, temporarily stopped executions due to problems with lethal injection. A federal district judge in California stopped the process in that state, and Governor Jeb Bush halted executions in Florida. In one case in the Sunshine State, a botched lethal injection took thirty-four minutes to kill the prisoner, who was clearly in pain, while officials sought to expedite the proceedings. Along with bungled lethal injections in Ohio, the actions in California and Florida lent credence to the proof presented in Abu-Ali's lethal injection case in Tennessee, which lost in the state courts. Despite compelling trial testimony in that case, the Tennessee Supreme Court found the chances of cruel and unusual punishment "less than remote." Perhaps now a federal court would be willing to consider the flawed lethal injection protocol and do so in time to halt E. J. Harbison's February 22, 2007, execution in Tennessee.

On January 16, 2007, the Tennessee Supreme Court set Philip's sixth execution date: May 9, 2007. When I visited Philip on the evening of January 18, 2007, we discussed the latest execution date. He was not surprised by the actions of the Tennessee Supreme Court. He had pending litigation in federal court in Memphis as well as in the Sixth Circuit Court of Appeals in Cincinnati, but he was not optimistic about the course of those appeals. Indeed, he spent most of the time discussing a civil case that he was bringing against O. C. Smith. I had found Philip a very good Chicago lawyer, Steve Tomashevfsky, who was representing him in this action. Even if the remaining actors in the Memphis charade of justice remained unscathed by Philip's case, he looked forward to getting Smith into court and putting him on the stand to face examination by a superb lawyer. It was one thing for Smith to conduct his charade unchallenged before a clemency board or to act out his bizarre pantomime in barbed wire with a bomb on his chest. Let him face an excellent lawyer armed with facts, studies, and expert testimony. Then we might get to the truth of the matter.

Philip's case not only proved Oscar Wilde's saying, "The Truth is rarely pure and never simple," but it also established that truth could be found despite long odds. The only question remaining was if justice would flow forth from the truth.

E. J. Harbison's lawyers filed a lethal injection suit in the federal district court of Nashville. The legal landscape had changed dramatically since the Tennessee Supreme Court's injudicious appraisal of the unconstitutionality of lethal injection being "less than remote." In addition to California and Florida, a North Carolina state judge had halted four executions scheduled there in order to examine the lethal injection protocol.

This scenario lent an interesting context for the status conference that Judge Aleta Trauger held in Nashville on the lethal injection petition filed on behalf of E. J. Harbison. After hearing what the parties had to say in court, she asked them to join her in chambers. In a discussion about the issue, she suggested the attorney general contact Governor Bredesen and have him halt executions until the matter could be fully studied by competent professionals. This would give the governor an opportunity to address the problem before the courts became involved. The attorney general, Bob Cooper, replied he would not do so, because the Tennessee lethal injection protocol had no problems whatsoever. This reasoning was offered despite the fact that Tennessee followed the exact same protocol that existed in Florida, California, and North Carolina. Judge Trauger set a February 14 date for an evidentiary hearing on the lethal injection process in Tennessee.

At three o'clock on February 1, 2007, Governor Phil Bredesen held a press conference to announce he was halting all executions until the execution protocol had been examined and remedied. He designated the commissioner of corrections, George Little, to appoint a commission and deliver a report to him by May 2, 2007.

The evening of February 1 I visited Philip. He was glad about the moratorium on executions for the four men with pending execution dates, but he was leery of his own situation. "I don't think it's an accident this report comes out May second .They can still try and get me on May ninth. I have a bad feeling about the governor. I feel like a target is on my chest."

The euphoria of the afternoon that had been generated by the halting of the four scheduled executions was a distant memory in light of Philip's concern about his situation. There was pending litigation in his case, but the legal prospects were not good. Indeed, his best claim for relief could be a lethal injection petition.

As was so often the case for Philip, it was a waiting game. This vigil on execution dates was not an easy position to maintain. At this point it was primarily about enduring. Philip just endured the wait. William Faulkner, in his Nobel Prize acceptance speech, spoke eloquently on the element of enduring in Southern character. He would appreciate the aspect of enduring that Philip now manifested for the sixth time under a death warrant.

With the help of Liz Garrigan, the editor of the *Nashville Scene*, the *Scene* filed a Tennessee Public Records Act request demanding the state turn over all documentation pertaining to the development of the new lethal injection protocol. On March 1, 2007, the state of Tennessee replied with a pile of dated documents, including the execution manual for electrocution and lethal injection. Interestingly, they also included information stating that the state's Department of Corrections had consulted with the Federal Bureau of Prisons on developing a new protocol for lethal injection. The Tennessee commission held two daylong meetings in late February to review the execution protocol. The state denied any public access to notations from the meetings under attorney-client privilege. Liz Garrigan, along with *Scene*'s lawyer, began readying the lawsuit to obtain the information.

In my visits with Philip, he described feeling like "a cruise missile is aimed at me." Given that Governor Bredesen had now postponed all other scheduled executions prior to Philip's, it was an understandable feeling. The report of the execution protocol committee was due no later than May 2, a mere seven days before Philip's execution date.

The lethal injection mandate Governor Bredesen issued directing the Department of Corrections to "fix" the lethal injection protocol by May 2 had consumed the department. A public hearing on the issue was held on Thursday, April 5, 2007.

As a minister of the Christian gospel, I was struck that the public hearing on lethal injection had been scheduled on Maundy Thursday. On the day Christians designate to reflect on the betrayal, arrest, and impending crucifixion of Jesus of Nazareth on Good Friday, the state of Tennessee was soliciting public suggestions about its killing machinery. Four of us spoke at the hearing: two lawyers, myself, and Harmon Wray, a fellow traveler in the fight against the death penalty for thirty-two years. It was difficult to see this public forum as little more than a formality. A series of secret meetings had been held by the commission that was hearing our testimony. It seemed likely that they had already decided whatever they were going to do in designing a new protocol and that this hearing was simply a public courtesy.

On April 12 I took the Rev. Jim Lawson to visit Philip and Abu-Ali on death row. Jim had been teaching at Vanderbilt University after retiring from his Methodist church in Los Angeles. Hiring him had been Vanderbilt's doing penance for expelling him from the Vanderbilt Divinity School because he had led the nonviolent training for the sit-in movement in downtown Nashville in 1960. Now he was back teaching at the university.

Abu-Ali was in good spirits and we had a delightful visit. He informed Jim of the history of his case and his religious journey. As he outlined his spiritual pilgrimage from black nationalist/Christian to a man who had woven several religious traditions into a spiritual path, he suddenly stopped. Looking directly at Jim, he said, "The only time I see black ministers out here is when Joe brings them out. That's one of the reasons I moved away from the Christian church." Jim, a Methodist minister wearing his clerical collar, nodded. We closed our visit with a prayer led by Reverend Lawson. As we awaited Philip's arrival, I briefly highlighted his case for the minister and also discussed his May 9 execution date. Jim was struck that this was Philip's sixth death warrant.

Philip came into the small visiting room and we hugged. I introduced him to Jim, and Philip explained his case to him. We talked a lot about clemency. Philip didn't want to go through another clemency hearing. He had already been through two hearings that were charades of justice. This time he had decided to send some religious tapes to the governor and "let the Holy Spirit work with him."

Philip was his own most eloquent spokesperson. By refusing media requests (limiting it to one interview with CNN) and not pursuing clemency, he was circumscribing the opportunity to get his story out. Although there was a residual base of Tennesseans who supported him from two prior near-executions over five years ago, the public needed to be reeducated on the case. But as I listened to him speak, I knew the reality was that Philip was emotionally exhausted and simply couldn't do any more.

Reverend Lawson reminded Philip of chapter 3 in the book of Exodus. It was the story of Moses being summoned by God to be a spokesman for the Lord and lead the people out of bondage. The minister pointed out two salient facts: (1) Moses felt inadequate and did not wish to do it, and (2) after seeing the Hebrew people suffer, God was moved to act. God acted through Moses. Jim went on to talk about his experience with God through the civil rights movement and said that God had worked through people in that movement in order to accomplish the justice He desired. Jim thought that God might be using Philip and his case to advance the cause of justice against the death penalty.

As I listened to Philip and Jim converse, I realized that Philip was weary in an existential sense. The pressure of the sixth death warrant was exacting its inevitable emotional toll. The machinery of killing was designed to destroy a person physically, but the subtle ways it eroded a person emotionally were less understood. Dr. George Woods had provided insight into this process with a report written during Philip's fourth death warrant. Now Philip was going through the sixth death warrant with more caging, strip searches, the repeated threat of imminent doom, and the ennui of death row. In a seeming contradiction, Philip wanted it all to be over it even as he wanted to continue to live. He had been tortured to the brink of emotional exhaustion and subsequent insanity.

I tried to speak to his exhaustion, but mostly I just listened. Listening seemed to be the most important thing I could do in the visit. As the visit wound down, I asked Jim Lawson to close with a prayer. He articulated a powerful prayer of comfort and compassion. We then embraced Philip and left the prison. The execution date of May 9 would arrive in three weeks.

***

STATE OF TENNESSEE
DEPARTMENT OF CORRECTION
RIVERBEND MAXIMUM SECURITY INSTITUTION
7475 COCKRILL BEND INDUSTRIAL ROAD
NASHVILLE, TENNESSEE 37243-0471
TELEPHONE (615) 350-3100 • FAX (615) 350-3400

April 19, 2007

Reverend Joe Ingle
5711 Old Hickory Boulevard
Nashville, TN 37218

Dear Reverend Ingle:

Records of the Tennessee Department of Correction reflect that on May 11, 1981, inmate Phillip Workman was convicted of First Degree Murder and sentenced to Death regarding Shelby County case #B812090. An order has been received rescheduling inmate Workman's execution for May 9, 2007. The execution is scheduled for 1:00 a.m. on that date.

Pursuant to TCA 40-23-116, a priest or minister who prepares a condemned prisoner for death may witness the execution. As you have been selected by inmate Workman to provide spiritual guidance during his confinement on Death Watch, you may be present at the carrying out of such death sentence.

The Tennessee Department of Correction needs to know if you are interested in viewing the legal execution of inmate Workman. In order to expedite this process, please sign and date on the respective line below indicating your intentions. Afterwards fax the letter with your signature to my office at the Riverbend Maximum Security Institution at 615/350-3400. If you plan to attend, provide a telephone number where you may be contacted day or night. Further, you should be at the Riverbend institution by 12:00 midnight and bring your notification letter with you, along with a picture ID. Upon arrival at the facility, please present the letter to the Checkpoint officer. If you have any questions regarding this matter, please feel free to contact me by calling 615/350-3100, extension 3103, for further information.

Sincerely,

Ricky J. Bell, Warden

RJB/md

I will attend. _____✓_____   Signature _____   Date _5/7/09_
                                        Telephone No. _72-42-3/179_

I will not attend. _____   Signature _____   Date _____

On April 23, 2007, the American Bar Association (ABA) released its report reexamining the death penalty in Tennessee and calling upon Governor Bredesen to extend his moratorium on executions until the entire system, not just the lethal injection protocol, could be remedied in light of the ABA study. In a press conference at the legislative plaza, Karen Mathis, the ABA president, noted too many blacks receiving the death penalty, woefully inadequate defense counsel, and a system that was fundamentally broken. The 334-page ABA report, titled "The Tennessee Death Penalty Assessment Report," was an in-depth analysis of the administration of the death penalty in Tennessee in twelve areas:

1. Collection, preservation, and testing of DNA and other types of evidence;
2. Law enforcement identifications and interrogations;
3. Crime laboratories and medical examiner's offices;
4. Prosecutorial professionalism;
5. Defense services;
6.The direct appeal process;
7. State post-conviction relief proceedings;
8. Clemency proceedings;
9. Jury instructions;
10. Judicial independence;
11. Racial and ethnic minorities;
12. Mental retardation and mental illness.

In no category was Tennessee's administration of the death penalty found to be adequate, and numerous recommendations for reform were advocated in the report. The silence from the governor, who had been briefed about the report in advance by the writers of the study, was ominous.

In response to the petition by the *Nashville Scene* under the Tennessee Public Records Act, chancellor Claudia Bonnyman held a hearing on April 25, 2007, to determine whether or not the Tennessee Department of Corrections should be compelled to produce the notes, e-mails, and documents generated by the lethal injection commission. Since the DOC commission was operating with state tax dollars, the inner workings of the group should be made public under the TPRA. Chancellor Bonnyman heard the arguments from both sides. She then summarized each party's position and indicated that she had read all the briefs and opinions submitted to the court. She announced she would have a decision in an hour.

Chancellor Bonnyman returned as promised and read her decision from the bench. In her comments, the chancellor clearly indicated that she grasped the issues involved in the case as well as the scope of the law. She found for the plaintiff, the *Nashville Scene*, and ordered the DOC to yield all documents and e-mails that had been written in preparation of the revised lethal injection protocol. The state indicated they would need to consult with the commissioner of corrections, the attorney general, and the governor before deciding on an appeal. The parties agreed to file their respective proposals on how to proceed by the close of court on April 26, 2007.

***

About two weeks before Philip's scheduled execution, I picked up Jim Lawson and we drove out to death row in my pickup truck. When we arrived in Unit 2, Philip was completing a visit with one of his lawyers. He waved us inside the small visiting room as soon as the lawyer left. We exchanged hugs and sat down for a visit.

Philip gestured at the legal papers next to him and said, "That's the papers to keep them from doing an autopsy. I don't want my body to be desecrated. They know how to kill me, so they don't need to do that. We'll file it in federal court."

Philip informed us that his brother Terry was coming down for a visit Sunday. He was planning to tell Terry that he didn't want him to witness the execution. "In that situation, you have to be strong. Seeing my family there, that would make it hard. I know Terry wants to be there, but I really don't want him to be there. I have to be strong, and seeing him just wouldn't help me." Philip smiled and looked at me. "But you know Terry. He takes a notion to be stubborn. But he's just going to have to go with me on this one. If I have to, I'll talk to the warden."

Jim and I had entered death row with its recycled air, leaving behind a lovely, cool spring afternoon with pansies blooming brightly outside the Unit 2 door. We were now plunged into a conversation with a man who was anticipating the state's killing him in less than two weeks. Philip was gearing himself up, trying to muster the strength to endure yet another trip to deathwatch. Meanwhile, his case remained in the routine appellate posture before the Sixth Circuit Court of Appeals without even an expedited briefing schedule. But there was no stay of execution in place. So we had this surreal appearance of a normal appellate course of events grinding against the personal reality of a man preparing for his extinction by the state of Tennessee. The clash of realities lent a dissonance to the occasion, almost a disassociation of reality.

"It looks like I'm headed to deathwatch," Philip said. "With Judge Donald waiting to issue the certificate of appealability, the Sixth Circuit won't have time to process the case. Plus with the lethal injection protocol coming out May second, that's only a week before my execution. That is going to be litigated, so it looks like I'll be over there when it's decided. I'm not going to pack my stuff. There are six of them that come and get you. They can pack it themselves. The one good thing is I get to use the phone lying on my bed while I'm on deathwatch. That's the way I like to talk. Here you have to stand and talk through the bars. At least I'll be comfortable talking on the phone." Philip smiled. "Of course, I'd just as soon not have the opportunity to be comfortable on the bed using my phone." We all chuckled.

Philip was wrestling with some particular scriptures and we discussed them. He loved the King James version of the Bible, and he had several editions along with one that was annotated by Helen White, the Seventh-Day Adventist teacher of one hundred years ago. He liked to be sure that his understanding of the words in the Bible was as clear as possible.

Suddenly, Philip looked directly into my eyes and said, "Where am I going to be buried?"

We had discussed this several years ago under his last trip to deathwatch, and now I reminded him of what we had discussed.

"I can't remember what we decided," he said. "There was just so much going on."

So I told him the decisions we had arrived at and asked if that was still agreeable. He nodded that it was okay. Then I asked, "You want to be buried, not cremated, right?"

Philip vigorously replied, "No cremation. That's just desecration of the body."

Philip then discussed the prophet Isaiah and his death. Some televangelist had explained Isaiah's death and maintained he was buried in a tree, which was later cut down. Jim Lawson and I assured

Philip that such a description was nowhere to be found in the Bible. Jim explained it was probably a legendary account the preacher had taken at face value. I had an earthier description of it in mind, but I held my tongue.

Philip seemed comforted by Jim's pastoral presence. Jim listened well, and when it came time to pray our final prayer with Philip, he articulated the spirit of the prisoner, what he was experiencing, and offered it to God. It was a deeply moving spiritual moment. We hugged Philip, and then after a visit with Abu-Ali, Jim closed with another powerful prayer.

***

As the calendar moved inexorably toward May 9, Philip's family wished to come for a final visit. His brother Terry visited on April 9. His daughter, Michelle, and her son, Cody, also wished to visit, as did Philip's nephew, Larry, and his family. Philip called me at home the evening of April 29 to discuss the visits. If they could come before he was moved to deathwatch, seventy-two hours prior to the execution, he would relent his initial reluctance and visit with them. I told him I would work it out with Warden Bell.

On the legal front, Judge Donald of Memphis had denied the stay of execution request but issued a certificate of appealability indicating the appeal had merit. The case was forwarded to the Sixth Circuit Court of Appeals. It would go before a panel of judges composed of two Republicans and one Democrat. The rejection rate of death row cases in the Sixth Circuit was over 90 percent when the panel had a Republican majority. Philip had yet to have a Republican judge vote favorably on his case at any level, including the Sixth Circuit Court of Appeals.

In preparing for the final family visits, I talked with Terry Workman. He mentioned he would be at the motel where he usually resided on his visits to Philip. I offered that maybe that would bring us good luck. He responded, "What we need is justice. All we've ever wanted in this case is a little justice."

On April 30, 2007, the Department of Corrections released its revised lethal injection protocol. To no one's surprise, the chemical cocktail ingredients remained the same: (1) *sodium thiopental*, which is highly unstable and should not be used as an anesthetic but is so utilized; (2) *pancuronium bromide*, which is the paralytic agent that freezes all muscles, thus creating a chemical veil over the killing so that while the prisoner might be experiencing a painfully gruesome death no one would know, because he has been paralyzed by this chemical; (3) *potassium chloride*, which delivers a maximum amount of pain to the cardiovascular system as it stops the heart.

Of course, this chemical cocktail was administered by untrained, unprofessional, non-credentialed correctional personnel. They utilized a long tube (some twenty-one feet in length) and a complicated delivery system that made Rube Goldberg's creations look simple. Additionally, the legislature and the Tennessee Veterinary Association had prohibited the use of pancuronium bromide in the euthanasia of animals. So it was legal to kill a human being but not an animal with this chemical concoction in Tennessee.

Governor Bredesen issued the following statement upon publication of the revised execution protocol: "As this completes the work that I asked the commissioner to undertake, the moratorium on executions will expire on schedule on May 2, 2007." So much for the death penalty reform recommendations of the ABA. So much for Philip Workman. And so it goes.

***

As Philip neared deathwatch once again, the family visit was scheduled for Saturday, May 5, before Philip was moved to deathwatch in the early morning hours of Sunday. In a meeting with warden Ricky Bell, as we arranged the visits we also discussed the legal situation and what would be happening in the institution regarding Philip's family. Terry Workman would visit on Sunday.

Philip's lawyers filed an appeal of the 60(b) petition into the Sixth Circuit Court of Appeals on May 1. Another petition that contained the appeal of the *error coram nobis* petition generated from Judge Colton's court included Dr. Wecht's unchallenged testimony that the bullet could not have come from Philip's gun. The lethal injection petition challenging the state's revised execution protocol would be filed before Judge Todd Campbell in the federal district court of Nashville. It was a race to the wire with the May 9 execution date and no stay of execution in effect.

When I visited Philip on the afternoon of May 5, he was jaunty. For a guy with an execution scheduled in four days, he was in remarkably good spirits. He informed me of the administrative procedures the lethal injection petition had to clear before it could be filed in federal court. The DOC had twenty-four hours to respond at each administrative level, so it probably could not be filed until Monday, May 7. After surveying the legal landscape, Philip said he would be headed for deathwatch again before a final decision would be reached.

We reviewed the family visits and who would be coming when. There would likely be the normal tensions that exist between family members at a time like this, but I thought these visits would be good for Philip and his family. He would be moved to deathwatch in the wee morning hours of Sunday, May 6, and Terry would visit that afternoon.

Given the degree of evidence in Philip's case, including—

- Dr. Cyril Wecht's uncontroverted testimony that the slain police officer's wound could not have been caused by Philip's bullet;
- Lieutenant Keenan's testifying during clemency that he had found the fatal bullet when at trial Terry Willis had testified that *he* was the person who found it;
- Harold Davis, the only eyewitness, recanting his testimony;
- A computer enhancement of the crime scene revealing that an evidence cup had been placed at the scene and probably covered the fatal bullet despite the crime scene diagram not recording the placement of that bullet; and
- Dr. O. C. Smith's bogus tests and testimony in clemency, and his bizarre act of wrapping himself in barbed wire with a bomb on his chest and blaming Workman supporters for the deed

—one would think a stay of execution certainly would be coming from somewhere. However, despite Philip's believing he would get a stay of execution, I saw only politics at work, not justice. I had seen so much go wrong that should have gone right in Philip's case, not to mention other death penalty cases I had been involved with across the South, that I was steeling myself for the politics of killing rather than justice. Any relief had to come through the Sixth Circuit Court of Appeals, where Philip had never garnered a Republican vote and that at this juncture was an overwhelmingly Republican appointee court.

The Sixth Circuit Court of Appeals panel voted 2–1 against Philip's 60(b) petition on May 4. Two Republicans voted against him and one Democrat voted for him. However, in the federal district court of middle Tennessee, Judge Todd Campbell issued a stay of execution based on the lethal injection protocol, setting a May 14 date for a hearing. The state appealed Judge Campbell's decision to the Sixth Circuit.

Becca and I had spent Friday night and Saturday in Atlanta watching the Dodgers play the Braves. This trip had been planned for months; I am a Dodger fan from childhood, and Philip encouraged me to go, telling me he would be all right. I received a phone call at the ball park Friday night learning of Philip's stay of execution from Judge Campbell. We returned to Nashville on Sunday, and Philip called me at home that night, May 6, to discuss the legal rulings. He reiterated his belief that the Republicans were "Pharisees" in the sense that they had ulterior motives and were not primarily interested in upholding the law. "The right wing talks about activist judges, but it's the Republican judges that are the activist judges. They don't enforce the law; they just want to get people executed."

Philip talked about his family's visits on Friday evening and Saturday. He had enjoyed them, especially the children. He noted it had been a bit crowded, but "I sure did enjoy having those Workman kids climb all over me." He had not yet been moved to deathwatch, because he had an intact stay of execution. The lawyers expected to know by noon Monday whether or not the stay of execution would hold.

On Monday, May 7, the Sixth Circuit Court of Appeals panel, composed of two Republicans and one Democrat, voted 2–1 to lift the stay of execution and the temporary restraining order issued by Judge Campbell that had set May 14 as a hearing date on Philip's lethal injection claim. Judge Cole, in his dissent, eloquently summed up the majority opinion of the Republican judges in the case:

> The majority's opinion rests on a profound jurisdictional defect: There is no appealable order before the Court. The district court issued a temporary restraining order [TRO], not a preliminary injunction. It is well established that "[a]n order granting, denying or dissolving a temporary restraining order is generally not appealable" . . . TROs have the modest purpose of preserving the status quo to give the court time to determine whether a preliminary injunction should issue . . . The short duration of a TRO—no more than 10 days under Rule 65(b)—is one of its chief distinctions from a preliminary injunction. Indeed, as this Court recently acknowledged, "[t]he rationale for this rule [i.e., the non-appealability of TROs] is that TROs are of short duration and usually terminate with a prompt ruling on a preliminary injunction, from which the losing party has an immediate right of appeal" . . .
>
> The district court's TRO cannot be magically transformed into a preliminary injunction, which *is* an appealable order, even though the State and the majority of this Court may wish it. This makes the majority's heavy reliance on the unpublished decision in *Alley v. Little* . . .—which involved a preliminary injunction—entirely inapposite. True, in certain situations not applicable here, courts will treat TRO's as appealable preliminary injunctions. For instance, if a TRO is extended beyond the 10 day limit provided for in Rule 65(b), then it may be treated as a preliminary injunction . . . This is not an issue here because the district court's order sets a preliminary injunction hearing date on May 14, 2007, and specifies that the TRO will dissolve at that date.
>
> . . . The TRO does not interfere with the State's conviction of Workman; it does not interfere with the State's ultimate imposition of the death sentence; and it does not indefinitely preclude the State from executing Workman. The TRO does no more than

prohibit Workman's execution on May 9, so that the district court may determine—a mere five days later—whether a preliminary injunction should issue. I cannot conclude that the State's interest—whether described as avoiding delay or achieving finality—is so compelling as to necessitate what is manifestly a TRO as a preliminary injunction . . .

Because I believe that there is no doubt that the district court issued a TRO and not a preliminary injunction, I would deny the State's appeal for lack of jurisdiction.

After learning of what the Republican majority on the panel wrote, I recalled that one of these judges (Eugene E. Siler Jr.) had distorted Colonel Fackler's research in the initial opinion, then when confronted with that manipulation, marked out the references to Fackler and reissued the opinion unchanged. This judge, now supplemented by Jeffrey Stuart Sutton, a Republican former attorney general of Ohio, was not objective and had decided long ago that Philip Workman must be killed no matter what the facts stated. This latest opinion on lethal injection, which treated a temporary restraining order as a preliminary injunction so that they would kill Philip before a hearing on the merits of a flawed lethal injection process was to take place, merely confirmed that reality. Now their decision would pass onto the entire Sixth Circuit, which was packed with other Republican appointees. Philip had no chance before those judges.

***

As I arrived at Riverbend Maximum Security Institution on the afternoon of Monday, May 7, there was no doubt the state of Tennessee was preparing for an official killing. The state highway patrol was assembled, creating a paramilitary presence and a preliminary checkpoint before entering the driveway leading to the prison. After passing muster with my ID and designation on the official list of visitors, I drove into the parking lot. Another checkpoint stopped me, and the guard ascertained again that I was in fact who I claimed to be. He then directed me to a parking space.

After parking my truck, I proceeded to the warden's office. I had a brief visit with warden Ricky Bell, who provided me with a soft drink. I was then escorted by a guard to Building 8, where deathwatch and the execution chamber were housed. After being buzzed through consecutive doors, I signed into the deathwatch log book. I then turned, entered a foyer through another solid metal door, and saw Philip through the glass of the non-contact visiting booth. Terry and Michelle were visiting him. He waved me into the visiting booth.

Philip was garbed in medical whites issued for those on deathwatch. The white shirt and white pants with a blue stripe down the leg gave the aura of visiting someone in a hospital. Rather than dying naturally from some physical condition, however, Philip was to be murdered on a gurney in thirty-six hours, and we were all acutely aware of that fact no matter how he might be dressed.

He was having a tough time. The rapidity of the changing events, even though he had girded his loins for this possibility, had surprised him. Michelle had been crying. Terry maintained his usual stoical demeanor while masking a breaking heart. Philip was trying to be strong. He noticed my soft drink can and said, " Don't let them see you with that." I grimly laughed and told him the warden had given it to me. He shook his head.

Philip went over his wishes for the next twenty-four hours and confirmed that I would be with him on deathwatch outside his cell. I told him that the warden had said I would have to leave by 11:00 P.M., some two hours before Philip's execution. He wondered why that was the case, since I had been outside his cell to within thirty-five minutes during his last deathwatch. I reminded him that we had had to get a court order to do that and that this time we were spread too thin legally to fight that battle again. He nodded.

Philip spoke firmly about not wanting anyone he loved being in the execution chamber. He needed to be strong at that time, and he didn't want to look into the witness room and see Terry or me there. "I can't be weak. If I saw you, I would break," he said. Terry and I agreed to honor his wishes, relieved because we did not want to be witnesses. However, if Philip needed us, we would have been there for him.

He reviewed the fast actions of the Sixth Circuit Court of Appeals. I agreed that it was quite unusual and that it looked like they were "clearing the decks." His reply was telling: "They're not clearing the decks. They're trying to clear *me*." As usual, he had come to the heart of the matter.

Terry, Michelle, and I concluded our visit with Philip at 4:00 P.M. with a final prayer, placing our hands against the window to meet his hands on the other side of the glass. He invoked the "hedge of protection" prayer he always prayed for his loved ones. I echoed it for him: "O Lord, place a hedge of protection around Philip. Support him with your strong right arm. May he feel your grace and strength. Deliver him from those who seek to kill him, and bring him safely through this ordeal." Then it was time to go.

After exiting the prison, Terry, Michelle, and I lingered around our vehicles to talk. We discussed our plans. Terry would join me with Kelley Henry, one of Philip's lawyers, for an event at the Belcourt Theater for the public. It would be one last review of the evidence demonstrating Philip did not kill Lieutenant Oliver featuring his lawyers and me talking about the case.

There was an unreality about the entire process leading up to Philip's execution. The press and the public had dwelled in a land of make-believe, not thinking this execution could actually happen. Now, with the rulings from the Sixth Circuit Court of Appeals, there was a sudden awareness that Philip could indeed be killed and that this sixth death warrant would be the fatal one.

The sparse turnout at the Belcourt event underscored the surreal nature of the proceedings. Although the press was now comprehending the gravity of the situation, the news was just dribbling out to the public as many came home from work. It was a striking contrast from Philip's last near-execution, when ten thousand people had written the governor, hundreds had mobilized at the time of the scheduled execution, and the Belcourt Theater had been packed.

THE TWENTY-THIRD CIRCLE

Tuesday dawned fair and cool. The lively coolness of April had extended into May. This was welcome after a bizarre March of 80-degree-plus temperatures ushering in premature blooming of plants and trees. The early glory of spring had been hammered with three consecutive nights of 20 degrees or lower. Spring shriveled before the eyes, and an ugly brown blighted many plants and trees.

Philip's situation seemed to be changing like the weather. After an early promising beginning, the killer judges were at hand to terminate the proceedings. Tuesday, May 8, brought a swirl of activity that culminated with my going out to the death house at 9:00 P.M. to be with Philip until 11:00 P.M. The official killing would take place at 1:00 A.M. on May 9.

Due to the sudden turn of events, much of my time not spent with Philip and his family was spent making funeral arrangements. Locating a funeral home, deciding with Philip again where to bury him, the type of funeral service he desired, the entire flurry of events had a frenetic yet simultaneous suspended-animation feeling. To have a conversation with a healthy, vigorous fifty-three-year-old man about his imminent killing and burial underscored the unreality of events. Of course, it was just confirmation of what the death certificate would state after the execution when it listed Philip's cause of death: "Homicide." Even the state of Tennessee would acknowledge that it had murdered Philip. It was a cold, political, calculated, and egregious display of wanton power despite the fact he had killed no one and thus under Tennessee law was not even subject to the death penalty. Memphis and state officials, along with judges, framed and conspired to kill Philip knowing full well he was innocent of Lieutenant Oliver's murder. Indeed, Oliver's own daughter had said she did not believe Philip killed her father.

Thus, the dissonance between truth and reality vibrated through me as I made my way back to deathwatch that Tuesday. I was stunned. Although I was functioning and taking care of the tasks at hand, I had a feeling of dislocation. It was like being in a cocoon. Signing various logbooks, hand-stamped, searched, escorted to deathwatch, the entire chain of events I knew so well was simply unreal. I could not comprehend that after seventeen years of visits, the last ten of them on a weekly basis, I was making my final visit to my friend, my brother.

The guards led me back to the cell. Philip was on the telephone finishing a conversation with his daughter, Michelle. These were the good-bye calls, the calls made to a loved one for a final expression of love and appreciation. He motioned for me to sit down.

Philip was wan. In his deathwatch whites, without his ever-present baseball cap with its words from Job, because deathwatch prohibited him wearing a cap, he was drawn. Even though the news from the U.S. Supreme Court had not come yet, he knew he was to be killed in four hours.

Wiping away tears from his eyes, he told me, "That was hard. That was Michelle. I just hope she can make it through. I also talked to Bubba [his nephew, who had brought his own children to visit on Saturday]. I sure did enjoy those Workman children climbing all over the place." He mustered a smile through the tears at the memory.

Philip wiped his nose with a paper towel, brushed the tears from his face with his sleeve, and looked at me through the bars. "Can you help me with these telephone calls?" he asked. "I just don't know if I can do anymore, and there are people to talk to. I just haven't had enough time since they brought me over here yesterday. You usually have seventy-two hours, but this has all been so compressed because of the lifting of the stay of execution yesterday."

I replied, "Philip, you know I will help you. How do you want me to do it?"

Philip smiled, snuffled, and said, "Let's just take some time here. See if I can get myself back together. Let's just talk for a while."

So two friends talked. The conversation unrolled, easily but painfully, until Philip looked up and said, "Okay, I've got to call Lori [a friend of his for some fifteen years]. You have to do this one with me. I want you to start it." I nodded and he dialed the number through the bars, thrusting the phone to me, and I heard it ring.

Lori was on the line immediately. "Lori, it's Joe. Philip and I are sitting here drinking some great grapefruit juice and wish you were here."

She caught my inflection. "Oh, it sounds like a party."

I nodded to Philip. "Yes, Lori, a party it is. The grapefruit juice seems to be all gone, but I understand they will give us as much as we want. Why don't you come over?"

Lori chuckled at my humor, knowing that when a prisoner is on deathwatch the authorities go out of their way to please the prisoner. The last thing they want is a dust-up over some minor thing. Above all, the killing machinery must operate smoothly.

As I chatted with Lori, Philip was composing himself. He washed his face in the lavatory and wiped it dry. He sat back down and took some deep breaths. As he moved around, Lori asked how he was doing and I answered as positively as I could. I explained that he was hoarse from all the conversation with the phone calls of the last few hours and said, "So don't be alarmed if he doesn't sound like himself." I told her he was literally talked out. Philip nodded, which indicated he was ready to talk. I passed the phone back to him through the bars, and he began his conversation with Lori. I flipped open my Bible and began reading passages, seeking guidance and consolation.

When Philip finished speaking with Lori, he came up off the bed and stood up. He went back to the lavatory and grabbed some paper towels. As he passed the stainless-steel toilet, tears or mucus fell onto the rim of the toilet. He noticed and took a paper towel and wiped the toilet rim all the way around. Philip, the original neat freak, the guy who washed his cell down for the next guy before each trip to deathwatch, was meticulous to the end. He could not stand to have stained the toilet rim. I commented on it and we both smiled.

Philip had one last telephone call to make, the one to Terry, who was in a nearby motel. Terry and I had agreed to rendezvous after I left Philip at 11:00 P.M. We would remain in a room in the administration building of the prison until either the U.S. Supreme Court stopped it or the execution took place.

As Philip and his brother talked, I recalled my conversations with Terry through the years. Philip had lived with Terry and his wife when Philip was sixteen. Then their daddy came to bring Philip home. Terry allowed Philip to go back with his dad but later regretted that decision. He thought things might have turned out differently if Philip had stayed with him rather than returning to an abusive father. It was the path not taken, and I encouraged Terry to let that go, because he had believed he was doing the right thing. He didn't know how abusive his father was to Philip, and who knew what was to come?

Philip completed the telephone call. He came over and we held hands through the bars. We prayed. As we prayed, each taking turns as the Spirit moved him, the tears dripped from our faces onto our hands. Each teardrop was a visible symbol of the love of Christ that united us in Philip's hour of suffering. It was also a manifestation of the utter heartbreak we experienced.

Philip mentioned that for his last words while strapped to the gurney, he would quote the words spoken by the apostle Stephen as he was stoned by the crowd. He then went on to talk about his funeral and his gravestone. His words ran through me like daggers, but I felt no pain. Indeed, my tears had ceased. I was there but not there. My subconscious had insulated me because the pain was too great. The cocoon-like state was complete. I was fully functioning but traumatized beyond emotional overload in such a way that I was inured to all that occurred around me.

Philip was concerned about being brave through the killing procedure. He reiterated that was why he could not have either Terry or me there. Then he asked a startling question: "You know I have false teeth?" I just looked at him and he continued. "I take pride in my appearance, and I'm wondering"—he hesitated momentarily and then plunged ahead—"how am I going to make a final statement if the drugs hit me and my head flops over and my teeth come out?"

I had immersed myself in learning about the chemical protocol for lethal injection in Tennessee. The old version and the updated protocol were virtually identical. I knew how the cruel, painful, and unnecessary process worked. As unusual as the question seemed from Philip, I had a ready answer. "Philip, it's a three-drug protocol," I said. "They are given sequentially. You will be paralyzed before it kills you. Your head won't flop over, because you will be immobilized. Don't worry about your teeth. They will be fine."

I was reminded of General J.E.B. Stuart, the Confederate cavalry leader in the Army of Northern Virginia during the Civil War. As he lay mortally wounded at Spotsylvania Courthouse in Virginia, he uttered his final words: "Do I still look pretty in the face?" Philip, too, wanted to die with dignity.

Of course, I also knew that the sequence of drugs meant that when Philip was paralyzed by the pancuronium bromide, he would be unable to communicate the horrific pain he could be experiencing from the combination of the other two drugs. This was the reason why pancuronium bromide had been outlawed in Tennessee for euthanizing animals.

In seminary, I had taken a course on death and dying. Although it had been valuable, nothing in that course, or in my subsequent reading of the literature, prepared me for working with someone who was being officially murdered, which is a completely different dynamic. There is nothing natural about the process. Death is a natural process, a winding down of the body, but killing is coerced and unnatural. Rather than a gradual depletion or sudden heart attack, state killing is a tormenting process, both mentally and physically. The healthy person is informed of how he will be killed and when he will be killed, and then several dry runs occur (five in Philip's case) when the process is stopped by the courts or governor, only to be resumed again. In a phrase, state killing is simply *civilized torture*.

When Philip came to death row in 1982, Kenny Campbell had befriended him at the old Tennessee State Prison. Kenny and Philip became close through the years, and when Kenny received a new sentencing hearing and obtained a life sentence some fifteen years after they met, he and Philip had remained in touch even though Kenny was transferred to the Morgan County Prison in eastern Tennessee. Philip now told me he had a message to share with Kenny, and I told him I would deliver it to his old friend.

Don Johnson was also a close friend who remained on death row. Don had come within four days of execution in October 2006. Don and Philip were very close, and Philip conveyed a message for Don, which I promised to deliver in the next few days.

Philip and I held hands again and prayed. He uttered a poignant and beautiful prayer for my daughter, who was undergoing teenage difficulties. His compassion in reaching out to her and our family in his direst hour enabled pain to penetrate my shocked, insulated state of mind. He invoked, as he did during our weekly visits in the closing prayer, the Lord "to place a hedge of protection around Amelia, Becca, and my brother [meaning me]. Keep this family safe and guard them. Keep the hedge of protection around them."

He then prayed for those who sought his death. Although clearly suffering, with tears rolling down his face and onto our hands as we held them together through the bars, he bore no ill will to those who sought to kill him. Finally, he offered a prayer for his own family—and, for the first time, himself.

Philip rose and fetched another paper towel. He blew his nose and wiped the tears away. He splashed cold water on his face in the lavatory. He came back over and we spoke again. He asked, "What should I put on my gravestone? It seems like something should come to me, but I just can't think. What do you think?"

The image of him from all our weekly visits loomed in my mind. "The Job quote on your baseball cap," I said. "What is it? Job 13:15?" He smiled. "The Lord must have put that on your heart. That's it."

We prayed some more and talked. The time was slipping away. Soon it was 11:00 P.M. There was no doubt in my mind that this was a Gethsemane experience. As the gospel writers described Jesus in the garden, prior to his arrest and subsequent execution he had agonized in prayer with God. Jesus prayed, "Father, if you are willing, remove this cup from me; yet not my will but your will be done." Six years before this evening, Philip had been on his knees beseeching God at the rear of his cell as the execution drew nigh. He had obtained an unexpected stay of execution forty-five minutes before his killing. This time, however, we knew there would be no last-minute reprieve. He shared his agony with me as we held hands and wept. The Lucan gospel writer wrote about Jesus wrestling with God as follows: "In his anguish he prayed more earnestly, and his sweat became like great drops of blood falling down on the ground." So it was with Philip. Just like Jesus, an innocent man facing extermination, Philip knew his murder was at hand. That knowledge caused profound anguish. It was not *his* will to die, but if it was God's will, he would go faithfully.

The guards made some not-so-subtle noises of rattling handcuffs and keys outside the barred door behind me. Philip and I continued to pray and talk. Our foreheads touched through the bars, and I felt the four-inch scar the Memphis police had caused when they hit Philip on the head as he tried to surrender, precipitating his flight with blood cascading down his face and the police then accidentally shooting Lieutenant Oliver. That leaning of heads together made the experience so intimate it seemed beyond real. I knew we had to part.

At 11:10 we stood facing each other. I embraced his shoulders through the bars. He grabbed me under my arms. It was a cruel mockery of the posture we had assumed when he had received the unexpected stay of execution six years earlier and shortly before his execution. He spoke first. "You are my brother."

I affirmed, "You are my brother, too."

Philip said, "I love you."

And I replied, "I love you too."

Earnestly, Philip spoke his last words to me: "I'll see you."

"I'll see you," I responded firmly.

We squeezed each other and I turned to leave. A rattling of keys and the door swung open. I looked back over my shoulder at my weeping brother. I gave him the thumbs-up as my heart finished breaking.

At this point, I was completely encased in the moment, and the pain had driven me beyond the experience of it into a state of shock. I automatically went through the emotions of signing out and being escorted back to the administration building. Many of the guards were dressed in uniforms of the killing color: black.

After ten minutes Terry Workman joined me, and we walked to a small room to await word from the warden about the course of events. Terry and I talked about the U.S. Supreme Court. Philip had fallen just one vote shy there the last time he'd filed for an appeal. It continued the pattern of his case frequently being one vote short at a critical juncture. We also discussed how the various family members were dealing with the ordeal. Although he appeared stoic, pain emanated from Terry.

The logistics of our situation soon proved uncomfortable. The witnesses to the execution were in the room behind us. Although we could not hear their conversation, we could hear laughter. Whether it was nervous or vindictive, we could not tell, but the sound of it coming through the wall was disconcerting. Finally Terry looked up and said, "I can understand someone being for the death penalty. What I can't understand is someone not having some respect at a time like this."

I responded, "Terry, none of this is about respect. It's all about power and control." My hands gestured at our environment as I continued, "There is no respect here. It's all about killing Philip."

A short time later, the warden opened the door and informed us that the U.S. Supreme Court had denied Philip's appeal. Philip was once again one vote short. The warden asked me if I wanted to join the other witnesses and proceed to the execution chamber. Recalling my promise to Philip, I told him I would stay with Terry. I asked the warden to let us know when it was over, and he said he would do so.

Terry and I prayed. We both had words to share with the Lord. We both wept. I found myself once again asking for a hedge of protection around Philip.

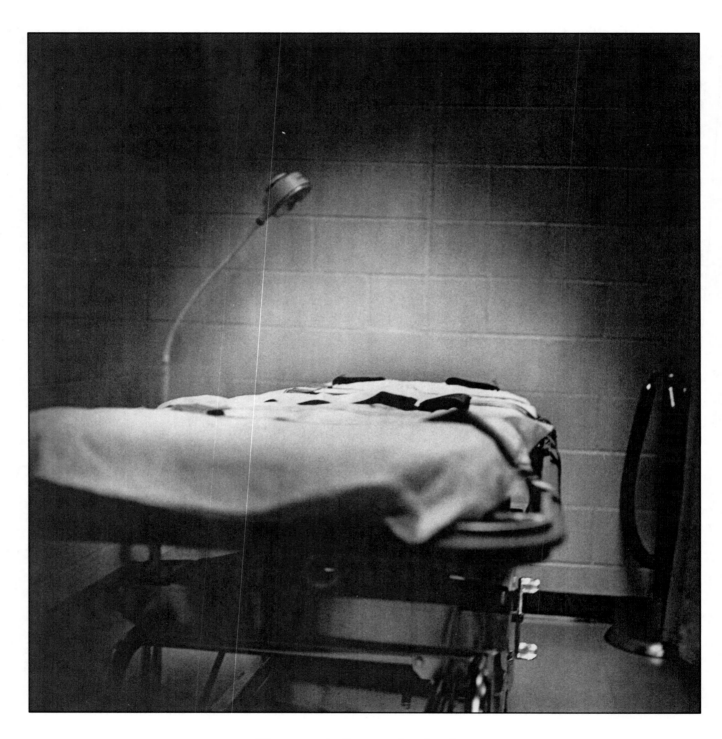

The gurney in the execution chamber.

THE TWENTY-FOURTH CIRCLE

The following account of the execution was written by Sarah Kelley for the *Nashville Scene* and published on May 17, 2007. It is used here with their permission:

WITNESS TO AN EXECUTION:
Evidence Suggesting Philip Workman Didn't Fire the Shot That Killed a Cop Was Not Enough to Stop His Lethal Injection

It's almost 1 A.M., the time Philip Workman is scheduled to die by lethal injection. Seven media witnesses wait inside a beige cinder-block room deep in the bowels of Riverbend Maximum Security Institution. The minutes slowly tick by and finally someone says what others have been thinking: "Maybe there's been a last-minute stay of execution."

But then a corrections officer guarding the room abruptly stands and announces, "It's time." Two officers escort the group through a set of steel doors and into a cramped room where several rows of chairs face three windows. Black blinds are drawn, obstructing the view of preparations inside the death chamber. The only sounds on the other side are an occasional clink or rattle.

At 1:20 A.M. Wednesday, May 9, a voice bellows over a speaker to test the sound. Suddenly two men raise the blinds and quickly exit the stark death chamber. There, in the middle of the room, 53-year-old Philip Workman lies strapped to a gurney.

On the night of Aug. 5, 1981, Philip Workman walked into a Wendy's restaurant in Memphis armed with .45-caliber semi-automatic pistol. The 28-year-old IV cocaine user robbed the restaurant at gunpoint and walked out with a bag of cash. But unbeknownst to Workman, an employee had tripped a silent alarm during the holdup, and police officers were waiting outside.

Exactly what ensued between Workman and police in the dark parking lot that night is unclear. The only certainty is that *someone* shot and killed Memphis Police Lt. Ronald Oliver.

Police claimed it was Workman who fired the single bullet that struck Oliver, although no ballistics evidence was ever presented to support this theory. At trial, the state's case rested almost entirely on the testimony of a single witness who testified he saw Workman "coolly and deliberately" shoot Oliver at close-range. Public defenders did little to prove otherwise, and Workman was convicted of first-degree murder and sentenced to death.

Years later, however, post-conviction lawyers uncovered evidence suggesting police pinned the shooting on Workman to cover up a tragic case of friendly fire, but it was not enough to save him. Although some say he's still to blame regardless of whether the deadly bullet came from his gun, the state's felony murder statute at the time would not have allowed him to be charged with first-degree murder or sentenced to death if he did not fire the shot.

"I have never experienced a case with this many twists and turns, cover-ups and lies. This case started out with a lie in 1981," says Kelley Henry, an assistant federal public defender who began working on the case in 2000. "It started out with police discovering a horrible truth—that one of their officers had accidentally killed one of their own." And from there, the lies simply spiraled out of control, she says, but by the time these lies were discovered, it was too late. No one wanted to hear it.

The state's primary witness eventually recanted, saying police told him to lie and even coached him on what to say. Two former Memphis cops also came forward with information suggesting it was, in fact, a fellow officer who shot Oliver. Two renowned forensic pathologists reviewed post-conviction evidence and said Workman's gun could not have been the source of the fatal bullet. Even Oliver's daughter, Paula Dodillet, has voiced skepticism about the prosecution. In a 2005 short-film about the case called "Deadly Silence," Dodillet says, "My belief and my feelings are that Mr. Workman did not kill my father . . . I know it's odd for me to be saying this, but it seems like there are a lot of questionable things related to this case."

In 1990, a new lawyer began representing Workman in his appeals. Christopher Minton, an assistant federal public defender in Nashville, was the first to question the credibility of the prosecution's star witness, Harold Davis.

"As far as Philip knew at trial, Harold Davis was there. Philip was led to believe that Harold Davis was telling the truth, so there is testimony from Philip saying, 'Well, I guess I shot the officer,'" Henry says during an interview one week before her client's execution. As for his trial testimony, Henry says Workman was strung out on cocaine during the robbery and that his memory of what happened was fuzzy. And although he did not remember shooting Oliver, he took the word of police and the state's key witness.

During trial Davis claimed he watched Workman shoot Oliver in the chest from about three feet away. He also testified that he left his car in the Wendy's parking lot that night, which is what first tipped off Workman's post-conviction lawyers that something was amiss. A review of crime scene photos in 1990 clearly shows Davis' car is not parked outside the restaurant.

Workman's lawyers also learned that before the night-shift officers headed out on patrol that evening, they were told a black male was suspected in a string of fast-food restaurant robberies in the area. "They would have assumed he was a suspect, but he's not even mentioned in the report," Henry says of Davis, a young black male. "Instead, they let him leave the scene?"

Workman's lawyers spent years trying to find Davis, a drifter with a history of drug abuse, but to no avail. And although the defense couldn't find him, they nonetheless argued during appeals that he lied as part of a police cover-up. Just days before Workman's first execution date in April 2000, the 6th U.S. Circuit Court of Appeals stayed the execution to consider the claims. The court split 7–7, however, and Workman's appeal was denied. Four more execution dates eventually were set and then stayed, and in one case Workman was within 42 minutes of lethal injection when the Tennessee Supreme Court ruled a lower court should consider the perjury claims, as well as ballistics evidence.

Before a 2001 hearing on the evidence was set to begin in the same Memphis courtroom where Workman was convicted, lawyers finally located Davis and, during an interview with the defense, he tearfully confessed to lying at the trial.

Davis later testified at the hearing that he lied about witnessing the shooting. A friend of Davis' also testified that they were together and nowhere near the crime scene the night Oliver was killed. A member of the jury that convicted Workman told the judge he would not have found the defendant guilty of first-degree murder or sentenced him to death had this evidence been presented at trial, and four other jurors signed affidavits echoing those remarks.

Despite the new evidence, the judge denied Workman a new trial, and another execution date was set. As for Davis' testimony, the judge said neither he nor his friend were credible witnesses, even though Davis passed a polygraph test indicating he was telling the truth about his past perjury. Not to mention he was the state's star witness in the first trial.

Davis still maintains he lied at trial. One week before Workman's execution, Davis sent an emotional video-recorded message to Gov. Phil Bredesen, saying: "I am talking to the governor to beg and plead for Philip Workman's life. I feel like Philip has been on death row probably in large part because of what I did and what I said, which turned out not to be true . . . All I'm asking, governor, is that you allow Philip the chance to redeem his life here on this earth, just as God has given me a chance."

Warden Ricky Bell stands just a few feet from the gurney, hands clasped in front of him, resting on his black suit jacket. After the blinds are raised he asks the condemned for any last words. It's 1:21 A.M. when Workman, staring up at the ceiling, says, "I have prayed to the Lord Jesus Christ not to lay charge of my death to any man."

Workman is secured to the gurney by four black straps across his body, and by leather restraints fastened around his ankles and wrists. He wears a white jail-issued uniform, which blends with the sterile surroundings—white sheets, concrete walls, tile floors and fluorescent lights. The room is vacant, with the exception of Workman and the warden. On the wall opposite the media witness room there is a small one-way mirror. On the other side the execution team administers the deadly cocktail of three chemicals, which are injected through a tube that's fed through a tiny hole in the wall and inserted into Workman's right arm. Workman is still, except to occasionally purse his lips as though he is thirsty.

Two silent minutes pass and at 1:23 A.M. Workman struggles to loudly proclaim, "I commend my spirit into your hands Lord Jesus Christ." His chest rises as though he is taking in a deep breath. He exhales, blinks several times, then closes his eyes. Workman's head tilts slightly to the left and he does not open his eyes or move again.

As the minutes elapse, Workman's face becomes flush. A few more silent minutes pass and his face turns blue, then ashen. Meanwhile, the warden stands in the same spot with his left hand grasping his right in front of him. He stares straight ahead showing no emotion, occasionally rocking back and forth in place.

Seventeen minutes into the execution Workman is pale white. Suddenly, the warden moves from his position as another man enters the room. The pair close the black blinds without a word. Then a man's voice comes over the speaker: "This concludes the execution of Philip Workman. Time of death, 1:38 A.M."

After discovering the state's key witness lied at trial, Workman's lawyers continued to chisel away at the government's case, finding what they call even more instances of perjury, deception and prosecutorial misconduct.

At Workman's trial, Terry Willis, a mechanic who worked at an auto parts store next to the Wendy's, testified that the day after the shooting he found a shiny piece of metal he thought was a ball bearing. He later realized that maybe what he found in the parking lot had something to do with the shooting the night before and he called police, who told him to put the item—which really was a bullet—back where he found it.

"That becomes the bullet the prosecutor argues to the jury at trial is the bullet that killed Lt. Oliver," says Henry, who adds that as a mechanic, Willis would have easily known the difference between a bullet and a ball bearing.

After the prosecution asserted this was the bullet that killed Oliver, an FBI agent testified that in fact the bullet had no traces of blood or tissue. The testimony was a surprise to prosecutors, who in turn waffled on whether it really was the death bullet, saying in the end it didn't really matter.

In 2001, Workman's lawyers reviewed crime scene photographs that ran in *The Commercial Appeal* and noticed an evidence marker near the spot where Oliver was shot. On subsequent diagrams by the state, that marker is not represented. Henry believes that is where the real bullet that killed Oliver was found that night, and that the bullet likely was thrown out to cover up who really fired the fatal shot.

In addition, Henry says the ammunition belt carried by one of the officers on the scene that night was inexplicably checked out of the evidence room at police headquarters for several hours the day after the shooting.

The first and only expert ever to testify under oath regarding ballistics was Dr. Cyril Wecht, a forensic pathologist hired by the defense nearly two decades after trial. After reviewing X-rays of the entry and exit wounds caused by the fatal bullet (records withheld from the defense for years), Wecht concluded a .45-caliber could not have been used to kill Oliver. That's because such bullets are designed to mushroom inside the body, and therefore do not typically exit. If by chance such a bullet does leave the body, the exit wound would be larger than the entry wound, which was not the case with Oliver. A second expert, Dr. Kris Sperry, chief medical examiner for the state of Georgia, signed an affidavit outlining similar findings.

Two former Memphis police officers eventually came forward with information Henry says further proves Workman did not shoot Oliver. In 2005, former Officer Charlotte Creasy told the defense she was directing traffic near the crime scene the night of the shooting when a hysterical woman approached and said she just saw a policeman shoot a fellow officer outside the Wendy's. Creasy claimed she relayed the information to her commander at the time, and that he told her to forget about it. Several witnesses maintain she has said this for years, although the information wasn't brought to the attention of the defense until two years ago, at which point Creasy was herself serving time for issuing false driving certificates, making her claim seem less than credible.

Matthew Ian John, a former Memphis officer turned lawyer, swore in an affidavit dated October 5, 2005, that during his police academy training, the shooting of Oliver was taught as an example of friendly fire.

Lawyers for Workman contend that if all of this evidence had been disclosed sooner, their client would have certainly been granted a new trial. "Then Workman would have won, there's really no doubt," Henry says. "Essentially, if the evidence is hidden long enough then the state wins."

Struggling to hold back tears, Henry speaks to a handful of reporters present for a press conference two days after the execution. She describes the last phone call she received from Workman at about 8 P.M. Tuesday, at which point it was clear there was little hope for a last-minute reprieve. Henry says he spoke individually to everyone in her office who worked on his case to relay his appreciation. Then, she says, before hanging up the phone, Workman said he forgave those responsible for putting him to death.

And although Workman maintained until his death that he did not kill Oliver, he nonetheless took responsibility for the situation that led to the shooting. Workman—who became a born-again Christian on death row—often said he agonized about what happened to Oliver.

"The state of Tennessee killed a good, Christian man," Workman's older brother, Terry Workman, tells the crowd. "The state of Tennessee killed a man that did not commit the crime they say he did. I know this for a fact." He goes on to relay details of the last time he saw his brother. After spending four hours together, much of that time spent praying, they said their final goodbye. Glancing back as the door was closing, Terry Workman recalls, "I saw tears well up in his eyes and I knew he knew what was going to happen to him that night."

The Rev. Joe Ingle, Workman's spiritual advisor, then describes the final few hours he spent with Workman, but not before relaying his own anguish about what happened. He says it's not the facts that put one of his best friends into the grave, but the myth that he was a cop killer, which he called "an utter and complete fabrication."

Several days earlier, Ingle spoke to a small crowd at the Belcourt Theatre to discuss details of the case and raise awareness about the upcoming execution. During that gathering he stated his belief that there had been a cover-up from the beginning, first by fellow officers, then by the prosecution. He also shared his disbelief and outrage that a story created out of whole cloth could lead to this.

Ingle, who frequently counsels death row inmates, first met Workman 17 years ago. They developed a deep friendship, and for the past 12 years, the two met almost every week. In the hours before his death, Ingle says he was the last person who loved Workman to be with him.

For two hours, Ingle sat in a chair outside Workman's cell. The two held hands through the bars, and leaned forward so their heads touched as they prayed. "I could feel his tears and my tears running off our faces and dripping onto our hands," he says, stopping for a moment to regain his composure. When it was clear their time together was almost up, Ingle recited a prayer that Workman often said at the end of their weekly sessions. "I asked God to put a hedge of protection around Philip Workman," he says, turning his head for a moment as he sobs. "But it was not to be, and it broke my heart, and it's still broken.

Bunk left empty in holding cell on death watch.

PURGATORIO

The associate warden opened the door to the room where Terry and I awaited news. He informed us that the execution had been completed. He asked if we wished to leave now and offered an escort for us. Terry and I conferred. We requested to remain in the room until the witnesses to the execution had left the building. He agreed to notify us when that was the case. Soon we heard the witnesses in the foyer of the administration building a few feet from our room. After some ten minutes, the babble calmed down and the only sound was of the guards exiting the prison. The associate warden came by and informed us we could leave with no problem. He provided a guard escort to our trucks. Terry and I agreed to meet back at his motel room.

Driving back to the motel, I felt disconsolate and exhausted. Arriving at Terry's room, I entered and joined Terry; his wife, Shelley; and Terry's daughter and her husband. The television was turned on, reporting from outside the prison. I had no stomach to listen and we just talked. The conversation was of Philip, what he meant to us all, and we all had quite a bit of anger to vent. After a half hour of conversation, I bid them good-bye. We would confer the next day to discuss the funeral. I went home and crashed in Becca's arms. There was not much to say. I finally fell asleep.

The rest of May 9 unspooled with phone calls to Terry and to the funeral home and discussions with lawyers. It became clear as the day progressed that the issue of what would happen to Philip's body would be the next subject of litigation. Although the state of Tennessee had argued the constitutionality of the lethal injection protocol and won in the courts, the state now wanted to demonstrate the proof of its legal victory by doing a full autopsy on Philip's body. This was in direct opposition to Philip's written declaration that he did not wish an autopsy because he believed it to be an act of "desecrating" his body. Federal district court judge Todd Campbell set a hearing for May 14 on the matter. In the meantime, he gave specific orders to the medical examiner, the inestimable Dr. Bruce Levy, that he not undertake any penetration or probing of Philip's body.

In contrast to the cold-blooded calculation of the state and its lust for power even beyond death, the Nashville homeless population had been flooded with pizzas during the night. The state had refused Philip's last request to donate his last meal—a vegetarian pizza—to the homeless in Nashville, but the Department of Corrections stated they did not "donate to charity" and refused the request. This was a curious statement in light of their contributing thousands of dollars to a nonprofit victims' rights group founded by the governor's wife. CNN broadcast the story of Philip's request and the state's response from the DOC. The national broadcast prompted thousands of people throughout the country to order vegetarian pizzas for their homeless populations, and more than 170 pizzas came to the Nashville Rescue Mission in honor of Philip.

The thoughtfulness of Philip donating his final meal to the homeless and his final words forgiving those who killed him and commending his spirit to Jesus resonated throughout the community. The naked display of power by the state and the courts in pushing through the execution despite evidence of innocence and a flawed execution process stood in direct contrast to Philip's final witness.

***

On the morning of May 10 I went back out to Riverbend. I was stunned, in a state of shock, going through the motions of what had to be done. One of those things that needed doing was delivering Philip's final message to his friend Don Johnson on death row. I parked my pickup truck in the parking lot and clambered out into a beautiful May day complete with pellucid sky and a slight breeze. Although I noted the beauty of the day, it brought no feeling of joy or pleasantness. It just ran over my skin like the breeze.

I walked up the sidewalk to the glass doors leading into the administration building. The sun burnished the glass brightly, and I could not see through the doors to the other side. I just focused on putting one foot in front of another, repeating the message to myself from Philip to Don over and over again. I opened the first set of doors. I was on automatic pilot, not paying attention to those around me, so when I proceeded through the second set of glass doors into the hall way, I was surprised to see warden Ricky Bell. He was talking to someone, but he stopped the conversation, walked the five feet to me, and I stood transfixed at the sight of the man who had just killed my brother. He extended his hand and I shook it. It was a reflexive act without thought. We exchanged pleasantries about the weather, and I moved on to checkpoint.

The encounter would have shaken me if I'd had any emotions left to shake. Instead, as I proceeded through checkpoint with the metal detector, hand stamp, and pat down, I just thought how strange it was that I had shaken Warden Bell's hand. Then I walked down to Unit 2 and had my visit with Don Johnson.

Don and Philip were both Seventh-Day Adventists and shared a deep Christian faith. We talked about the events of the last forty-eight hours, the insanity of Philip's case, and a bit about the faith. I gave him Philip's message. He was grateful for it. We closed with prayer and I left. Still semi-somnolent as I discharged my duties regarding Philip, I returned home to telephone and inform the funeral home about the latest news from the courts regarding obtaining Philip's body.

Several days after Philip's execution, I let it be known that I was going to hold a press conference to set the record straight about Philip's case. I was still quite angry, as well as traumatized, but I felt a need to reiterate one last time what a miscarriage of justice we had just witnessed with his execution. Kelley Henry, one of Philip's lawyers, was kind enough to join me for the press conference.

There was a decent turnout for a non-news event. Kelley and I went over the blatant injustices, I was able to publicly state my grievances with the Memphis cabal against Philip, and the press conference generated some stories. I guess for me it was primarily cathartic. Kelley was her precise, articulate, and analytical self. I bared a little outrage. Some of my anger was at the press for so totally missing the importance of events leading up to the execution, although I retained enough common sense not to tell them that. Many of them assumed Philip would get another stay of execution, since he had done so five times previously and it didn't look like he was guilty of killing anyone. They, like many, underestimated the power and politics of state killing.

The state organization against the death penalty held a memorial service for Philip in an east Nashville church. I didn't have the heart to go, but Kelley Henry asked me so I went. She had been kind to me, and the least I could do was return the favor. Kelley and I shared a few words about Philip at the memorial service. Frankly, I could no longer tell if what I was saying made sense. I was emotionally spent. But I did note the sparse attendance. I guess everyone was still in a state of shock.

Word reached me that one of Phillip's dear friends who had visited him for more than ten years, someone he had called for a final time shortly before his execution, had been admitted to a local psychiatric unit. I made arrangements to visit her.

As I entered the local hospital and made my way to the locked psychiatric unit, I could not help but think that I could probably use a week or two of such treatment myself. I was still functioning but felt like a block of wood. As I entered a hallway of the hospital after clearing the locked door, I found the room of Philip's friend. She was lying in her bed and I went to her and hugged her. There were no words. We just held each other and the sobs came forth from her. My own eyes misted, but the tears would not come.

I pulled up a chair and we talked. She told me that after her final phone call with Philip, she had started losing it. She thought she could handle it, but she could not. She had been in the psychiatric unit for several days and was beginning to feel calmer. We had a relaxed visit. She wanted to know how it was with Philip at the end, and I put the best possible spin on it that I could. I wanted her to recover, and she need not dwell on the specifics of what happened to Philip. I had that cross to bear, and it was enough for one person. We reminisced over the years we had shared with Philip. We had some good laughter about the idiosyncratic things Philip would do on occasion. He was still a work in progress regarding his attitude toward women; he had a traditional Southern male view, and we joked about that attitude. Soon it was time for me to go, because I did not want to wear out my fragile friend. We shared a prayer and a good-bye hug.

Judge Campbell held the hearing about the autopsy but ruled against Philip's request to respect his body "as a temple of the Lord." Given the reality that any appeal of Judge Campbell would be to the same killer panel in the Sixth Circuit Court of Appeals that had repeatedly ruled against Philip, and did so twice in the four days prior to his execution, the prospect of appeal did not offer much hope. The five-day delay for filing an appeal gave us a bargaining chip. With each passing day the half life of the chemicals that killed Philip increasingly dissipated. The state wanted access to the composition of those chemicals in order to mount a defense against a lethal injection challenge from E. J. Harbison's lawyers. Hence, we brokered a deal with the medical examiner for a minimally invasive procedure termed a partial autopsy shortly before the five-day period for notice of appeal concluded. The medical examiner turned the body over for burial on Saturday morning, May 12.

The family held a graveside service, which I assisted with, on the afternoon of May 14. It was a hot May afternoon with a blue sky and a gentle breeze. Philip had requested a Seventh-Day Adventist minister talk about the afterlife, and we arranged for John Dysinger, who had visited Philip in prison, to speak. His family also provided lovely gathering music prior to the service. The Rev. Victor Singletary, a friend I had asked to help, led the service. Terry Workman spoke for the family. We sang "The Old Rugged Cross." I performed the commendation and committal, observing that we all go "from earth to earth, ashes to ashes, dust to dust." I invited those who wished to join me to come forward and place a spade full of dirt on Philip's coffin. I shoveled dirt onto the coffin. Others came forward to place earth on the coffin. When that final ritual was complete, the burial crew filled in the hole around the coffin.

I had arranged for the funeral to be videotaped for the guys on death row so that they could view it. It was important that they know that Philip was treated with dignity, respect, and honor by those who loved him. It was a decided contrast to the humiliation and abuse of power the state of Tennessee and the federal government inflicted upon him.

Philip's grave marker reads:

Philip R. Workman

June 1, 1953—May 9, 2007

THOUGH HE SLAY ME, YET WILL I TRUST IN HIM

Joe Ingle gazes at family photos at home.

EPILOGUE

In *A Rumor of War*, Philip Caputo writes, "At the very beginnings of Western civilization, it was the role of the battle singers, who sang their verses around the warriors' guttering fires, to wring order and meaning out of the chaotic clash of arms, to keep the tribe human by providing it with models of virtuous behavior—heroes who reflected the tribe's loftiest aspirations—and with examples of impious behavior that reflected its worst failing."

The Inferno: A Southern Morality Tale is the work of a battle singer. Only, like Caputo, I too have been in the cauldron where the worst and the best of people are exposed. It is no accident that Siegfried Sassoon, Wilfred Owen, John Laurence, and Philip Caputo, to name a few, battle singers all, provide meaning for me among the shards of slaughter that constitute America's killing machinery, which we label the death penalty.

My fellow battle singers have one great advantage in that their battle is over. Unfortunately, the grinding gears of the American death penalty machinery are still at work. Because I am a Southerner and dwell in the South, the belly of the death penalty beast, I do not expect to see the end of this barbaric institution in my lifetime. I celebrate the victories in other states where abolition has come, but I know all too well the fecund ground of race and class upon which my region has prospered.

The second distinction between my battle song and those of other battle singers is that to a significant degree mine is not public. My song is a report back to a society that has sent a segment of its population behind walls and bars, a chronicling of what happens in that private place rather than a public display. Indeed, our executions are secreted away, usually at night, as if the very act is shameful and not to be noticed.

The final difference between this battle singer and my predecessors is that their song presents a story that coheres. Even in a lost war like Vietnam, threads are discovered and woven so that misbegotten tragedy has produced the most battle singers of any of America's conflicts. The utter lack of meaning, the casual mendacity recorded in my *Inferno*, presents no great truth or consequence in this battle song. It is a sad, chaotic tale of one human being's entrapment, abuse, and ultimate destruction. There is no effort to "keep the tribe human by providing it with models of virtuous behavior" or "examples of impious behavior that reflected its worst failings." Rather, it is the story of people doing their jobs, menial and mundane, that ultimately result in a killing as a result of their actions in an official capacity. Of course, it is all done for the public good and in our names.

So, dear reader, I leave you in Purgatorio in this version of *The Inferno*. It is where I dwell. Unlike Dante, we have no Beatrice to lead us to Paradiso. We are dwelling in purgatory with the prospect of even more infernos looming ahead. What is not clear is how we can navigate, how we can chart a path for our souls that takes us beyond the death penalty by taking it to its demise and delivering us to paradise.

Although I do not see the way, my hope is with Dante, and with the late Bill Styron, who quoted him so movingly at the end of *Darkness Visible:*

E quindi uscimmo a riveder le stelle
And so we came forth, and once again beheld the stars.

NOT INNOCENT ENOUGH

Nanci Griffith, Charley Stefl, Thomm Jutz
(reprinted with permission)

What the hell was I doing there in that fast food parking lot?
They say I robbed the restaurant and a Memphis cop got shot.
I was trying to feed my habit, I was scared and I was high.
It was never my intention that anyone should die.

And just how many of us aren't innocent enough?
Just how many of us aren't innocent enough?
Just how many of us aren't innocent enough?
My name is Philip Workman and I'm not innocent enough.

It's not a long walk from a trailer park to a Tennessee cell block,
But I got saved behind these bars, soon I'll give my soul to God.
Reverend Joe is praying for me and the family left behind.
They say my bullet took his life but that bullet was not mine.

Oh, just how many of us aren't innocent enough?
Just how many of us aren't innocent enough?
Just how many of us aren't innocent enough?
My name is Philip Workman and I'm not innocent enough.

I had no money for a lawyer to fight the system from within.
There's no justice for the poor from the witness they brought in.
Circumstance and random chance, I never meant to do no harm.
Now that cop and I, we've both died from that needle in my arm.

And there were those who called for mercy in those final days.
Even the officer's daughter cried to grant me stay.
But I'm not innocent enough, I'm not innocent enough
I'm not innocent enough, I'm not innocent enough.

And just how many of us aren't innocent enough?
Just how many of us aren't innocent enough?
Just how many of us aren't innocent enough?
My name was Philip Workman, I was not innocent enough.

Selected Bibliography

Quotations in this book are from the sources listed below as well as many legal documents pertaining to Philip's case obtained through the Tennessee Public Records Act. Where written sources were unavailable, quotations have been followed as closely as possible based on my video transcriptions and personal recollections.

Blackmon, Douglas A. *Slavery by Another Name: The Re-Enslavement of Black Americans from the Civil War to World War II*. New York: Doubleday, 2008.

Campbell, Kenny. Handwritten notes.

Caputo, Philip. *A Rumor of War*. 1977; New York: Henry Holt, 1996.

Carroll, James. *Constantine's Sword*. New York: Houghton-Mifflin, 2001.

Gamble, Dixie. *Beyond Right and Wrong*. Film short. 2004.

Horn, Dan. "The Politics of Life and Death: An Inmate's Fate Often Hinges on Luck of the Draw." *Cincinnati Enquirer*, April 15, 2007.

Ingle, Joseph P. *Last Rights: 13 Fatal Encounters with the States Justice*. New York: Union Square Press, 2008.

———. *Slouching toward Tyranny: The Making of the Tyranny of the Majority in the United States of America*, forthcoming.

Laurence, John. *The Cat from Hué: A Vietnam War Story*. New York: Public Affairs, 2002.

Leung, Rebecca. "Terror at the Morgue." CBS *48 Hours* report. Aired April 23, 2005. Http://www.cbsnews.com/2100-18559_162-688910.html?tag=contentMain;contentBody.

Mauer, Marc. "Comparative International Rates of Incarceration: An Examination of Causes and Trends," Presented to the U.S. Commission on Civil Rights. The Sentencing Project, Washington, D.C. June 20, 2003. Http://www.sentencingproject.org/doc/publications/inc_comparative_intl.pdf.

Naomi Shihab Nye, "Kindness." In *Words under the Words: Selected Poems*. Portland, OR: Far Corner Books, 1995.

Sayward, Amy L., and Margaret Vandiver, eds. *Tennessee's New Abolitionists: The Fight to End the Death Penalty in the Volunteer State*. Knoxville: University of Tennessee Press, 2009.

Secours, Molly, and Dixie Gamble. "Deadly Silence." Short film. 2007. Http://www.youtube.com/watch?v=xoWvZXOBgmA.

Styron, William. *Darkness Visible: A Memoir of Madness*. New York: Random House, 1990.

"Tennessee Executions." *All Things Considered*. National Public Radio. April 3, 2000. Http://www.npr.org/templates/story/story.php?storyId=1072418.

Tuchman, Barbara. *The March of Folly: From Troy to Vietnam*. New York: Ballantine, 1985.

Workman, Philip. *Though You Slay Me*. Nashville: Canary Cottage Industries, 1999.

ACKNOWLEDGMENTS

In my visits with Philip Workman, one of his most heartfelt desires was that "my case make a difference for somebody else." To a remarkable degree, Philip wanted his case to help others and was not focused on his own plight. In order to fulfill this oft-stated concern, I have written this book.

As I have researched and written over the years of Philip's case and subsequent to his killing by the state of Tennessee, I have been aided by numerous people. Chris Minton was kind enough to read the final draft and offer suggestions. Don Dawson helped me identify some of the players. Margaret Vandiver was helpful in all questions to do with Memphis; her friendship through the years, from Florida to Tennessee and places in between, has been a godsend. Thanks also to Elizabeth Vandiver for sharing her Italian expertise.

On the technical front, Nanci Griffith made possible the transposition of tapes to DVDs of the clemency hearings for the website. Nanci's song about Philip, "Not Innocent Enough," is evocative of the case, and I thank her for granting her permission to reprint the lyrics here. Mary Catherine Nelson led me through the new world of print-on-demand and e-books so that the work may be accessible to as many readers as possible. Jill R. Hughes, my editor, was unstinting in her work to make this as fine and readable a book as was humanly possible. For all of these folks I am grateful while taking full responsibility for whatever mistakes may exist in the work.

I owe a debt of gratitude to Gigi Cohen, whose superb photographs grace this book. Gigi followed her artistic instinct and spent a significant amount of time with Philip Workman and me, photographing as she went. Her photos alone make this book worth purchasing, and I regret it is the nature of e-books that those who read it in that format do not experience the power of the photos as they appear in the book.

In my work with the condemned over the years, I have been blessed with the support of Becca, my wife, and many friends. That work and this book would not have been possible without them. In particular, Jeanne Ballenger and Irwin Venick, Bob and Nancy Brewbaker, Art and Betts Gatewood, Brad and Cindy MacLean, Marian Ott and Craig Philip, Bob and Lucy Pryor, Mike and Lisa Radelet, Jackie Shrago, and Margaret Vandiver contributed to bringing this work to its final fruition. For their support and friendship I am most grateful. I am also grateful to David Kendall for his legal review and his steadfast friendship.

The fact that I completed the final page of this effort on the Martin Luther King Jr. Day holiday is interesting. I did not set out to do that; it just ended up finishing on January 16, 2012. Some may regard this as a coincidence and others providential. I reserve judgment. But I do find it singularly appropriate given Dr. King's opposition to the death penalty and the fact that he was slain in Memphis, Tennessee.

Joseph B. Ingle

January 16, 2012

CPSIA information can be obtained at www.ICGtesting.com
Printed in the USA
LVOW032342300312

275550LV00001B/1/P